JT Paasch teaches philosophy as an adjunct professor for Georgetown University.

OXFORD THEOLOGICAL MONOGRAPHS

OXFORD THEOLOGICAL MONOGRAPHS

Divine Production in Late Medieval Trinitarian Theology

Henry of Ghent, Duns Scotus, and William Ockham

JT PAASCH

OXFORD
UNIVERSITY PRESS

OXFORD

UNIVERSITY PRESS

Great Clarendon Street, Oxford OX2 6DP

Oxford University Press is a department of the University of Oxford.
It furthers the University's objective of excellence in research, scholarship,
and education by publishing worldwide in

Oxford New York

Auckland Cape Town Dar es Salaam Hong Kong Karachi
Kuala Lumpur Madrid Melbourne Mexico City Nairobi
New Delhi Shanghai Taipei Toronto

With offices in

Argentina Austria Brazil Chile Czech Republic France Greece
Guatemala Hungary Italy Japan Poland Portugal Singapore
South Korea Switzerland Thailand Turkey Ukraine Vietnam

Oxford is a registered trade mark of Oxford University Press
in the UK and in certain other countries

Published in the United States
by Oxford University Press Inc., New York

© JT Paasch 2012

The moral rights of the author have been asserted
Database right Oxford University Press (maker)

First published 2012

British Library Cataloguing in Publication Data

Data available

Library of Congress Cataloging in Publication Data

Library of Congress Control Number: 2011942652

Typeset by SPI Publisher Services, Pondicherry, India
Printed in Great Britain
on acid-free paper by
MPG Books Group, Bodmin and King's Lynn

ISBN 978-0-19-964637-1

1 3 5 7 9 10 8 6 4 2

For August

Preface

This is a book about three things: theology, philosophy, and medieval scholasticism. It is about theology because it deals with the doctrine of the Trinity; it is about philosophy because it analyzes philosophical theories of that doctrine; and it is about medieval scholasticism because the theories it examines were authored by late thirteenth- and early fourteenth-century scholastics. I could not have completed a book of this sort without a great deal of help from a great number of people.

Richard Cross got me started on this project, and he taught me many wonderful things. In particular, he taught me about Scotus's Trinitarian theology, and I cannot think of a more capable teacher for such a difficult subject. Marilyn McCord Adams also deserves special mention. From working through the texts with me line by line, to offering detailed feedback on every draft of every chapter, the amount of time she freely gave throughout the duration of this project goes far and beyond the call of duty.

In addition, I want to thank Mark Henninger, the holder of the Isabella A. and Henry D. Martin Chair in Scholastic Philosophy and Politics at Georgetown University. Not only did the Martin Chair provide crucial funding during the later stages of this project, the final product would not have come to fruition without Professor Henninger's wisdom and expertise in early fourteenth century scholasticism.

Friends and family supported and encouraged this project as well. My parents, Tonja and Vik, Madhavi Nevader, Scott Williams, Joseph Jedwab, Dale Tuggy, Greg Spendlove, Tom Ward, Bernd Goerhing, and Sash Tehrani each provided support in all sorts of valuable ways. Finally, I owe a special debt of gratitude to Allyn, Bede, and Hattie, for they gave me love and support even when I spent too many days and nights in the books. This goes for Allyn especially. After listening to me talk about scholastic technicalities for so many years now, she probably knows more about medieval philosophy than she ever wanted to. Any errors or faults, of course, are my own.

Contents

PART II: HOW A DIVINE PERSON
IS A PRODUCER

Abbreviations

Adams, *Ockham*	Marilyn McCord Adams, *William Ockham*, 2 volumes. Notre Dame, Indiana: University of Notre Dame Press, 1989.
AL	*Aristoteles Latinus.* Edited by G. Vuillemin-Diem et al. Bruges, Paris, Leiden, Köln, et al., 1953–.
AW	John Duns Scotus, *God and Creatures: The Quodlibetal Questions.* Edited and translated by Felix Alluntis and Allan Wolter. Princeton, NJ: Princeton University Press, 1975.
Cross, *Duns Scotus on God*	Richard Cross, *Duns Scotus on God.* Aldershot, England and Burlington, Vermont: Ashgate, 2005.
De Prima Philosophia	Avicenna, *Liber de Prima Philosophia sive Scientia Divina, V–X.* Edited by S. van Riet. Leiden: Brill, 1980.
De Primo	John Duns Scotus, *A Treatise on God as First Principle*, second revised edition. Edited and translated by Allan Wolter. Chicago: Franciscan Herald Press, 1966.
Iunt.	*Aristotelis Opera cum Averrois Commentariis.* Edited by Johannes Franciscus Bagolinus et al. Venice: Giunta, 1562–1574.
Opera (Henry of Ghent)	*Henrici de Gandavo Opera Omnia.* Edited by Raymond Macken et al. Leuven: Leuven University Press, 1979–.
OPh (Scotus)	*B. Iohannis Duns Scoti Opera Philosophica.* St. Bonaventure, NY: St. Bonaventure University Press, 1997–2006.
OPh (Ockham)	*Opera Philosophica.* St. Bonaventure, NY: The Franciscan Institute, 1974–1988.

OTh	William Ockham, *Opera Theologica*. St. Bonaventure, NY: The Franciscan Institute, 1967–1986.
Quod. (Henry of Ghent)	*Quodlibeta*. Edited by Jodicus Badius [= "Bad"]. Paris, 1518. Reprinted by Louvain: Bibliothèque S. J., 1961.
Rep. I–A	John Duns Scotus, *The Examined Report of the Paris Lecture (Reportatio I–A)*, volume 1. Edited and translated by Allan Wolter and Oleg Bychkov. St. Bonaventure, NY: The Franciscan Institute, 2004.
Sent.(Aureol)	Peter Aureol, *Scriptum super Primum Sententiarum*, 2 volumes. Edited by Eligius Buytaert. St. Bonaventure, NY: St. Bonaventure University Press, 1952–1956.
Sent.(Lombard)	Peter Lombard, *Sententiarum Quatuor Libri*. Ad Claras: Quarrachi, 1882.
SQO	Henry of Ghent, *Summa Quaestionum Ordinariarum*. Edited by Jodicus Badius. Paris, 1520. Reprinted by St. Bonaventure, NY: The Franciscan Institute, 1953.
Vat.	John Duns Scotus, *Opera Omnia*. Civitas Vaticana: Typis Polyglottis Vaticanis, 1950–.
Wad.	John Duns Scotus, *Opera Omnia*. Edited by Luke Wadding. Lyons, 1639. Reprinted by Hildesheim: Georg Olms Verlagsbuchhandlung, 1968.

1

Introduction

As is well known, Christians believe that there are three distinct persons in the Godhead, and these are denominated respectively as the Father, Son, and Spirit. Yet despite being distinct, these three persons are also supposed to be one and the same God. On the face of it then, it would appear that Christians are supposed to believe that when it comes to the Godhead, three distinct things (persons) are also somehow one and the same thing (God).

As if that were not perplexing enough, Christians also believe that there is an internal process of origination that gives rise to these three persons. In particular, the Father is supposed to produce the Son, and then the Spirit is supposed to be produced either by the Father and Son together (which is how the Latin tradition puts it), or by the Father, but *through* the Son (which is how the Greek tradition puts it).[1] Either way, there are clearly supposed to be two productions

---

[1] Although the Latin and Greek traditions disagree about whether we should say the Spirit comes from the Father *and* the Son or *through* the Son, the difference between "and" and "through" is not necessarily clear, and indeed some Latin authors believed the difference to be merely verbal and not substantive. For instance, Robert Grosseteste was often quoted as saying "sententia graecorum est quod Spiritus Sanctus . . . non procedens a Filio sed a solo Patre, per Filium tamen; et videtur haec sententia contraria nostrae, qua dicimus Spiritum Sanctum a Patre et Filio procedere . . . unde propria est, de hac visa contrarietate disquirerent, pateret utrique tandem ipsam contrarietatem non esse veraciter realem, sicut est vocalis" (from *Notula super Epistolam Ioannis Damasceni "De Trisagion,"* Magdalen College, Oxford, MS 192, f. 215rb, as quoted by Scotus in *Ordinatio*, 1.11.1, n. 9 (*Vat.* 5: 3.1–8)). Even Peter Lombard says in *Sent.*, 1.11.2 (1: 208): "Sed cum non sit aliud Spiritum sanctum esse Patris vel Filii, quam esse a Patre et Filio, etiam in hoc in eandem nobiscum fidei sententiam convenire videntur [Graeci], licet in verbis dissentiant." In any case, this Latin/Greek disagreement makes no difference for the issues I will examine in this book, so the word "through" could easily be substituted for "and" wherever I say the Spirit comes from the Father *and* the Son.

within the Godhead: one which results in the Son, and another which results in the Spirit.

Moreover, these productions are traditionally thought to be eternal. So it is not as if, at some point in time long before the universe was created, the Father first produced the Son, and then five minutes later, the Spirit gets produced by the Father and the Son (or through the Son). On the contrary, there is supposed to be no point at which the Son or Spirit do not exist. Nevertheless, the tradition maintains that there is still some (non-temporal) sense in which the Father precedes the Son, and some (non-temporal) sense in which the Father and Son both precede the Spirit.

Given all that, one might wonder how this sort of divine production is even possible, and how it is supposed to work. To put it very generally, how exactly does one divine person produce another? When the Father produces the Son, or when the Father and Son produce the Spirit, what exactly is going on there?

In the late thirteenth and early fourteenth centuries, scholastic theologians dealt with these questions on at least two different levels. On one level, they focused on the specific details of the Son's and Spirit's respective productions. This involved questions like the following. Are the Son and Spirit produced in the same way, or in different ways? If the same way, how can they be distinguished? If different ways, which ways in particular? In short, what is the precise nature of the Son's production, and what is the precise nature of the Spirit's production?

In this respect, Augustine stands prominently in the background. In his *De Trinitate*, Augustine drew a number of analogies between the Trinity and the human mind, and he suggested that at least in some ways, the Son is produced similar to the way that our minds produce concepts, while the Spirit is produced similar to the way that our wills generate love.[2] Most scholastic thinkers adopted this Augustinian framework to some extent, but some saw it as little more

[2] See, for instance, Augustine, *De Trinitate*, 15, nn. 39–41 (*Corpus Christianorum Series Latina*, volume 50A, ed. W. J. Mountain and F. Glorie (Turnhout: Brepols, 1968), 516.49–517.52, 517.56–57, 517.1, 517.8–518.2, 518.22–24): "per quod uelut speculum quantum possent, si possent, cernerent trinitatem deum in nostra memoria, intellegentia, uoluntate. Quia tria in sua mente . . . profecto reperit illius summae trinitatis imaginem . . . deum patrem et deum filium . . . uideretur in memoria et intellegentia mentis nostrae . . . memoriae tribuens omne quod scimus etiamsi non inde cogitemus, intellegentiae uero proprio modo quandam cogitationis informationem . . . De spiritu autem

than a convenient analogy, while others took it quite literally and maintained that the Son and Spirit really are produced in the manner of concepts and love.[3]

Still, all of this remains on a level that is largely concerned with the specific details of the Son's and Spirit's respective productions. But late thirteenth- and early fourteenth-century scholastic theologians recognized that divine production needs to be investigated on another level, for to focus only on the Son's and Spirit's respective productions already assumes that a divine person can be produced in the first place, and that such a production can be explained in a coherent way. But that is not immediately obvious. Indeed, how *can* a divine person be produced?

This is not an easy question to answer. In our own lives, we typically produce things by constructing them out of materials, but it is hard to see how that could help in the divine case. After all, God is traditionally thought to be entirely spiritual, so one would think that there simply are no materials in the Godhead that could be used to construct a divine person in the first place.

But how can one thing produce another without using any materials? Is the Father just supposed to conjure up the Son out of nothing? If such a thing were even possible, wouldn't that mean that the Father creates the Son *ex nihilo*? And then wouldn't the Son be a lesser deity of sorts, for aren't all creatures in some sense lesser beings than their creator or creators?

Christians have typically rejected these options, for the earliest ecumenical Creeds (at least as they are traditionally understood) say that the Son is *not* created, and that the Son is *not* a lesser deity.[4] How, then, could the Father possibly produce a Son, without creating an

sancto nihil *in* hoc *aenigmate* quod ei simile uideretur ostendi nisi uoluntatem nostram, uel amorem seu dilectionem."

[3] The details of these debates are complex, and there is arguably a good portion of the material that we do not yet understand. Fortunately, there have been a number of studies that analyze some of the relevant texts and issues in detail. For a helpful summary of this scholarship, as well as the scholarship on medieval Trinitarian theology in general, see Russell Friedman, *Medieval Trinitarian Thought from Aquinas to Ockham* (Cambridge: Cambridge University Press, 2010), 178–86. There Friedman conveniently provides an annotated bibliography of some of the most important studies.

[4] For example, with respect to the claim that the Son is not created, the Nicene Creed says that "those who say [the Son] . . . came to be from things that were not [i.e. from nothing] . . . these the catholic and apostolic church anathematises" (*The Decrees*

inferior deity? And by extension, how could the Father and Son together possibly produce a Spirit without creating an inferior deity as well?

In the late thirteenth and early fourteenth centuries, scholastic theologians subjected these questions to detailed philosophical analysis. And indeed, it is not hard to see why. The schoolmen were highly trained philosophers as well as highly trained theologians, and they could see that there is a good deal at stake here. The issue brings to the fore questions about the full divinity of the Son and Spirit, as well as questions about the very nature of production in general.

Despite the importance of this issue though, it has not received much scholarly attention. In this book, I will look at what three important scholastic thinkers have to say about this topic, namely Henry of Ghent (*c*.1217–1293), John Duns Scotus (1265/66–1308), and William Ockham (1287–1324).[5] These authors serve as a particularly good entry point into this issue because their discussions

of the Ecumenical Councils, 2 volumes, ed. Norman Tanner (London: Sheed and Ward, and Washington, D.C.: Georgetown University Press, 1990), 1: *5). With respect to the claim that the Son is equal to the Father, the Nicene Creed also says that "We believe in . . . the Son of God . . . [who comes from the Father as] God from God, light from light, true God from true God" (ibid., 1: *5), and that of course is traditionally thought to imply that the Son is just as much God as the Father.

[5] The most noteworthy treatments of this issue that I know of are as follows. First, there is Michael Schmaus, *Der Liber Propugnatorius des Thomas Anglicus und die Lehrunterschiede zwischen Thomas von Aquin und Duns Scotus*, vol. 2 (Münster Westfalen: Verlag der Aschendorffsche Verlagsbuchhandlung, 1930), 59–106. Schmaus usefully summarizes how a number of medieval theologians deal with these questions, including Henry of Ghent, Duns Scotus, and even Ockham (briefly). Second, there is Friedrich Wetter, *Die Trinitätslehre des Johannes Duns Scotus* (Münster Westfalen: Aschendorffsche Verlagsbuchhandlung, 1967), 90–121, and 136–59. Wetter focuses only on Scotus, but he provides a far more comprehensive summary of Scotus's texts than Schmaus does. Unfortunately, both Schmaus and Wetter spend most of their time summarizing (or perhaps it would be more accurate to say "paraphrasing") the relevant texts, but there is little by way of detailed analysis. More recently, Richard Cross has offered a brief but helpful analysis of some aspects of Henry's and Scotus's positions in *Duns Scotus on God*, 172–6, and 203–9. I should mention that Stephen Dumont briefly touches on Henry's and Scotus's theories in "William of Ware, Richard of Connington, and the *Collationes Oxonienses* of John Duns Scotus," in *John Duns Scotus: Metaphysics and Ethics*, ed. Ludger Honnefelder, Rega Wood, and Mechthild Dreyer (Leiden: E. J. Brill, 1996), 59–85. Dumont does not offer an extensive philosophical analysis of Henry's and Scotus's arguments, but he does provide some useful context for Scotus's debates with Henry's followers. As for Ockham, apart from a few brief mentions in Schmaus (*Der Liber Propugnatorius*, 70–2), Ockham's take on this issue has not been analyzed in detail at all, so far as I know.

make up a single conversation. Of course, this was not a conversation that happened face to face, for Henry, Scotus, and Ockham belonged to successive generations. But Scotus does respond directly to Henry's ideas, and Ockham responds directly to the ideas of both Henry and Scotus. So taken all together, these discussions make up a tightly integrated debate which offers a convenient glimpse into late thirteenth- and early fourteenth-century scholastic philosophical theology.

Before I get into the details of this debate, I want to spend the rest of this chapter clarifying the way that Henry, Scotus, and Ockham understand the problem. As they see it, to ask how one divine person can produce another first involves asking a broader question: how can anything produce anything? In this regard, Henry, Scotus, and Ockham found the respective theories of Aristotle and the Persian philosopher Avicenna to be particularly important.

1.1. ARISTOTLE ON PRODUCTION

In the *Physics*, Aristotle describes a well-known argument which concludes that coming-into-being is impossible. According to this argument, if something *x* begins to exist at a particular point in time *t*, then one might assume that *x* did not exist before *t*. However, that would mean that *x* would have been pure nothing at that point, and since nothing can come from nothing, one could not end up with an *x* at *t* if there was nothing there before *t*. So, one might think, *x* must have existed *before t*. But if that is right, then *x* would not *begin* to exist at *t*, for it already existed beforehand.

There is, then, no way to explain how *x* comes to be. Either there was no *x* before, in which case one could not end up with an *x*, or there was an *x* before, in which case *x* would already exist. However you think about it, there is just no way for anything to come into being, and so even though it may appear to us as if various things come to be, this can be nothing more than an illusion.[6]

---

[6] Aristotle, *Physics*, 1.8, 191a27–34 (*AL*, 7, 1.2: 35.16–36.8; *Iunt.*, 4: 41vH-I, 42rC): "et dicunt neque fieri eorum que sunt nullum neque corrumpi, propter id quod necessarium est fieri quod fit aut ex eo quod est aut ex eo quod non est, ex his autem utrisque impossibile est esse; neque enim quod est fieri (esse enim iam) et ex eo

A crucial assumption here is that something cannot come from nothing, and this, of course, is intuitively plausible. Imagine a sculptor sitting in her studio with no materials in front of her. It is hard to imagine how she could conjure up a statue out of nothing, for one cannot start with nothing and get something out of it. Hence:

(T1) For any x,
     x cannot be produced from nothing.

Aristotle accepts T1 wholeheartedly, for he agrees that if we start with absolutely nothing, we cannot get anything out of it. However, Aristotle points out that the aforementioned argument assumes that things which come to be are either *entirely* non-existent beforehand, or they exist *completely* beforehand, and this is a mistake. When a sculptor makes a clay statue, it is true that her statue does not exist before she makes it, but it is not true that she starts with absolutely nothing. On the contrary, she starts with some clay, and then she fashions that clay into a statue.

For Aristotle then, although it is true that we cannot conjure things up out of nothing, we can take something that already exists and transform it into something new. In other words, production is possible so long as the product is made from pre-existing materials—i.e. something that already exists but which has not yet been transformed into the desired product.[7] Thus, Aristotle insists that:

quod non est nichil utique fieri; subici enim aliquid oportet. Et sic consequenter contingens augmentantes neque esse multa dicunt sed tantum ipsum quod est. Illi quidem igitur talem accipiebant opinionem propter ea que dicta sunt." See also *De Caelo*, 3.1, 298b15–18 (*Iunt.*, 5: 174rB): "Quidam enim ipsorum auferebant omnino generationem et corruptionem, nihil enim eorum quae sunt, aut generari aiunt aut corrumpi, sed solum videri nobis, ut Melisso atque Parmenidi"; *Metaphysics*, 1.3, 984a30–984b1 (*AL*, 25, 3.2: 20.237–241; *Iunt.*, 8: 3vM–4rA; *AL*, 25.2: 14.16–21): "Verum quidam unum esse dicentium, quasi ab ea questione devicti, ipsum unum immobile dicunt esse et naturam totam non solum secundum generationem et corruptionem . . . verum et secundum aliam mutationem omnem"; ibid., 1.5, 986b27–30 (*AL*, 25, 3.2: 26.393–396; *Iunt.*, 8: 5vK; *AL*, 25.2: 20.12–15): "Parmenides autem magis videns visus est dicere. Nam preter ens non ens nichil dignatus esse, ex necessitate ens opinatur unum esse et aliud nichil; de quo manifestius in Phisicis diximus."

  [7] Aristotle, *Metaphysics*, 7.7, 1032b30–1033a1 (*AL*, 25, 3.2: 144.343–346; *Iunt.*, 8: 173rB, 174vG; *AL*, 25.2: 134.18–20): "Quare, sicut dicitur, impossibile factum esse, si nichil preextiterit. Quod quidem igitur pars ex necessitate existet, palam; materia namque pars, inest enim et fit hec"; *Physics*, 1.7, 190b1–5 (*AL*, 7, 1.2: 32.4–7; *Iunt.* 4: 37rC): "quod autem et substantie et quecumque alia cum sint ex quodam subiecto fiant, consideranti fiet utique manifestum. Semper enim est aliquid quod subicitur, ex

(T2) For any *x* and *y*,
        if *x* produces *y*,
        x cannot produce *y* without any materials *m*.

It is important to emphasize that Aristotle thinks this is the *only way* to produce something. After all, since he fully accepts the idea that things cannot come from nothing (T1), he cannot allow any cases where a production starts from nothing. The only way to produce something is to start with pre-existing materials. In Aristotle's universe, creation *ex nihilo* is just flat-out impossible.[8]

This means, so far as Aristotle is concerned, that only material things can be produced, for they are material and hence *made* from materials.[9] And for Aristotle, all the things we see coming into being and passing away here on earth are like this. Plants, animals, stones, steam, and so on—all of these are generated, broken down, and

---

quo fit quod fit, ut plante et animalia ex semine"; ibid., 190a14–15 (*Iunt.*, 4: 35vI; *AL*, 7, 1.2: 30.17–31.2): "Determinatis autem his, ex omnibus, quae fiunt, hoc est accipere, si aliquis inspexerit, sicut dicimus, quod oportet semper aliquid subici, quod fit. Et hoc, etsi numero est unum, et forma quidem non unum"; ibid., 191a4–11 (*AL*, 7, 1.2: 34.11–12, 15–18; *Iunt.*, 4: 40rD, 40vG): "et ostensum est quoniam oportet subici aliquid contrariis et contraria duo esse . . . Subiecta autem natura scibilis est secundum analogiam. Sicut enim ad statuam es aut ad lectulum lignum aut ad aliorum aliquod habentium formam materia et informe se habet priusquam accipiat formam, sic ipsa se ad substantiam habet et hoc."

   [8] Aristotle, *Physics*, 1.8, 191b13–14 (*AL*, 7, 1.2: 37.5–6; *Iunt.*, 4: 43rE): "Nos autem et ipsi dicimus fieri quidem simpliciter nichil ex eo quod non est"; *Metaphysics*, 12.7, 1072a20 (*AL*, 25, 3.2: 256.237–238; *Iunt.*, 8: 316vL; cf. *AL*, 25.2: 212.21–22): "Quoniam autem ita contingit [viz. quod omnis productus est de materia], et si non sic, ex nocte erit et simul omnium et ex non ente [quod est absurdum, secundum Aristotelem]"; *De Caelo*, 3.2, 302a4–9 (*Iunt.*, 5: 199rD): "Aliud enim ex alio corpus fieri est possibile, ut ex aere ignem, omnino autem ex nulla alia praeexistente magnitudine est impossibile, maxime enim ex corpore, potentia existente, actu fiet corpus, sed, si id, quod potentia est corpus, nullum est aliud corpus actu prius, vacuum separatum erit [quod est absurdum manifestum, secundum Aristotelem]."

   [9] Aristotle, *Physics*, 1.7, 190b10–19 (*AL*, 7, 1.2: 32.11–15, 33.3–4, 6; *Iunt.*, 4: 37vI, 38vG, 38vL, M): "Omnia autem que sic fiunt manifestum est quoniam ex subiectis fiunt. Quare ostensum ex dictis est quoniam quod fit semper compositium est, et est quidem aliquid quod fit, est autem aliquid quod hoc fit . . . Manifestum igitur est, sicut sunt cause et principia eorum que natura sunt, ex quibus primis sunt et fiunt . . . quod fiat ex subiecto et forma"; *Metaphysics*, 8.1, 1042a25–31 (*AL*, 25, 3.2: 169.24–30; *Iunt.*, 8: 209vM, 210rE–M[=F]; *AL*, 25.2: 158.5–11): "Nunc autem de confessis substantiis tractabimus. Hee vero sensibiles; sensibiles autem substantie omnes materiam habent. Est autem substantia quod subicitur, aliter quidem materia; materiam vero dico que non hoc aliquid ens actu potestate est hoc aliquid. Aliter vero ratio et forma, quod hoc aliquid ens ratione separabile est. Tertium vero quod est [compositum] ex hiis, cuius solius generatio et corruptio."

regenerated as natural processes transform the earth's materials in
various ways.

However, at the most fundamental level of decomposition, the
materials themselves cannot be generated. For if the earth's basic
matter were itself produced, it would have to be made from further
materials (by T2), and those materials would have to be made from
still further materials, and so on ad infinitum. Since this cannot go on
forever, Aristotle concludes that the basic matter that makes up the
earth and everything in it could not ever have been produced. Rather,
it must have always been there.[10]

So although earthly substances can be generated out of various
materials, the ultimate matter from which all those substances are
made cannot. On the contrary, it always exists, forever being transformed. In Aristotle's universe, plants, animals, stones, steam, and
other such things are forever coming into being and passing away as
natural processes continually transform the earth's materials in various ways. There is no beginning or end to this process, just as there is
no beginning or end to the earth's matter.[11]

---

[10] Aristotle, *Metaphysics*, 7.8, 1033b3–4 (*AL*, 25, 3.2: 145.379–381; *Iunt.*, 8: 175vI;
AL, 25.2: 135.26–27): "Si igitur et hoc facit ipsum [viz. materiam], palam quia similiter
faciet, et ibunt generationes in infinitum"; ibid., 12.3, 1069b35–1070a4 (*AL*, 25, 3.2:
248.61–66; *Iunt.*, 8: 297vK-L; *AL*, 25.2: 206.11–16): "Postea quia nec fit materia nec
species, dico autem ultima [materia et species]. Omne namque transmutat aliquid et
ab aliquo et in quid. A quo quidem, primo movente; cuius vero, materia; in quod vero,
species. In infinitum ergo sunt, si non solum es fit rotundum sed et ipsum rotundum
aut es; necesse est itaque stare"; *Physics*, 1.9, 192a25–34 (*AL*, 7, 1.2: 40.6–16; *Iunt.*, 4:
46vG-I): "Corrumpitur [viz., materia] autem et fit est quidem sic, est autem sic non.
Secundum quidem enim quod est in quo, secundum se corrumpitur; quod enim
corrumpitur in hoc est, privatio; in quantum autem est secundum potentiam, non
per se, sed incorruptibilem et ingenitam necesse est ipsam esse. Sive enim fiunt, subici
oportet aliquid primum ex quo inest; hoc autem est ipsa natura, quare erit ante fieri
(dico enim materiam primum subiectum unicuique, ex quo fit aliquid cum insit non
secundum accidens); et si corrumpitur, in hoc adibit ultimum, quare corrupta erit
antequam corrumpatur."

[11] Aristotle, *De Generatione et Corruptione*, 1.3, 318a9–11 (*AL*, 9.1: 18.12–14; *Iunt.*,
5: 351vH): "Nunc autem ut in materie specie positam causam dicamus, propter quam
semper corruptio et generatio non deficit naturam"; ibid., 318a24–29 (*AL*, 9.1: 19.4–8;
Iunt., 5: 351vM): "Quocirca propter huius corruptionem alterius esse generationem et
huius generationem alterius esse corruptionem inquietam necesse est esse transmutationem. De generationem quidem igitur esse et corruptionem similiter semper circa
unumquodque entium, hanc existimandum sufficientem omnibus causam"; ibid.,
319a19–22 (*AL*, 9.1: 22.17–21; *Iunt.*, 5: 353vG): "et quoniam generationem esse
continue causa ut materia subiectum, quoniam transmutativum in contraria; et est
alterius generatio semper in substantiis alterius corrupto et alterius corruptio alterius
generatio."

Aristotle also believes that the earth is surrounded by concentrically rotating celestial spheres (each of which, presumably, has a body and a soul). The sun, moon, planets, and stars are embedded in these various spheres, so they are carried around the earth as these spheres rotate. All of these heavenly bodies are made of a special material (often called "ether"), but this cannot be produced any more than the earth's matter can. Thus, Aristotle maintains that these heavenly bodies are also eternal. Like the earth, they were never produced, but rather always have been and always will be in existence.[12]

Further, Aristotle believes that each celestial sphere is governed by a distinct immaterial being—a spirit.[13] But since spirits are altogether free of materials, they cannot be constructed out of materials, so Aristotle concludes that they cannot be produced either. Like the earth and the celestial spheres, these spirits are just "there," as it were, forever governing their respective heavenly bodies.[14]

Hence, the only things in Aristotle's universe that actually come into being and pass away are the things that do so here on earth. Everything else simply exists, always and forever, without ever being

---

[12] Aristotle's remarks about the heavens are somewhat cryptic, but see *Metaphysics*, 12.1–8, 1069a18–1074b14 (*AL*, 25, 3.2: 246.1–264.422; *Iunt.*, 8: 290vG-334rD; *AL*, 25.2: 204.1–219.17), especially chapter 8, 1073a14–1074b14 (*AL*, 25, 3.2: 260.310–264. 422; *Iunt.*, 8: 326rA-334rD; *AL*, 25.2: 215.16–219.17).

[13] For more on this, see P. Merlan, "Aristotle's Unmoved Movers," *Traditio* 4 (1946): 1–30; and Harry Wolfson, "The Plurality of Immovable Movers in Aristotle and Averroes," *Harvard Studies in Classical Philology* 63 (1958): 233–53.

[14] As Aristotle puts it in *Metaphysics*, 12.6, 1071b20–22 (*AL*, 25, 3.2: 254.199–255. 202; *Iunt.*, 8: 314rC; *AL*, 25.2: 211.13–16): "Oportet igitur esse principium [viz., motor unuscuiusque coeli] tale cuius substantia actus. Amplius igitur tales oportet esse substantias sine materia; sempiternas enim esse oportet, si et aliud aliquid sempiternum; actu igitur"; *De Caelo*, 1.9, 279a19–23 (*Iunt.*, 5: 67rA): "Extra autem coelum quod neque est, neque contingit esse corpus ostensum est. Manifestum igitur est quod neque locus, neque vacuum, neque tempus est extrinsecus. Quapropter neque quae illic sunt, nata sunt in loco esse, neque tempus ipsa facit senscere, neque ulla transmutatio ullius eorum est, quia super extima disposita sunt latione, sed inalterabilia, et impassibilia, optimam habentia vitam, et per se sufficientissimam, perseverant toto aevo." Aristotle also maintains, as I mentioned above, that the celestial spheres cannot be produced either, even though they are composed of (a special kind of heavenly) matter. All the celestial spheres do is rotate in circles eternally. Cf. *Metaphysics*, 12.2, 1069b25–26 (*AL*, 25, 3.2: 248.47–50; *Iunt.*, 8: 296vL; cf. *AL*, 25.2: 205.26–206.1): "Omnia vero materiam habent quecumque transmutantur, sed aliam [materiam habent]; et sempiternorum quecumque non generabilia mobilia autem latione, verum non generabilem habent [materiam], sed unde quo [materiam]."

produced.[15] And indeed, that makes perfect sense within the confines of Aristotle's theory of production, for as he sees it, the only way to produce something is to do it with materials. Consequently, the only things that can be produced in the first place are material beings of the sort that we encounter here on earth.

1.2. AVICENNA ON PRODUCTION

The great Persian philosopher Avicenna adopts much of Aristotle's picture of the universe. That is, he agrees that here on earth, terrestrial beings are forever generated and broken down as natural processes transform the earth's materials in various ways, and he agrees that the earth is surrounded by concentrically rotating celestial spheres, each of which is governed by its own spirit.

However, Aristotle believes that, apart from the particular things that are continually being generated here on earth, everything else in the universe is eternal and therefore was never produced. But Avicenna believes the universe eternally flows out of or emanates from God, perhaps similar to the way that someone from that era might have thought that heat always emanates from the sun.

That being said, Avicenna does not think everything flows *directly* out of God. Rather, it happens in a hierarchical manner, which runs as follows.[16] At the top of the hierarchy is God, and God is the sort of

---

[15] Aristotle, *De Caelo*, 2.1, 283b26–30 (*Iunt.*, 5: 95vH-I): "Quod igitur neque factum sit universum coelum, neque contingat ipsum corrumpi, quemadmodum quidam dicunt, sed sit unum, et sempiternum, principium quidem et finem non habens universi aevi, habens autem et continens in seipso infinitum tempus, et ex dictis licet accipere fidem, et per opinionem eam, quae ab aliter dicentibus, et generantibus ipsum effluxit. Si enim sic quidem sese habere contingat, eo autem modo, quo illi dicunt, non contingat, magnum utique habebit et hoc momentum ad fidem de immortalitate ipsius, et sempiternitate." See also *Physics*, 8.1, 250b10–252b6 (*AL*, 7, 1.2: 277.1–284.3; *Iunt.*, 4: 338rB-348vL). For other Aristotelian texts on the world's eternity that were commonly cited and discussed in the Middle Ages, see Richard Dales, *Medieval Discussions of the Eternity of the World* (Leiden: Brill, 1990), 39–49. On medieval cosmology in general, see Edward Grant, *Planets, Stars, and Orbs: The Medieval Cosmos, 1200–1687* (Cambridge: Cambridge University Press, 1996).

[16] The *locus classicus* for Avicenna's discussion of the universe's emanation is his *De Prima Philosophia sive Divina Scientia* (otherwise known as *The Metaphysics of the Healing*), book 9, chapter 4. For more detailed discussions of emanation, see Seyyed Houssein Nasr, *An Introduction to Islamic Cosmological Doctrines*, revised edition

thing that necessarily exists. That is, God exists entirely on his own account, and not on account of something else. God does not flow out of anything else, God is not made from anything else, and God does not come from anything else in any other sort of way. Rather, God always has and always will exist, without being produced in any way.[17]

Nevertheless, a separate spirit flows out of God, and this is the spirit that will govern the outermost celestial sphere.[18] This spirit is called the "First Intelligence," and for reasons I will discuss below, it is a little less perfect than God, and a little bit different in kind. In other words, the First Intelligence is an imperfect likeness of God.

Next, two types of things flow out of the First Intelligence. The first is the celestial sphere it will govern (or more precisely, the body and soul of that sphere), and this is the outermost sphere that encircles the earth.[19] The second is yet another spirit, called the "Second Intelligence," and this spirit is an imperfect likeness of the First Intelligence, just as the First Intelligence is an imperfect likeness of God.[20]

(Boulder, Colorado: Shamhala, 1978), Part III, especially 197–214. For a more recent treatment, see Herbert Davidson, *Alfarabi, Avicenna, and Averroes on Intellect: Their Cosmologies, Theories of the Active Intellect and Theories of Human Intellect* (Oxford: Oxford University Press, 1992), especially 74–83.

[17] Avicenna, *De Prima Philosophia*, 9.4 (476.40–45): "Iam certum est nobis ex supradictis quod necesse esse per se unum est et . . . quod esse omnium quae sunt est ab eo et quod non potest habere principium ullo modo nec causam, scilicet nec a qua est res, nec in qua est res, nec per quam est res, nec propter quam est, ita ut ipse sit propter aliquid."

[18] Avicenna, *De Prima Philosophia*, 9.4 (479.87–480.10): "quoniam ipse [viz., id quod est necesse esse per se] est agens omne quod est hac intentione quia ipse est ens a quo fluit quicquid est . . . igitur ea quae primo sunt ab eo—et haec sunt creata—non possunt esse multa nec numero . . . quoniam id quod sequitur ex eo, est ab eius essentia . . . Si enim provenirent ab eo duae res discretae . . . illae non provenirent nisi ex duobus modis diversis in eius essentia . . . iam autem prohibuimus hoc antea et ostendimus destructionem eius. Manifestum est igitur quod primum eorum quae sunt a causa prima unum numero est . . . Unde . . . primum causatum est intelligentia pura . . . et ipsa est prima intelligentiarum separatarum."

[19] Strictly speaking, Avicenna believes that Intelligences produce their inferiors through acts of understanding. In this case, it is through understanding different aspects of itself that the First Intelligence produces the body and soul of its celestial sphere. Avicenna, *De Prima Philosophia*, 9.4 (483.85–91): "Igitur ex prima intelligentia . . . inquantum intelligit seipsam, sequitur ex ea forma caeli ultimi et eius perfectio et haec est anima, et propter naturam essendi possibile quae est ei et quae est retenta inquantum intelligit seipsam, est esse corporeitatis caeli ultimi quae est contenta in totalitate caeli ultimi."

[20] As I mentioned in the last note, Intelligences produce their inferiors through acts of understanding, but here it is through its understanding of God that the First

This process is then repeated. From the Second Intelligence flows its celestial sphere (the next innermost sphere), as well as a Third Intelligence; from the Third Intelligence flows its own celestial sphere and a Fourth Intelligence; and so on down the line.[21]

Note, though, that each emanation results in an inferior Intelligence, so there is a loss of power with each emanation. By the time we get to the Tenth Intelligence, there is not enough power for any further celestial spheres or Intelligences to flow out of it.[22] Still, something similar happens: from the Tenth Intelligence flows the earth and its inhabitants (or more precisely, the earth's matter, and then the specific forms and souls that we find in it).[23]

Terrestrial beings, in turn, can "produce" other things, but only with the use of pre-existing materials. That is, terrestrial beings only have enough power to transform the earth's materials, but nothing can flow out of them in the way that, say, the Second Intelligence flows from the First Intelligence. Thus, the process of emanation runs

Intelligence produces another Intelligence. Avicenna, *De Prima Philosophia*, 9.4 (483.85–87): "Igitur ex prima intelligentia, inquantum intelligit primum [viz. id quod necesse esse per se], sequitur esse alterius intelligentiae inferioris ea."

[21] Avicenna, *De Prima Philosophia*, 9.4 (483.81–82): "Sub unaquaque autem intelligentia est caelum cum sua materia et sua forma, quae est anima [caeli], et intelligentia inferius ea"; ibid., (483.91–484.99): "Unde ipsa et id quod est commune virtuti sunt sic quod ex ipsa sequitur intelligentia, et ex eo quod est commune virtuti, inquantum appropriatur sibi ipsi secundum modum suum, sequitur sphaera prima cum suis partibus duabus, scilicet materia et forma . . . Similiter est dispositio in intelligentia et intelligentia, et in caelo et caelo, quousque pervenitur ad intelligentiam agentem quae gubernat nostras animas"; ibid., (487.89–488.92): "Iam igitur vere manifestum est quod ex omni intelligentia superiore in ordine, secundum hoc quod intelligit primum, provenit esse alterius intelligentiae inferioris ea, sed, secundum hoc quod intelligit seipsam, provenient circuli per se tantum."

[22] Davidson, *Alfarabi, Avicenna, and Averroes on the Intellect*, 76: "What an intelligence emanates depends on its nature and power. As intelligences succeed one another, their power diminishes, and because the active intellect stands low in the hierarchy its power is no longer sufficient to emanate eternal beings like those emanated by the intelligences above it." The "active intellect" that Davidson speaks of here is the final Tenth Intelligence.

[23] Davidson, *Alfarabi, Avicenna, and Averroes on the Intellect*, 76: "While the active intellect [i.e. the Tenth Intelligence] cannot fully imitate the intelligences above it and eternally emanate the body of a celestial sphere, the soul of a celestial sphere, and an additional incorporeal intelligence, it does emanate lesser analogues. The active intellect is (1) the emanating cause of the matter of the sublunar world, (2) the emanating cause of natural forms appearing in matter, including the souls of plants, animals, and man, and (3) the cause of the actualization of the human intellect."

out of steam, as it were, so that it stops with the earth and its inhabitants.[24]

Although Avicenna's universe looks very much like Aristotle's in some respects (i.e. the earth is surrounded by rotating celestial spheres, etc.), Avicenna departs from Aristotle insofar as he adds his hierarchical scheme of emanation to explain how the universe comes into being. This has important implications for what Avicenna would say about a general theory of production.

First of all, in Avicenna's universe, things can and do get produced without the use of pre-existing materials. For instance, the Intelligences, the celestial spheres, and even the earth's matter flow directly out of their producers, but none of these are constructed from pre-existing materials. So Avicenna would say (contra Aristotle) that it is, in fact, possible to produce something without materials.

However, one could also infer from this that if you do produce something without materials, you are creating it from nothing. This seems quite plausible, for surely that is just what creation *ex nihilo* means: you start with nothing (no materials), and then you end up with something. If that is right, then producing something without materials really amounts to creating it:

(T3) For any x and y,
    if x produces y,
    x creates y from nothing iff
    x produces y without any materials m.

The second point to note is that in Avicenna's universe, everything that gets produced without materials is inferior to its producer. For example, the First Intelligence is inferior to God, the Second Intelligence is inferior to the First Intelligence, the celestial spheres are inferior to their governing Intelligences, and so on. Anything which emanates from another is a lesser sort of being than that from which it emanates.[25]

---

[24] Avicenna, *De Prima Philosophia*, 9.4 (487.80–84): "Et hoc est post completionem esse omnium caelestium, et sequitur semper intelligentia post intelligentiam, quousque fiat sphaera lunae, et deinde fiant elementa et aptantur recipere impressionem unam in specie, multam numero, ab intelligentia ultima."

[25] Avicenna, *De Prima Philosophia*, 9.4 (486.63–64): "causae vero datrices esse sunt perfectiores in esse, recipientes vero esse sunt inferiores in esse"; ibid., (487.86–89): "Oportet igitur ut, ex unaquaque intelligentia, fiat intelligentia inferior ea et esset tunc

The idea here, I think, can be stated very generally like this: if you produce something without materials, then you create it (by T3), and creatures are typically inferior to their creators. This too seems quite sensible. Just think of many of the world's great creation myths—the things that get created are usually lesser beings than the god or gods who create them. So also in Avicenna's scheme of emanation. If you produce something without materials, then of course you create it, in which case you will end up with an inferior product. Hence:

(T4) For any *x* and *y*,
       if *x* produces *y*,
       y is inferior to *x* if
       x produces *y* without any materials *m*.

For Avicenna then, although it is possible to produce something without materials, the result will be created (T3), and it will be an inferior being (T4). In that sense, Avicenna presents a very different theory of production than Aristotle. For while Aristotle thinks products can only be constructed from materials, Avicenna thinks the whole universe is created without any pre-existing materials at all, albeit in a hierarchical manner that results in successively inferior beings.

1.3. BASIC PROBLEMS: CREATION AND SUBORDINATION

When applied to the Trinity, Aristotle's and Avicenna's respective theories of production generate two closely related problems. First, there is a creation problem: how can one divine person produce another without creating him? Second, there is a subordination problem: how can one divine person produce another without ending up with an inferior deity?

quousque possint fieri substantiae intelligibiles divisibiles multae numero propter multitudinem [recipientium] causarum, et usque huc perveniunt."

Consider the following. One would think, first of all, that since the Son and Spirit are spiritual, they cannot be made from any materials whatsoever:

(T5) For any divine persons x and y,
   if x produces y,
   x cannot produce y with any materials m.

But Aristotle claims that the only way to produce something is to do it with materials, and if that were true, then the Father would not be able to produce the Son at all:

(1) For any x and y,
   if x produces y,
   x cannot produce y without any materials m.
   [Aristotle's T2.]

(2) The Father cannot produce the Son
   with any materials m.
   [From T5.]

(3) Therefore, the Father cannot produce the Son.
   [From (1) and (2).]

Henry, Scotus, and Ockham obviously must reject this conclusion, for it contradicts their belief that the Father does, in fact, beget a Son.

In order to avoid this problem, one could follow Avicenna's lead and give up Aristotle's idea that the only way to produce something is to do it with materials. Of course, that is very easy for Henry, Scotus, and Ockham to do, for they accept the Christian doctrine that God creates the world *ex nihilo*, so they believe (like Avicenna and unlike Aristotle) that it is possible to produce something without materials.

Nevertheless, one could point out (just as Avicenna did) that if you produce something without materials, surely you create it from nothing, and that could easily be applied to the divine case as well:

(1*) For any x and y,
   if x produces y,
   x creates y from nothing iff
   x produces y without any materials m.
   [Avicenna's T3.]

(2) The Father cannot produce the Son
   with any materials m.
   [From T5.]

(3*) Therefore, if the Father produces the Son,
       the Father must create the Son from nothing.
       [From (1*) and (2).]

Henry, Scotus, and Ockham cannot accept this conclusion either, for as I said earlier, the Creeds say that the Father does not create the Son (and by extension, the Spirit is not created either). Instead then, Henry, Scotus, and Ockham must maintain that:

(T6) For any divine persons *x* and *y*,
       if *x* produces *y*,
       x does not create *y* from nothing.

Moreover, if the Son (for instance) were created, then one could argue that he would therefore be inferior to the Father:

(1**) For any *x* and *y*,
       if *x* produces *y*,
       y is inferior to *x* if
       x produces *y* without any materials *m*.
       [Avicenna's T4.]

(2)   The Father cannot produce the Son
       with any materials *m*.
       [From T5.]

(3**) Therefore, if the Father produces the Son,
       the Son will be inferior to the Father.
       [From (1**) and (2).]

But Henry, Scotus, and Ockham cannot accept this conclusion any more than the others, for the Creeds say the Son is equal to the Father (and the same goes for the Spirit). Hence, these authors must alternatively maintain that all the divine persons are equal:

(T7) For any divine persons *x* and *y*,
       if *x* produces *y*,
       x and *y* are equal in perfection.

Henry, Scotus, and Ockham thus need to find a way to explain how the Son and Spirit can be produced without being created as lesser deities.

1.4. POINTS OF AGREEMENT

When Henry, Scotus, and Ockham try to solve the creation and subordination problems I discussed in the last section, there are certain points they agree upon, and which they take as given. In a sense, these points set the theological boundaries for any scholastic debate about the Trinity at the time, and indeed, they had already been canonized by the Fourth Lateran Council of 1215.

First of all, Henry, Scotus, and Ockham agree that the divine persons share a constituent, which they typically refer to as the "divine essence." Now, to call this an "essence" might be misleading to our modern ears, because today we often think about essences in the abstract (e.g. as the list of features that make something what it is). But in this context, the divine essence is not abstract in this way. On the contrary, it is a concrete *thing*, i.e. a real constituent that exists in each divine person.

Further, the divine essence is the most perfect and most potent entity in the universe—so much so, in fact, that it makes the persons all-powerful, all-knowing, and so on. As a loose analogy, we might think of it as an extraordinary power pack that bestows super powers on its possessors (which, in this case, are the divine persons).

That being said, the divine essence is not partitioned or multiplied in the persons. That is, it is not divided up amongst the persons, as if each person had their own portion of it, nor is it replicated in each person, as if there were three discrete instances of it. Rather, the whole of this one divine-essence-thing exists in each and every divine person, and it is numerically the same in all of them.[26] Thus:

(T8) For any divine persons x and y,
  (i) the divine essence D_1 is a constituent of x,
  (ii) the divine essence D_2 is a constituent of y, and
  (iii) D_1 and D_2 are numerically identical.

---

[26] Lateran IV, n. 2 (Tanner, *Decrees*, 1: 232.17–25): "Pater enim ab aeterno Filium generando, suam substantiam ei dedit . . . ac dici non potest, quod partem suae substantiae illi dederit et partem retinuerit ipse sibi . . . sed nec dici potest, quod Pater in Filium transtulerit suam substantiam generando, quasi sic dederit eam Filio, quod non retinuerit ipsam sibi . . . Patet ergo, quod sine ulla diminutione Filius nascendo substantiam Patris accepit, et ita Pater et Filius habent eandem substantiam."

18

Introduction

Yet over and above the divine essence, the persons are related to each other in unique ways. To borrow some traditional Latin metaphors, the Father is said to "beget" the Son, whereas the Father and Son are said to "breathe" the Spirit.[27] On this particular configuration, there is something unique about each person: the Father is the only one of the three who "begets," the Son is the only one who is "begotten," and the Spirit is the only who is "breathed."[28]

Consequently, the Father has a unique paternal relationship with the Son, and this was known as his fatherhood (*paternitas*). Similarly, the Son has a unique filial relationship with the Father, and this was known as his sonship (*filiatio*). The Spirit's relationship with the Father and Son is harder to label, for neither Latin nor English has a good term for it. But we can follow the scholastics here in calling it "passive spiration" (*passiva spiratio*), for that just means "being breathed."

Medieval theologians call these unique divine relationships the "personal properties" of the persons. The Latin word for "property" (*proprietas*) can either refer to a particular characteristic of something, or it can refer to someone's private property, just as it does in modern-day English. Both meanings apply nicely to the divine case: a personal property is something that belongs only to one divine person, and to nobody else.[29]

All in all then, each divine person includes two constituents: (i) the shared divine essence, and (ii) a unique personal property. Of these,

---

[27] Or, as Lateran IV puts it, n. 1 (Tanner, *Decrees*, 1: 230.5–8): "Pater a nullo, Filius autem a solo Patre ac Spiritus sanctus ab utroque pariter . . . Pater generans, Filius nascens et Spiritus sanctus procedens."

[28] Note that there is not a distinct "breather" here, for that is something the Father and Son do together.

[29] Here I am characterizing the personal properties as relationships, and indeed, that was one traditional scholastic view. However, there was some debate about what these personal properties actually are. Scotus and Ockham, for instance, famously consider the view that the personal properties might be absolute (non-relational) constituents rather than relationships. For more on this, see Schmaus, *Der Liber Propugnatorius*, 482–550; Wetter, *Die Trinitätslehre*, 283–342; Marilyn McCord Adams, "The Metaphysics of the Trinity," *Franciscan Studies* 66 (2008): 112–40; Richard Cross, *Duns Scotus on God*, 195–202; and Richard Cross, *Duns Scotus* (Oxford: Oxford University Press, 1999), 65–7. For the relevant texts in Scotus and Ockham, see book 1, distinction 26, of their respective *Ordinationes*. Nevertheless, when it comes to the issues I examine in this book, Scotus and Ockham assume that the personal properties are relationships just as I have characterized them here, so I will follow suit throughout.

the divine essence makes each person divine, while their personal properties make them the unique persons that they are by distinguishing them from the other persons.[30] For instance, the Father is divine because of the divine essence, but he is the Father because of his unique fatherhood. Similarly, the Son is also divine because of the divine essence, but he is the Son because of his unique sonship. In general then:

(T9) For any divine person x,
    x is constituted by
    (i) the divine essence D, and
    (ii) a unique personal property F.

Nevertheless, the personal properties are not like entirely distinct extra parts that are stuck onto the divine essence. Likewise, the persons are not like larger objects that are made up of all those extra parts. On the contrary, Henry, Scotus, and Ockham believe that everything in the Godhead is, to use their terminology, *really the same* as the divine essence itself.[31]

To use a spatial analogy, we might think of the divine essence as if it "overlaps" everything in the Godhead. That is, the divine essence does not occupy a mere portion of the Father, Son, and Spirit. Rather, it occupies the whole of them, and that includes their personal properties. So each divine person is "filled to the brim," as it were, with the very same divine essence, so much so that everything in them can be said to be really the same as the divine essence itself. Hence:

(T10) For any divine person x and any personal property F,
    (i) x is really the same as the divine essence D, and
    (ii) F is really the same as D.

---

[30] Lateran IV, n. 1 (Tanner, *Decrees*, 1: 230.15–17): "Haec sancta Trinitas secundum communem essentiam [est] individua et secundum personales proprietates [est] discreta."

[31] Lateran IV, n. 2 (Tanner, *Decrees*, 1: 232.4–10): "Nos autem ... credimus ... quod una quaedam summa res est [viz., essentia divina] ... quae veraciter est Pater et Filius et Spiritus sanctus, tres simul personae ac sigillatim quaelibet earundem, et ideo in Deo Trinitas est solummodo non quaternitas, quia quaelibet trium personarum est illa res, videlicet substantia, essentia sive natura divina."

Of course, one might wonder about this. How could the divine
persons in any sense be the same as the divine essence, but yet also
be distinct from each other? Or, to put it more generally, how could
any one thing (e.g. the divine essence) be really the same as three
distinct things (e.g. the divine persons)? And indeed, this is one of the
perennial difficulties for Trinitarian theology in general.[32] In the
context of this study though, it would take us too far afield to get
into the various ways that medieval theologians tried to solve this
particular difficulty. For our purposes here, the point to note is just
that everything in the Godhead is, at least in some sense, supposed to
be really the same as the divine essence.

Finally, scholastic thinkers like Henry, Scotus, and Ockham agree
that the divine essence is not produced, and it does not do any
producing. This is not to say that the divine essence plays no role in
divine production (as we shall see in Part II of this book), but it is to
say that the divine essence does not play the role of the producer or
the product. On the contrary, it is the *persons* who produce each
other.[33] Thus:

(T11) For any divine person *x*,
     (i) the divine essence *D* does not produce *x*, and
     (ii) *x* does not produce *D*.

As I mentioned already, these points are common ground for
Henry, Scotus, and Ockham. Whatever else these scholastic theologians might want to say about divine production, they take these
points as given (and, in fact, they take them to be points of
canonized doctrine that are demanded by the Fourth Lateran
Council). So, in a manner of speaking, these are the boundaries
of the playing field.

---

[32] Or, as Ockham nicely puts it when he asks how there could be one God when
there are also three divine persons, *Ordinatio*, 1.2.10 (*OTh* 2: 359.12–16): "Difficultas
istius quaestionis oritur ex identitate divinae essentiae cum relatione [e.g., paternitate
vel filiatione] et cum persona, quia si essentia et relatio et persona sint simpliciter una
res numero indistincta, difficile est videre quomodo sunt plures relationes et plures
personae et non plures essentiae."

[33] Lateran IV, n. 2 (Tanner, *Decrees*, 1: 232.11–13): "[essentia divina] non est
generans neque genita nec procedens, sed est Pater qui generat, Filius qui gignitur
et Spiritus sanctus qui procedit."

1.5. CONCLUSION

Henry, Scotus, and Ockham each want to explain how the Son and Spirit can be produced without being created as lesser deities, given the above mentioned points of agreement. In the rest of this book, I will examine how each of these authors attempt to do that in detail.

For conceptual clarity, I have divided this study into two parts. In the first part, I consider how a divine person is supposed to be *produced*. What are the ingredients, as it were, that go into a produced person? Are there any materials, or at least something that plays the role of materials? If not, what other sorts of ingredients are there, if any?

In the second part, I consider how a divine person is supposed to be a *producer*. When one divine person produces another, do any of the producing-person's ingredients play some role in the process? If so, what exactly is their function? And how do the answers to any of these questions solve (or fail to solve) the creation and subordination problems I discussed above?

As we shall see, Henry, Scotus, and Ockham subject all of these questions to detailed philosophical analysis, and they offer creative solutions that are worthy of careful study by any philosopher, theologian, or historian who concerns themselves with the scholastic tradition of philosophical theology.

Part I

How a Divine Person is Produced

2

Change and Production

When Henry, Scotus, and Ockham focus their attention on explaining how a divine person is produced, they look to the best theories of production that were available at the time. Since Aristotle offered one of the most comprehensive of such theories, Henry, Scotus, and Ockham naturally turn there for inspiration. In this chapter, I want to briefly outline the Aristotelian theory of production with which these authors work. In the rest of Part I, we will see how they do (and do not) apply this model to the production of a divine person.

2.1. AN ARISTOTELIAN MODEL OF CHANGE

Medieval Aristotelians believe that earth, air, fire, and water are the most elemental kinds of material substances that occur in and upon our planet. After all, more complex substances like metals or living organisms eventually decay into the four elements, whereas the four elements do not appear to decay into further, even simpler kinds of substances (or so it might seem to someone who lived before the days of microscopes).

Yet despite the fact that the elements cannot decay into simpler kinds of substances, it would appear to be a naturally occurring fact that they can be transformed into *one another*. For instance, when fire heats water, it causes the water to evaporate, at which point the water is transformed into air. The question, then, is this: how exactly does this sort of transformation happen?

According to Aristotle, such transformations occur analogous to the way that lumps of clay are transformed into statues. A lump of clay becomes a statue when it loses its lump form and acquires a statue form. Similarly, water becomes air when its constituent material loses the form of water and takes on the form of air. Thus, elemental transformations involve some constituent matter acquiring a new elemental form.

Aristotle also models more complex transformations on the same pattern, but with the elements serving as the materials for further substances. Thus, when the elements are mixed together in various ways, they can take the form of (say) clay, bronze, or even organic tissue. Organic tissue, in turn, can take the form of an organic body, and organic bodies can take the form of various kinds of living organisms.

So on this Aristotelian theory, any material substance is a lump of some kind of constituent material that exists under the form of that particular kind of substance, where the material is called its "matter," and the form is called its "substantial form." Material substances are thus composed of (i) matter and (ii) at least one substantial form. Further, a lump of matter is transformed from one kind of substance into another when it ceases to have one substantial form and comes to have another substantial form.

Aristotle even thinks sexual reproduction works this way. As he sees it, when living organisms reproduce, the father's seed causes the material in the mother's menses to take the form of an embryo or fetus, and that can eventually develop into a full-grown adult. Thus, by Aristotle's reckoning, even living organisms come to exist when a lump of material acquires a substantial form.

Note that on this theory, individual substantial forms determine the *identity* of material substances. That is, a material substance is the particular substance that it is so long as it has its individual substantial form. Hence, a material substance begins to exist when a lump of material acquires its particular (substantial) form, and it ceases to exist when its material loses that form.

However, once a material substance does exist, and up until the time that it perishes, it can undergo further changes that do not affect its identity. Indeed, we know from experience that material substances gain and lose various features throughout their lives, without ceasing to be who or what they are.

For instance, Socrates can go to the beach and get a tan, but he is still Socrates when he gets that tan, and he is still Socrates when he later loses his tan. Similarly, Socrates can grow upwards and outwards, but again, he is still Socrates when he grows to a certain height or develops a certain girth.

Medieval Aristotelians consider these sorts of changes to be incidental changes (or "accidental changes," as some put it) in the sense that they do not affect (and hence are incidental to) the identity of the substances that undergo them. Again, Socrates is still Socrates whether he gets a tan or not. By contrast, when a material substance is generated or perishes, that is a *substantial* change, for it involves a whole substance coming to exist or ceasing to exist.

Nevertheless, incidental changes follow the same pattern as substantial changes. A substantial change occurs when a lump of material *x* gains or loses a substantial form *F*, and an incidental change occurs when a material substance *x* gains or loses an incidental form *F*. Thus, be it a substantial change or an incidental change, the basic pattern is the same: change is the process whereby something *x* gains (and/or loses) a form *F*.

Aristotle also believes that change involves a passage from potentiality to actuality. For instance, when Socrates gets a tan, he goes from *potentially* being tanned to *actually* being tanned. Similarly, sculptors transform lumps of clay from *potential* statues into *actual* statues. So change begins with a potential state of affairs, and it ends with an actual state of affairs.

This is an important point, because part of what it means for a recipient to be in a state of potentiality is this: it has the *capacity* to be changed in a certain way. And indeed, not every recipient can be changed in just any way whatever (spirits, for example, cannot get tans). A change requires the right kind of recipient, namely one that has the real capacity to receive the relevant sort of form.

2.2. CATEGORIZING CHANGES

Aristotle identifies four different types of change, but we will only be concerned with three of them. First, there is substantial change, i.e. the kind of change that occurs when a substance comes to exist, and as we have seen, this occurs when a recipient acquires a new substantial form. Second, there is quantitative change, i.e. growing or shrinking, and this occurs when a recipient acquires a new size. Third, there is qualitative change, i.e. a change in something's qualities, and this occurs when a recipient acquires a new quality such as a new color or temperature. (The fourth kind of change is locomotion, i.e. change in place, but as I said, we can ignore that here.)

Notice that these three types of change follow the same basic pattern discussed above—a capable recipient x acquires a new form F. However, these three types of change can be distinguished and classified by the type of "form" that the recipient acquires. In substantial changes F is a substantial form, in quantitative changes F is a new size, and in qualitative changes F is a new quality.

Medieval Aristotelians also discuss another, secondary type of change, and that is a change in something's relationships. For instance, if I were to paint one of my kitchen chairs white, that would make it similar (in color) to my white kitchen walls. This would involve a change in the chair's relationship with the walls, for the chair would go from not being similar to being similar (in color) to the walls.

Now, I say that changes in relationships are a secondary type of change because medieval Aristotelians believe they typically presuppose a change in something's substance, size, or qualities. In the case of my freshly painted kitchen chair, its new found similarity (in color) with the walls presupposes a change in its own qualities (it's become white). Nevertheless, changes in relationships still follow a pattern similar to that of other changes. For whereas other changes occur when a recipient x acquires a new form F, a change in relationship can similarly be said to occur when a recipient x acquires a new relationship R.

2.3. PRODUCTION

As Henry, Scotus, and Ockham see it, production involves bringing something into existence. However, the notion of production as "bringing something into existence" needs to be qualified in three important ways. First, I should stipulate that for our purposes here, production does not extend beyond the immediate product and its constituents, for although countless things may be a consequence of any one thing being produced, this should not be taken to imply that the producer of that one thing produced all those other things too.

(Hitler's parents did not produce the Holocaust; they only produced Hitler.)

Second, production does not extend to things whose constituents are united in merely trivial ways. Any number of items can be heaped together arbitrarily, but in this context, the immediate product of a production must be something whose constituents are bound together more tightly than that, i.e. in such a way that they constitute not an arbitrary heap, but rather some sort of integrated and internally unified entity. Hence, my parents did not produce the aggregate of me and this desk where I am now sitting. Rather, they just produced me.

Third and finally, in this context, production does not necessarily imply any reference to time. Of course, many productions do occur at particular points in time, and many productions involve the passage of time, but Henry, Scotus, and Ockham do not think that all productions happen in time, or that all productions involve the passage of time. Indeed, as I pointed out in the Introduction, divine production is supposed to be entirely eternal. So for our purposes here, we should think of production in a sense that is neutral to any temporal reference.

Nevertheless, even when production is understood with these qualifications, it is still a very broad notion that encompasses a variety of cases. For instance, medieval Christians believe that God creates the world out of nothing, and that counts as a production insofar as God thereby brings the world into existence. Similarly, medieval Aristotelians hold (as we have seen) that terrestrial substances generate other terrestrial substances through substantial change, and that counts as production too, for on the Aristotelian theory, that is how terrestrial substances typically come into existence.

Still, one might wonder about the forms that the recipients of Aristotelian change acquire: are *they* produced? As an analogy, consider a sculptor who makes a bronze statue. Even though the statue comes to exist through this process, doesn't the statue's *shape* come to exist through this process as well? Likewise for substantial change: doesn't the substantial form of the new substance get produced as a part, so to speak, of the new substance too?

Henry, Scotus, and Ockham debate this. As they put it, in what sense is the form of the product a *terminus* of that product's production? Like the English word, the Latin word *terminus* can refer to the end point or extremity of something. For instance, the termini of any given processes are the start and end points of those processes, just as the termini of any given relationship are the things that are related by that relationship. Similarly then, the termini of any given production would stand at either side of that production, i.e. on the side of that which produces, and on the side of that which is produced.

So when Henry, Scotus, and Ockham wonder about the sense in which the form of a product is a *terminus* of that product's production, the question is: in what sense does the form of that product stand on the produced side of that production? Is the form produced separately and then somehow attached to the product, or does the form come to exist some other way? Does the form play any special role in the product's production, and if so, which role in particular? As we shall see, Henry, Scotus, and Ockham give different answers to these questions, and those answers have important ramifications for their respective claims about divine production as well.

2.4. DIVINE PRODUCTION

With all of that said, let me turn to the question that will occupy us throughout the rest of Part I, namely: what is involved when a divine person is *produced* by another divine person? According to the Aristotelian model I discussed in this chapter, substances come to be when a lump of some kind of material acquires a substantial form. But how does this apply to divine production? What, if anything, plays the role of the materials, and what, if anything, plays the role of the form? If nothing plays the role of matter and form in the Godhead, then how exactly does divine production happen? And how does any of this help solve the creation and subordination problems I discussed in section 1.3? In the following chapters, we will see how Henry, Scotus, and Ockham each attempt to answer these questions.

3

Henry of Ghent

In this chapter, I want to look at the way that Henry of Ghent answers the following question: how exactly is a divine person produced? Henry's answer to this question is quite striking, and as we shall see in the following chapters, it provokes a vigorous reaction from Scotus and Ockham.

3.1. SOLVING THE CREATION PROBLEM

As I explained in section 1.3, one of the problems that Henry is trying to solve is a creation problem: how does one divine person produce another without creating him? After all, it seems very plausible to assume that since the divine persons are immaterial, they cannot be produced with any materials:

(T5) For any divine persons x and y,
     if x produces y,
     x cannot produce y with any materials m.

But if a product were produced without any materials, then surely it would be created from nothing (*ex nihilo*):

(T3) For any x and y,
     if x produces y,
     x creates y from nothing iff
     x produces y without any materials m.

Therefore, if the Son (for instance) were produced without materials, he would be created, and that contradicts the Nicene Creed's claim that the Son is not created:

(T6) For any divine persons x and y,
      if x produces y,
      x does not create y from nothing.

In order to explain how a divine person can be produced without being created, Henry will have to reject one of the above three claims. Of course, he is not going to reject the last one, for that comes straight out of the Nicene Creed, so he will have to reject one of the first two. But which one?

Henry discloses his answer in his critique of Peter Lombard (d. 1160) on this very issue. In his *Sentences*, Peter asks whether the Son is produced from nothing, and he of course says no. According to Peter, the Son is not produced from nothing, he is produced from something. As the Nicene Creed puts it, "the Son is begotten from the substance of the Father."[1]

But what does it mean to say that the Son is produced from the Father's *substance*? As Peter sees it, this does not mean that the Son is *made* from the Father's substance, as if that "substance" were some sort of material stuff out of which the Father could fashion the Son.[2] On the contrary, Peter maintains that to say the Son is produced from the Father's substance just means that the Son is produced *by* the Father, who *is* a substance.[3]

As far as Henry is concerned, Peter has not said enough to show that the Son is uncreated. After all, creatures are produced by a substance too (God), but creatures are still created *ex nihilo*. So, thinks Henry, if we only say that the Son is produced by a "substance," then we still leave open the possibility that the Son could be created as well.

The only way to show that the Son is uncreated, argues Henry, is to show that the Son is produced from some sort of materials (or at least something that plays the role of such materials).[4] Otherwise the Son

---

[1] Tanner, *Decrees*, 1: 5/*5.

[2] Lombard, *Sent.*, 1.5.2 (1: 110): "Filium et Spiritum Sanctum non esse de nihilo, sed de aliquo, nec tamen de aliqua materia."

[3] Lombard, *Sent.*, 1.5.2 (ibid.): "«Filius substantiae Patris», id est Filius Patris substantiae, id est, qui est substantia."

[4] Henry of Ghent, *SQO*, 59.2 (*Bad.* II f. 144vT): "Unde cum Magister Sententiarum exponit eam [viz. 'Pater generat Filium de sua substantia'] sic, id est de se qui est substantia, quaero ab eo an ly 'de' significat circumstantiam quasi materiae, an principii activi. Si principii [activi], tunc aequivoce exponit, quia ly 'de sua substantia'

would be produced without any ingredients whatsoever, in which case he would quite literally be made "from nothing."

For Henry then, T3 is true (even for the Godhead), and T5 is false. Still, T5 is extremely plausible. Indeed, how could anything immaterial (like the divine persons) possibly be produced with "materials" of any description? Henry recognizes that he must explain how anything in God could be (or at least be like) materials. In the next section, I will look at Henry's attempt to do just that.

3.2. DIVINE BEGETTING AND TERRESTRIAL BEGETTING

As I have noted already, the Nicene Creed says that "the Son is begotten from the substance of the Father." Now, for an Aristotelian theologian (like Henry), this easily could have brought Aristotle's theory of substantial change to mind, for the word "begotten" is the very word that Aristotle used to describe the process by which living organisms and other terrestrial substances are produced—namely, the process whereby a lump of matter acquires a substantial form.

Perhaps it is not surprising then to find Henry insisting that divine production is analogous to this Aristotelian kind of terrestrial begetting. More precisely, Henry insists that just as terrestrial begetting involves a lump of matter, a substantial form, and a substance composed of both, divine production similarly involves the divine essence, a personal property, and a person constituted by both:

> In the case of natural [i.e. terrestrial] production, there are [certain] things that we can use for our purposes concerning divine production.

---

non notat ibi nisi circumstantiam quasi materiae. Cum enim haeretici quaerebant si Pater generat Filium, aut ergo de aliquo aut de nihilo, aut de substantia sua aut de aliena, non erat eorum intentio quaerere nisi secundum quod ly 'de' notat circumstantiam quasi causae materialis." Scotus summarizes Henry's position nicely in *Ordinatio* 1.5.2.un., n. 54 (*Vat.* 4: 42.6–13): "Et si respondeatur sicut Magister videtur respondere in littera, quod est de substantia Patris, id est de Patre, qui est substantia,—arguitur quod ista expositio non sit sufficiens, quia tantum exponit 'de' ut notet rationem principii originantis vel efficientis; et posito quod hoc modo sit de Patre, adhuc restat quaestio utrum de aliquo vel de nihilo sicut de materia vel de quasi-materia, et cum non de nihilo sit (quia hoc modo creatura est de nihilo), ergo de aliquo, et stat argumentum."

> In [terrestrial] production, there are three different things to consider...
> namely [i] the matter... [ii] the form... and [iii] the composite consti-
> tuted from both...In divine production, there are three things that...
> correspond [to these three], namely [i] the divine essence, [ii] a personal
> property, and [iii] the...person who contains both in himself.[5]

So, for instance, when the Father produces the Son, the divine essence
plays the role of a lump of matter, sonship plays the role of a
substantial form, and the Son is thereby like a begotten substance
constituted by both (and a similar account can be given for the Spirit's
production). Hence, on Henry's view:

(T12) For any divine persons x and y,
      if x produces y by a production P,
      the divine essence D in y
      is (like) a lump of matter m.

(T13) For any divine persons x and y,
      if x produces y by a production P,
      the personal property F in y
      is (like) a substantial form F.

(T14) For any divine persons x and y,
      if x produces y by a production P,
      y is (like) a composite substance
      composed of a lump of matter m
      and a substantial form F.

However, in order to map terrestrial begetting onto divine production
in this way, Henry knows that he needs to provide some mapping
rules. That is, he needs to explain the precise sense in which the divine
essence plays the role of matter, as well as the precise sense in which a
personal property plays the role of a form.

To do that, Henry focuses on the fact that when one living organism begets another, the lump of matter in the offspring is not

---

[5] Henry, *SQO*, 54.3 (*Bad.* II f. 84rE): "Est ergo sciendum quod in exemplo
productionis naturalis est invenire ea quibus uti possumus ad intentum nostrum
circa productionem divinam. Est enim in productione considerare tria...scilicet,
subiectam materiam...et ipsam formam...et compositum constitutum in esse ex
utroque...est invenire tria correspondentia...in productione divina, videlicet ipsam
divinam essentiam et proprietatem personalem, et ipsum...personam ambo illorum
in se continentem."

produced (it exists already).[6] The form, on the other hand, comes to exist along with the offspring. As an analogy, consider how sculptors make clay statues. A sculptor does not produce the lump of clay in her statue, but she does cause its shape to come to exist as she fashions her clay into the statue.

An important distinction is at play just underneath the surface of this analogy: some constituents (typically forms) are produced in products, but others (typically matter) are not. For convenience, let me call the former "produced constituents" and the latter "unproduced constituents." An unproduced constituent is any constituent of a product that is not produced by the production that brings the product itself into existence (though the constituent in question may have been produced by some other production). For example, the clay in a statue, the bricks in a wall, the flour and eggs in a cake, or any other constituent of a product that is not produced by the production that brings the product it belongs to into existence—all of these are unproduced constituents of their respective products.

Of course, an unproduced constituent comes to reside *in* the product through that product's production.[7] To use our statue analogy again, even though a sculptor may not cause the clay in her statue to exist, she certainly causes it to reside in her statue in the sense that, by making her statue from this particular lump of clay, she causes that clay to become a constituent *of* her statue. After all, if she had decided to make her statue with something else, that lump of clay would still be sitting in her studio unused, and it would not be part of her statue.

Yet even though the clay becomes a constituent of the statue, the point is that it is not produced by the production that brings the statue itself into existence. And for that reason, the clay is an unproduced constituent of the statue. Let me therefore define an "unproduced constituent" in the following way:

(T15) For any *x*, *y*, and *F*,
  F is an unproduced constituent of *y* =$_{df}$ iff
  (1) *x* produces *y* by a production *P*,

[6] Henry, *SQO*, 54.3 (*Bad.* II f. 84rE): "materia vero tanquam ingenita et incorruptibilis, in composito solum habet esse per generationem, nullo tunc modo generatur in ipso, nisi largissime loquendo de generatione."
[7] Henry, *SQO*, 54.3 (*Bad.* II f. 84rE): "quicquid est in ipso [viz. producto] etiam habet esse in ipso per actum productionis."

> (ii) F is a constituent of y, and
> (iii) x does not produce F by P.

A produced constituent, by contrast, is any constituent of a product that does come to exist precisely through that product being produced. The shape of a statue, the substantial form of a living organism, and other such things typically come to exist when something produces the products to which they belong. And indeed, they would not exist without the production in question. Hence:

> (T16) For any x, y, and F,
> F is a produced constituent of y $=_{df}$ iff
>   (i) x produces y by a production P,
>   (ii) F is a constituent of y, and
>   (iii) x produces F by P.

Of course, in typical cases of terrestrial begetting, the matter counts as an unproduced constituent of the product, whereas the form counts as a produced constituent of the product. After all, at the lowest level of decomposition, the matter of living organisms does not come to exist through the process by which those organisms are begotten, but their forms do.

Henry then points out that something similar happens in divine production. As I explained in section 1.4, Henry accepts the common view of his time that each divine person includes two constituents, namely the divine essence and a unique personal property such as fatherhood or sonship. Consequently, when the Father begets the Son, he produces something that has two constituents (the divine essence and sonship), much like how living organisms produce offspring that also have two constituents (matter and form).[8]

Further, the Son has one produced constituent and one unproduced constituent, just as living organisms do. Consider sonship first. This comes to exist through the Son's production, and it does not exist on account of any other production. It is not as if the Father produces sonship by another productive act and then attaches it to the Son. On the contrary, sonship comes to exist solely through the

---

[8] Henry, *SQO*, 54.3 (*Bad.* II f. 84rE): "consimiliter in productione divina quisquis est productus in Deo habet esse suum per actum productionis, et etiam quicquid est in ipso."

Son himself being produced.[9] For this reason, Henry thinks we can say (at least in some sense) that sonship is "produced" through the Son's production.[10] Hence, it counts as a produced constituent of the Son (and the same would apply to the Spirit's personal property too):

(T17) For any divine persons x and y,
      if x produces y by a production P,
      the personal property F in y
      is a produced constituent of y.

Now consider the divine essence. Unlike sonship, the divine essence does not come to exist through the Son's production. As I explained in section 1.4, Henry and his contemporaries believe that the divine essence is not produced:

(T11) For any divine person x,
      (i) the divine essence D does not produce x, and
      (ii) x does not produce D.

Consequently, when the Father produces the Son, he cannot *produce* the divine essence; he can only *share* it with the Son. Thus, the divine essence counts as an unproduced constituent of the Son, much like how the basic matter in a living organism counts as an unproduced constituent of that organism:[11]

(T18) For any divine persons x and y,
      if x produces y by a production P,
      the divine essence D in y
      is an unproduced constituent of y.

---

[9] Henry, *SQO*, 54.3 (*Bad.* II f. 84rE): "quoniam proprietas [sicut filiatio] non solum habet esse in persona producta [sicut Filio] per ipsam productionem, sed etiam simpliciter habet esse per illam [productione], quia in illa [viz. Filio] habet esse absque [aliqua alia] productione."

[10] Henry, *SQO*, 54.3 (*Bad.* II f. 84rE): "Propter quod forte aliquo modo posset proprie vel saltem magis proprie quam de essentia, aut minus improprie dici quod proprietas [sicut filiatio] producatur in persona producta [sicut Filio], ut quod filiatio generetur non simpliciter secundum se, sed tantum in Filio."

[11] Henry, *SQO*, 54.3 (*Bad.* II f. 84rE): "[divina] essentia vero per productionem habet esse in producto, sed non habet esse simpliciter per productionem, quia absque productione passive habet esse in producente... Nullo autem modo proprie dici posset quod essentia produceretur etiam in producto, ut quod deitas generaretur in Filio, sed solummodo quod haberetur in ipso per generationem, et ita quod proprie dicitur essentia communicari Filio per generationem."

Henry's mapping rules are therefore the following: the divine essence is like a lump of matter insofar as it is an unproduced constituent of the Son, sonship is like a form insofar as it is a produced constituent of the Son, and the Son himself is like a composite substance insofar as he is constituted from both. And the same mapping rules would apply to the Spirit as well.[12]

So according to Henry's model, a divine person is produced much like a living organism or other terrestrial substance: the Father, for instance, produces the Son by taking the divine essence and giving it the form of sonship. Of course, living organisms and other terrestrial substances are usually made from distinct lumps of matter, but since there is just one divine essence in God, it would seem Henry is proposing that we think of the divine persons as three substances who are simultaneously constituted from the very same lump of matter.[13] To use an analogy proposed by Augustine (which Henry does not, so far as I know, ever explicitly use), we might think of the divine persons as three gold statues all made of the same lump of gold at the same time, where the divine essence is like the gold, and the personal properties are like each statue's particular shape.[14]

---

[12] Henry, *SQO*, 54.3 (*Bad.* II f. 84rE): "Dicimus ergo quod quemadmodum in productione naturali materia est subiectum generationis, inquantum est in potentia ad formam et per hoc ad compositum generandum de ea; sic in productione divina, puta in generatione Filii, et consimiliter in spiratione Spiritus Sancti, ipsa divina essentia est quasi subiectum generationis, et ut aliquid in potentia, licet necessario semper coniuncta actui ad generandum de ea personam constitutam ex essentia [divina] et proprietate [e.g. filiatione]."

[13] Interestingly, Jeffrey Brower and Michael Rea have proposed a similar theory. See their "Material Constitution and the Trinity," *Faith and Philosophy* 22 (2005): 57–76. Cf. also Jeffrey Brower, "Abelard on The Trinity," in *The Cambridge Companion to Abelard*, ed. Jeffrey Brower and Kevin Guilfoy (Cambridge: Cambridge University Press, 2004), 223–57; and Michael Rea, "Sameness without Identity: An Aristotelian Solution to the Problem of Material Constitution," *Ratio* 11 (1998): 316–28. However, Brower and Rea base their theory on constitution relationships, whereas Henry bases his theory on production relationships.

[14] Augustine, *De Trinitate*, 7.6, n. 11 (*Corpus Christianorum Series Latina*, volume 50, ed. W. J. Mountain and F. Glorie (Turnhout: Brepols, 1968), 264.74–77): "Non itaque secundum genus et species ista dicimus sed quasi secundum communem eandemque materiem. Sicut ex eodem auro si fierent tres statuae, diceremus tres statuas unum aurum."

3.3. THE TERMINUS OF PRODUCTION

As I mentioned in section 2.3, another important question here is this: in what sense does the form of a product count as the *terminus* of that product's production? Now, it might be tempting to take the Aristotelian model of begetting (where substances are generated when a lump of matter acquires a new substantial form) and argue that, in order to beget a material substance, all a begetter needs to do is produce a substantial form. After all, the matter already exists, so only the form needs to be produced. Thus, one might be tempted to think that a begetter primarily produces the form, whereas the whole composite ends up getting produced secondarily—as a by-product, so to speak, of producing that form in the lump of matter.

According to Henry though, it is the other way around. At one point in the *Metaphysics*, Aristotle claims that it is not forms that are produced, but rather the concrete things that possess those forms.[15] And taking this as his inspiration, Henry echoes Aristotle's language by saying that when one living organism or other terrestrial substance begets another, the whole offspring is produced in a primary sense, while its substantial form is produced only in a secondary sense.[16]

This means, I take it, that living organisms and other terrestrial substances do not primarily beget forms. Rather, they beget whole organisms or substances. Of course, the forms come to exist in those organisms and substances too, but only as a part of the productive process. By analogy, when a sculptor makes a statue out of clay, it is not as if she first produces the shape and then attaches it to the clay. On the contrary, she simply makes the statue, and the shape comes to exist as part of that process.

For Henry then, the whole product is the terminus of production in a primary sense, whereas that product's form can be considered as a terminus of production only in a secondary or derivative sense. For clarification of this idea, we might look to Henry's later *Quodlibet*

---

[15] Aristotle, *Metaphysics*, 7.8, 1033b16–18 (*AL* 25, 3.2: 146.393–395; cf. *AL* 25.2: 136.11–13; *Iunt.*, 8: 176vH): "Palam igitur ex dictis quia quod quidem ut species aut ut substantia [viz. forma] dicitur non fit, synodus autem secundum hanc dicta fit."

[16] Henry, *SQO*, 54.3 (*Bad.* II f. 84rE): "ita quod secundum determinationem Philosophi VII *Metaphysicae* [1033b16–18], compositum generatur per se et primo, secundo vero forma [generatur] in composito."

15.7, for there he makes this point more perspicuously.[17] In that context, Henry considers the view that living organisms beget their offspring by doing nothing more than generating the form:

> A fifth [view about begetting] comes from those who propose [that begetters are mere] givers of forms, so that begetting is the production of a form not *from* matter, but only *in* matter, as if begetting were nothing other than the creation of a form in matter.[18]

Henry goes on to reject this view. Strictly speaking, he says, it is not *forms* that are begettable and perishable. Rather, it is *whole substances* that are begettable and perishable. Thus, producers do not generate forms alone, nor do they generate any part of a form (not even an embryonic "seed," so to speak, that might grow into a form). Rather, material substances beget whole substances, and their forms only come to exist as part of that process:

> A sixth [view about begetting] comes from those who propose that in begettable and perishable things, there is nothing of the form, nor any 'seeds' [of forms], nor any form at all, that is begettable and perishable. So begetting is not of a form by itself (just as it is not of matter) but rather only of the composite of matter and form ... just as the Aristotelians proposed, and their position, I believe, encapsulates the true method of natural begetting.[19]

All of this makes it clear that on Henry's view, the whole product of a production qualifies as the terminus of that production in the most primary sense because it comes to exist through that production, and it is that which the producer produces but which is not itself a

---

[17] For the dating of Henry's works, see José Gómez Caffarena, "Cronología de la *Suma* de Enrique de Gante por relación a sus *Quodlibetos*," *Gregorianum* 38 (1957): 116–33; and ibid., *Ser participado y ser subsistente en la metafísica de Enrique de Gante* (Roma: Pontificia Università Gregoriana (Analecta Gregoriana, 93), 1958), 270.

[18] Henry, *Quod.*, 15.7 (*Opera*, 20: 39.93–95): "Quintus [positio circa generatione] est ponentium datores formarum et generationem esse, non productionem formae de materia, sed in materia tantum, quasi generatio non esset aliud quam creatio formae in materia" (the emphases in the translation are mine).

[19] Henry, *Quod.*, 15.7 (*Opera*, 20: 39.99–114): "Sextus [positio circa generatione] est ponentium quod nihil formae aut seminarium eius nec omnino forma aliqua in generabilis et corruptibilibus quin sit generabile et corruptibile, et quod generatio non est per se formae sicut nec materiae, sed solius compositi ex materia et forma ... prout posuerunt peripatetici, quorum positionem puto continere verum modum generationis naturalis."

constituent of some further composite that is produced through that same production:

(T19) For any x and y,
     y is the terminus of a production P
     in a primary sense $=_{df}$ iff
     (i) x produces y by P, and
     (ii) y is not a constituent F
     of some z that x produces by P.

The form of the product, on the other hand, qualifies as the terminus of its product's production only in a secondary or derivative sense because it comes to exist *in* the product as part of the process whereby that product is produced, and according to T16 above, that is just what a produced constituent is. So:

(T20) For any x, y, and F,
     F is a terminus of a production P
     in a secondary sense $=_{df}$ iff
     (i) x produces y by P, and
     (ii) F is a produced constituent of y.

We can easily apply this to divine production as well: when one divine person produces another, Henry would say that the produced person is the terminus of that production in a primary sense, while the personal property is a terminus of that same production only in a secondary sense.[20] For instance, when the Father produces the Son, the Father performs just one act of production, and the Son himself is the terminus of that production in the most primary sense. The Son's sonship is a terminus of that production only in a secondary or derivative sense because although it is produced in some sense, it only comes to exist as part of the process of producing the Son. Thus, Henry would affirm that

(T21) For any divine persons x and y,
     if x produces y by a production P,
     y is the terminus of P in a primary sense.

(T22) For any divine persons x and y,
     if x produces y by a production P,
     the personal property F in y
     is a terminus of P in a secondary sense.

---

[20] See notes 9–11 above.

The divine essence, of course, is not produced at all, so by Henry's analysis, it would not be the terminus of production in any sense, for it does not come to exist as the result of divine production any more than a lump of matter comes to exist as the result of begetting a living organism. Hence:

> (T23) For any divine persons x and y,
>   if x produces y by a production P,
>   the divine essence D is not the terminus of P in any sense.

3.4. DISANALOGIES

Henry knows his model is imperfect, and he is careful to note a few disanalogies. First, he points out that a lump of matter is not, in and of itself, a complete substance. We might think of the matter from which a terrestrial substance is made as being like the raw material from which a complex artifact is made. In its raw form, it is "incomplete" in the sense that the structure, functionality, and other such features that the finished product has are lacking. The divine essence, however, is nothing like raw materials, for it is the most complete and most perfect entity in the universe. So unlike terrestrial begetting, divine production does not begin with anything like raw materials. Rather, it begins with a complete substance, namely the divine essence itself.[21]

In this respect, Henry points out that divine production is more like a qualitative change, for in the case of a qualitative change, a complete substance simply acquires a new quality. For instance, when the sun gives Socrates a tan, the sun takes Socrates, who is a complete substance in and of himself, and then it gives him a new tan color. So also in divine production: when the Father begets the Son, he takes the divine essence, which is a complete substance already, and he gives it sonship.[22]

---

[21] Henry, *SQO*, 54.3 (*Bad.* II f. 85vG): "Differt igitur productio divina summe a productione qualibet alia, quia illa [viz. in productione qualibet alia] vadit per transmutationem ad perfectionem, et in ipsa distat potentia ab actu; in ista [viz. in productione divina] vero nequaquam, differt specialiter a productione naturali quae est generatio: quia illa est de imperfecto substantialiter, ista vero est de perfecta substantia."

[22] Henry, *SQO*, 54.3 (*Bad.* II f. 85vG): "In quo plus convenit cum productione quae est alteratio, quia in illa subiectum quod est in potentia, est aliquid exsistens in actu."

Still, Henry believes (like many other medieval thinkers) that qualities are discrete things that are distinct from the substances that gain and lose them. Hence, when Socrates gets a tan, one thing (Socrates) combines with another thing (a tan color), and the two are really distinct. In the Godhead, however, the divine essence is really the same as the Son and his sonship (see T10 in section 1.4). Thus, the Son's production is unlike a qualitative change insofar as the Son's constituents are not really distinct.[23]

Henry next toys with another model: perhaps the divine persons are more like species than living organisms.[24] As is well known, medieval Aristotelians believe that every species includes two constituents: a genus that it shares with every other species in the same genus, and a unique specific difference that distinguishes it from other species in the same genus. For example, the human species includes animality and rationality, for humans are animals just like other animals, but they are the only animals that are rational.

However, Henry does not think that animality and rationality are two distinct *things* which are stuck together to make up the human species. On the contrary, animality and rationality are just different aspects of the human species.[25] And in this respect, Henry thinks the Son is analogous to a species, for the divine essence and sonship are not distinct things, just as animality and rationality are not distinct things either.

Still, Henry points out that there are plenty of other ways the divine persons are *not* like species. Most importantly, Henry believes that animality is differentiated into various species, whereas the divine essence is not divided up amongst the divine persons in any way. On

---

[23] Henry, *SQO*, 54.3 (*Bad.* II f. 85vG): "sed differt in hoc, quod subiectum in alteratione est in potentia ad aliquid re absolutum differens ab ipso: in productione autem divina nequaquam."

[24] Henry, *SQO*, 54.3 (*Bad.* II f. 85vG): "in quo divina productio convenit plus cum productione speciei ex genere."

[25] Strictly speaking, Henry believes that the genus and specific difference in a species are "intentionally distinct," but this does not involve a distinction between *things*. For more on Henry's intentional distinction, see Raymond Macken, "Les diverses applications de la distinction intentionelle chez Henri de Gand," in *Sprache und Erkenntnis im Mittelalter*, ed. Jan Beckmann et al. (Berlin: de Gruyter (Miscellanea Mediaevalia, 13), 1981), 2: 769–76; and Roland Teske, "Distinctions in the Metaphysics of Henry of Ghent," *Traditio* 61 (2006): 227–45.

the contrary, the divine persons share the numerically same divine essence (see T8 in section 1.4).[26]

In the end then, Henry sticks with his model of terrestrial begetting. Because the divine essence is an unproduced constituent and sonship is a produced constituent in the Son, Henry thinks it is best to say the divine essence plays the role of matter, and sonship plays the role of a substantial form. Likewise, the same holds good for the Spirit. In short, Henry believes that terrestrial begetting is the best analogy we have for understanding the mechanism of divine production.

3.5. CONCLUSION

All of this gives Henry a convenient way to explain the meaning of the Nicene Creed's statement that "the Son is begotten from the substance of the Father." For Henry, the "substance" of the Father is the divine essence, and that is like a lump of matter that makes up the persons. Thus, to say that the Son is begotten from the substance of the Father just means that the Son is "made," as it were, from the same entity that the Father is, namely the divine essence.

Now, one might think that Henry's theory would have met with considerable resistance from his contemporaries. After all, this is the age of high scholasticism, where God's immateriality was practically dogma. How, then, could anyone in the late thirteenth century dare to suggest that the divine essence is like something material, even as an analogy?[27]

---

[26] Henry, *SQO*, 54.3 (*Bad.* II f. 85vG): "quia in hac productione genus quod est sicut subiectum et materia, est in potentia ad aliquid absolutum: ut ad differentiam, quae sola intentione differt ab ipso; hic [viz. in productione divina] autem subiectum est in potentia ad aliquid respectivum, quod differt ab ipso sola ratione. Et licet ista productio sit magis similis divinem quam alia, in multis tamen aliis differt: quia productio speciei ex genere per differentiam procedit de incompleto ad completum, assumendo complementi determinationem, ut secundum aliud et aliud re descendat in aliam et aliam speciem, et sit tantum unum commune secundum rationem."

[27] As Scotus puts it in *Ordinatio*, 1.5.2.un., n. 93 (*Vat.* 4: 60.9–13): "quia omnes a tempore Augustini usque ad istud non sunt ausi in divinis nominare materiam nec quasi-materiam, cum tamen omnes concorditer dicerent cum Augustino quod Filius generatur de substantia Patris."

Surprisingly though, Henry garnered a healthy group of followers from the next few generations of scholastic theologians. Thus, for whatever reasons, Henry's theory was seen (by some at least) to be not just acceptable, but also essentially correct.[28] Nevertheless, like any theory, Henry's view had its critics, and Scotus was one of the most outspoken. It is to his criticisms that I turn next.

---

[28] According to the editors of Ockham's *Opera Theologica* (see *Ord.*, 1.5.2 (*OTh* 3: 49, note 1), and the references there), the list of Henry's followers on this issue includes: Richard Connington, Robert Cowton, Durandus of St. Pourcain, and even William Alnwick, Scotus's great disciple. We should also add Scotus's own putative teacher to this list, namely William of Ware. For more on Scotus's debates with William of Ware and Richard Connington on this issue, see Stephen Dumont, "William of Ware, Richard of Connington, and the *Collationes Oxonienses* of John Duns Scotus," in *John Duns Scotus: Metaphysics and Ethics*, ed. Ludger Honnefelder, Rega Wood, and Mechthild Dreyer (Leiden: E. J. Brill, 1996), 59–85.

4

Scotus against Henry

Henry construes divine production on analogy with Aristotelian begetting, i.e. where a lump of matter acquires a substantial form—with the divine essence playing the role of the matter, and a personal property playing the role of the form. Scotus, however, entirely rejects this theory, and in this chapter, I want to look at the most important criticisms that Scotus levels against Henry's view.

4.1. THE TERMINUS OF CHANGE AND PRODUCTION

As I explained in section 3.3, Henry thinks that when one living organism begets another, the whole product is the terminus of that production in the most primary sense, whereas the product's form is the terminus of that same production only in a secondary or derivative sense, for it comes to exist in the product merely as a part of the productive process.

But Scotus points out that change and production are defined differently, strictly speaking. Production is defined as the process whereby something comes to exist, while change is defined as the process whereby a recipient gains a form it was initially deprived of. So the point of production is to produce a *product*, and the point of change is to *introduce a form* into a recipient.[1]

---

[1] Scotus, *Ordinatio* [= *Ord.*], 1.5.2.un., n. 95 (*Vat.* 4: 60.19–61.2): "Productio enim est formaliter ipsius producti, et accidit sibi quod fiat cum mutatione alicuius partis compositi, ut patet [viz. quod mutatio est per accidens in productione] in creatione; mutatio formaliter est actus 'mutabilis' qui de privatione transit."

Given that, Scotus infers that change and production must have different termini, formally speaking, for the terminus of production is a whole product, while the terminus of a change is a recipient having a new form. As he puts it in the *Lectura*:

> Change and production have formally distinct termini, for the terminus of change is the form introduced in the matter, but the proper terminus of production is the whole composite ... for [when it comes to change and production] there are formally distinct termini in [what we might broadly call] the 'generation' [i.e. the change or the production]: the proper termini of change are 'being deprived of a form' and 'having a form', but the terminus of a production is the whole composite itself.[2]

Further, terrestrial begetting is a type of change, for terrestrial begetting occurs when a lump of matter acquires a substantial form. Hence, terrestrial begetting has the termini that are proper to change, for first the lump of matter is deprived of the intended form, and then it actually possesses that form.

However, as I pointed out in section 2.1, individual substantial forms determine the *identity* of material substances in the sense that any given material substance exists only so long as it has its individual substantial form. Consequently, the termini of the change (i.e. being deprived of the form and having the form) also correspond to the non-existence and the existence of the begotten substance.

Thus, while change involves "being deprived of a form" and "having a form," and while production involves a whole product that comes to exist, terrestrial begetting involves both: it involves the non-existence and existence of the begotten substance, as well as "being deprived of" and "having a form." As Scotus puts it in the *Reportatio*:

> The difference between begetting, production, and change is clear, for change is an act [that happens to] something which is changeable by itself, so its termini are 'not [having] such [a form]' and '[having] such [a form]'. Whence, that which now exists in a different way than it did before is said to be changeable. But begetting is not an act [that happens

---

[2] Scotus, *Lectura* [= *Lect.*], 1.5.2.un., n. 91 (*Vat.* 16: 444.28–445.16): "Et ideo alios terminos habet formaliter mutatio et productio, nam terminus mutationis est ipsa forma inducta in materia, sed terminus proprius productionis est totum compositum ... quia [mutatio et generatio] habent terminos formaliter distinctos in generatione [id est, in mutatione et generatione], nam termini proprie mutationis sunt privatio et forma, sed terminus productionis est ipsum totum compositum."

to] something changeable; rather, it is, by itself, the way to [acquire] a [substantial] form, just as perishing [is the way to become] deprived [of a substantial form]. Thus, the termini [of begetting] are 'existing' and 'not existing', that is, [to have a substantial] form and [to be] deprived [of a substantial form]. Production, however, is not the way to exist or not to exist [in this manner], nor [the way] to acquire or be deprived of a form, but rather [the way] into what is generated or produced. So production has for its proper terminus not a form but rather the [whole] composite.[3]

Thus, in terrestrial begetting, change and production coincide. That is, terrestrial begetting involves a *change* because it results in a lump of matter acquiring a substantial form it was initially deprived of, and it involves a *production* because it results in a material substance coming to exist. Formally speaking then, there are *two* termini in any given terrestrial begetting: the terminus of the change (i.e. the form), and the terminus of the production (i.e. the whole substance).

Scotus is therefore sometimes willing to say, as Henry does, that the produced composite is the terminus of the production in a primary sense, while the acquired form is the terminus of the same production in a secondary sense.[4] But he points out that the form plays a special role here. For any given terrestrial begetting results in a particular kind of material substance, and the (substantial) form of that substance is what gives it its nature—that is, the form is what makes that substance the particular kind of substance that it is.

Consequently, Scotus thinks there is an important sense in which the acquired substantial form *terminates* the process of begetting, for terrestrial begetting is not complete until the receptive lump of matter

---

[3] Scotus, *Reportatio I–A* [= *Rep. I–A*], 1.5.2.un., n. 75 (Wolter, 279–80): "Quod autem sit differentia inter generationem, productionem et mutationem, patet; quia mutatio est actus per se mutabilis et termini sunt non tale et tale. Unde illud dicitur mutabile quod se habet aliter nunc quam prius. Generatio autem non est actus mutabilis, sed est per se via ad formam, sicut corruptio ad privationem, et ita termini eius sunt esse et non esse, id est forma et privatio. Productio autem est via non ad esse vel non esse sive ad formam et privationem, sed ad genitum vel productum, ita quod habet pro per se termino non formam sed compositum."

[4] That Scotus is willing to call the composite the terminus in a primary sense and the form the terminus in a secondary sense is evident from the following comment in *Rep. I–A*, 1.5.2.un., n. 39 (Wolter, 269): "Dicendum quod in producto est distinguere terminum primum, id est suppositum [viz. totum productum], et terminum secundum, id est formalem terminum productionis [viz. formam producti]."

acquires the intended substantial form. For this reason, Scotus prefers
to say that the substantial form is not the terminus in a secondary
sense, but rather that the form is the *formal terminus* of production.
As he puts it in the *Lectura*:

> I say that in creatures, there is something that is produced, and that is
> the terminus of that production in a primary sense—it is the whole
> composite that is primarily produced or begotten, just as [the Philoso-
> pher] proves in *Metaphysics* VII [1033b16–18]. Similarly, there is some-
> thing that is formally in the product which is produced, and this is the
> formal nature under which the production terminates. This is the
> formal terminus of that production, and it is the form of the product.
> So in one sense, the form truly terminates the production . . . the form
> truly is a terminus of that production, even though the composite itself
> is the terminus in a primary and adequate sense.[5]

Further, the formal terminus of terrestrial begetting is not merely
something incidental—it is not a mere side-effect, so to speak—to the
produced substance. For since the substantial form is the constituent
that makes the produced substance the particular kind of substance
that it is, that form cannot be incidental to it at all. On the contrary, it
is absolutely essential for the production of that sort of product. As
Scotus explains in the *Ordinatio*:

> I say that a production has the [whole] product for its terminus in a
> primary sense, and I call this primary terminus here an adequate
> terminus. In this way, the Philosopher says in *Metaphysics* VII
> [1033b16–18] that the [whole] composite is what is primarily begotten,
> for it is what primarily gets its existence from the production, and this is
> adequate [for there to be a production]. Nevertheless, the form in the
> composite is the formal terminus of that begetting, but this is not an
> incidental terminus, as is apparent from the Philosopher's comment in
> *Physics* II [193b12–18] where he proves that a form is a nature: 'beget-
> ting is natural because it is the way into a nature, but since it is the way

[5] Scotus, *Lect.*, 1.5.1.un., nn. 27–8 (*Vat.* 16: 420.8–22): "dico quod in creaturis est
aliquid quod producitur, quod est primus terminus productionis, —et est totum
compositum quod primo producitur et generatur, sicut probatur VII *Metaphysicae*
[1033b16–18]; similiter, est aliquid formale in producto quod producitur, quod est
formalis ratio sub qua terminat productionem, et est formalis terminus productionis, et
haec est forma producti. Et quod sic forma uno modo vere terminat productionem . . .
forma vere est terminus productionis, sed tamen terminus primus adaequatus est ipsum
compositum."

into a form', and so on. That argument would mean nothing if the form were only an incidental terminus of that begetting.[6]

For Scotus then, although the whole composite is the terminus of production in the most primary sense, the composite's substantial form has a special role as the formal terminus of production: it gives the composite the intended nature, thereby terminating the process of production. We can thus define the formal terminus of production like this:

(T24) For any x, y, and F,
      F is the formal terminus of a production $P =_{df}$ iff
      (i) x produces y by P, and
      (ii) F is the (ultimate) substantial form of y.

With Scotus's notion of the "formal terminus" of production at hand, we can now turn to Scotus's critique of Henry's theory. As far as Scotus is concerned, when it comes to divine production, the divine essence must be the formal terminus of production. That is, the divine essence must play the role of the substantial *form* of the product, not the *matter* (as Henry claims).[7]

In short, whereas Henry claims with T12 that the divine essence plays the role of "matter" in divine production—

(T12) For any divine persons x and y,
      if x produces y by a production P,
      the divine essence D in y
      is (like) a lump of matter m.

—Scotus rejects Henry's T12 and replaces it with:

---

[6] Scotus, *Ord.*, 1.5.1.un., nn. 27–9 (*Vat.* 4: 25.13–26.9): "dico quod productio habet productum pro termino suo primo, et dico hic 'primum terminum' terminum adaequatum; et hoc modo dicit Philosophus VII *Metaphysicae* [1033b16–18] quod compositum primo generatur, quia est quod primo habet esse per productionem, hoc est adaequatum. In composito tamen forma est formalis terminus generationis, non autem terminus per accidens, sicut apparet per Philosophum II *Physicorum* [193b12–18], ubi probat formam esse naturam per hoc quod 'generatio est naturalis quia est via in naturam, est autem via in formam, ergo etc.',—quae ratio nulla esset si forma tantum esset terminus per accidens generationis."

[7] Scotus, *Lect.*, 1.5.2.un., n. 69 (*Vat.* 16: 436.7–9): "essentia est formalis terminus generationis et productionis Filii, igitur essentia non est materia nec quasi-materia generationis Filii sicut subiectum"; *Ord.*, 1.5.2.un., n. 64 (*Vat.* 4: 47.12–13): "essentia est terminus formalis productionis et generationis Filii, ergo non quasi-materia"; *Rep. I-A*, 1.5.2.un., n. 58 (Wolter, 274): "essentia divina est formalis terminus generationis Filii, non ergo est materia vel quasi-materia de qua producatur Filius."

(T25) For any divine persons *x* and *y*,
       if *x* produces *y* by a production *P*,
       the divine essence *D* is the formal terminus of *P*.

Scotus offers a number of arguments for why T25 must be true and T12 false, but in the following two sections I want to look at the two that are the most important.

4.2. DIVINE PRODUCTION IS NOT A MERE CHANGE IN RELATIONSHIP

The first argument I want to discuss begins with a point I mentioned in section 2.2, namely that the type of change depends on the type of form the recipient acquires. For instance, when Socrates gets a tan, he acquires a new color, and since colors are qualities, Socrates therefore undergoes a qualitative change. Similarly, when Socrates grows taller, he acquires a new size, and since sizes are quantities, Socrates therefore undergoes a quantitative change.

According to Henry, however, when the Father produces the Son, the divine essence plays the role of the matter, and sonship plays the role of the substantial form. Thus, on Henry's view, it looks as if sonship would be the formal terminus of the Son's production. But as I explained in section 1.4, a personal property like sonship is just a relationship, and as Scotus sees it, that would mean that divine production would be a mere change in relationship, not a genuine instance of begetting.[8]

---

[8] Scotus, *Lect.*, 1.5.2.un., n. 72 (*Vat.* 16: 436.24–437.6): "si essentia non esset formalis terminus productionis Filii, tunc generatio et productio Filii magis essent de genere relationis, et mutatio relativa, quia secundum Philosophum V *Physicorum* [224b6–8] mutatio est eadem specie cum termino, ut dealbatio cum albedine, et non cum ligno albo, quod est unum per accidens; si igitur terminus productionis Filii esset relatio, tunc esset illa productio ad-aliquatio, nec esset productio substantia, quod falsum est"; *Ord.*, 1.5.2.un., n. 69 (*Vat.* 4: 49.7–13): "aliter non esset ista productio generatio, sed magis esset mutatio ad relationem, quia productio ponitur in genere vel specie ex suo termino formali, sicut patet per Philosophum V *Physicorum* [224a26–30; 224b6–8],—sicut alteratio ponitur in genere qualitatis, qua ibi est forma quae est formalis terminus alterationis; ergo si formalis terminus huiusmodi productionis esset relatio, ista productio poneretur in genere relationis et non esset generatio"; *Rep. I–A*, 1.5.2.un., n. 63 (Wolter, 275): "mutatio et omnis per se productio ponitur per se in genere termini ad quem et praecipue in genere termini formalis, V *Physicorum*

This provides Scotus with a good reason to insist that the divine essence must be the formal terminus of divine production. For by Scotus's reckoning, divine production will only count as a genuine instance of begetting if the formal terminus is a substantial form (or at least something very much like a substantial form), and of course, the divine essence is at least much more like a substantial form than a personal property is. After all, the divine essence makes the persons divine, much like how my human form makes me human, whereas the personal properties are just relationships which distinguish the divine persons from each other.[9] Thus, as Scotus sees it, the formal terminus of divine production must be the divine essence, not a relationship like sonship.

4.3. THE SUBJECT OF INCOMPATIBLE PROPERTIES

The second argument I want to discuss is much more complicated than the first. As Scotus understands it, Henry proposes that the Father produces the Son by "imprinting" a form (sonship) in a lump of matter (the divine essence), perhaps similar to the way that a signet ring's shape gets imprinted in a lump of soft wax.

Scotus then asks: is the Son's form imprinted in (i) the divine essence *as such*, or is it imprinted in (ii) the divine essence *in some*

[224a26–30; 224b6–8], ubi exemplificatur de omnibus per se motu et mutatione, scilicet generatione et alteratione et augmentatione. Si igitur formalis terminus productionis Filii non est essentia sed relatio, tunc productio Filii non esset generatio, sed magis adaliquatio erit; igitur [divina essentia] non est quasi materia."

[9] Scotus, *Ord.*, 1.5.2.un., n. 68 (*Vat.* 4: 49.3–6): "in creaturis natura est formalis terminus productionis, non autem proprietas individualis vel hypostatica,—sicut patet II *Physicorum* [193b12–13], ubi habetur quod generatio est naturalis, sive dicitur natura, quia est «via in naturam»"; *Rep. I–A*, 1.5.2.un., n. 62 (Wolter, 275): "Philosophus II *Physicorum* [193b12–13] ostendit quod generatio est natura, quia est 'via in naturam' sive in formam; ergo natura est per se terminus formalis generationis et non proprietas individualis individuans naturam, cum natura non sit primus terminus generationis, sed compositum. Ergo multo magis natura vel essentia divina erit formalis terminus productionis et non relatio."

particular person (like the Father)?[10] Scotus argues that neither option is acceptable. Option (i) is no good because the divine essence as such is shared by all three persons, so if the Son were begotten from the divine essence as such, then the Son would be from all three persons, and that is absurd.[11]

Option (ii) is no good either, for the wax from which a seal is made is the very same wax in which the seal's form is imprinted. Consequently, if the Son were made *from* the Father's "wax," so to speak, then the Son's form would be imprinted *in* the Father's "wax." But then the Father's "wax" would have *two* forms (fatherhood and sonship), in which case the Father would be two persons, and that is also absurd.[12]

---

[10] Scotus, *Lect.*, 1.5.2.un., nn. 83–4 (*Vat.* 16: 441.22–442.3): "si essentia sit illud de quo producitur Filius, oportet quod hoc sit secundum aliquod esse ipsius essentiae, quia illud de quo generatur Filius oportet habere aliquod esse prout sibi imprimitur forma eius. Quaero igitur quid est illud esse quod habet essentia, secundum quod de ea producitur Filius: vel est esse quod est essentia de se, aut est esse incommunicabile in alia persona?"; *Ord.*, 1.5.2.un., nn. 72–3 (*Vat.* 4: 50.15–51.8): "essentiae ut de ea generatur Filius necesse est assignare aliquod esse, quia principiare aliquod verum ens—in quocumque genere principii—non convenit alicui nisi realiter enti. Quaero igitur, quod esse convenit essentiae ut ipsa est de quo per impressionem generatur Filius: aut praecise esse ad se, quod est essentiae ut essentiae . . . aut convenit sibi esse in aliqua subsistentia [e.g. in Patre]"; *Rep. I–A*, 1.5.2.un., n. 68 (Wolter, 276–7): "omne principium reale entis realis habet esse reale secundum quod principiat, alioquin illud quod principiat esset non-ens; essentia est principium reale et entis realis, scilicet in quantum est principium quasi materiale, et entis realis, scilicet Filii; ergo dat sibi aliquod reale esse. Ergo vel dat sibi esse ad se [viz. essentia qua essentia] vel esse ad [aliquam personam, viz. essentiam in persona sicut Patre]."

[11] Scotus, *Ord.*, 1.5.2.un., n. 73 (*Vat.* 4: 51.5–7): "[esse convenit essentiae ut ipsa est de quo per impressionem generatur Filius] aut [est] praecise esse ad se, quod est essentiae ut essentiae,—et tunc Filius est de essentia ut essentia, et hoc modo [Filius] est trium personarum"; *Rep. I–A*, 1.5.2.un., n. 68 (Wolter, 277): "sed [essentia] non dat sibi [viz. ad Filium] esse ad se [i.e. 'esse ad se' est 'esse divinae essentiae in se'], quia tunc Filius esset de substantia Patris secundum esse ad se; ergo [Filius esset] de substantia trium, eo quod substantia ad se non est plus unius personae quam alterius."

[12] Scotus, *Lect.*, 1.5.2.un., n. 84 (*Vat.* 16: 442.8–14): "Sed si hoc dicatur, quod Filius est de essentia Patris secundum esse in alia persona, ut in prima exsistens, tunc arguo sic: esse de quo est aliquid per impressionem, non potest intelligi sine esse in quo est aliquid, nec esse in quo est aliquid potest intelligi sine hoc quin sit illud. Si igitur est aliquid de quo per impressionem est Filius, ut substantia secundum quod est in Patre, tunc substantia secundum quod est in Patre necessario erit illud in quo est Filius"; *Ord.*, 1.5.2.un., n. 73 (*Vat.* 4: 51.8–52.4): "aut ingenita [persona est esse in quo filiationem imprimitur],—et si hoc, cum in intellectu eius quod est 'esse de quo aliquid producitur' includatur hoc quod est 'esse illud in quo forma inducitur', et in intellectu eius quod est esse in quo includatur habere illud quod est in eo, et per consequens esse formaliter per ipsum,—ergo si essentia ut est in Patre sit de quo Filius

To illustrate this latter claim, Scotus points out that if someone whitewashed a wall, that wall would be the very thing that has the resulting white color. Similarly, if sonship were imprinted in the Father's "wax," then the Father would be the very thing that has sonship, and so the Father would be a Son, just as the wall would be white. And while there is nothing absurd about a wall being white, Scotus thinks it would be absurd to say that the Father is also the Son.[13]

Since neither option (i) nor option (ii) is acceptable, Scotus concludes that the divine essence cannot function in any way as the material in which the Son's form is "imprinted." On the contrary, the divine essence must be more like the form of the Son, so again, the divine essence must be the formal terminus of divine production.

To clarify the details of this argument, allow me restate it as follows. In accordance with Scotus's own wording, let the Father's form of fatherhood be F, let the Son's form of sonship be S, let the divine essence as such be D, and let the divine essence in the Father be D_F.

(1) D is in all three divine persons.
(2) If the Son were "made from" D, then the Son would be from all three divine persons.
(3) The Son cannot be from all three divine persons.
(4) Therefore, the Son cannot be "made from" D.
(5) F is in D_F.
(6) If S were imprinted in D_F, then S would be in D_F.
(7) Therefore, S and F would both be in D_F.
(8) S and F cannot both be in D_F.
(9) Therefore, S cannot be imprinted in D_F.

generatur (et per impressionem, secundum eos), sequitur quod ipsa ut in Patre erit illud in quo notitia genita [viz. Verbum vel Filius] imprimitur, et ita essentia ut in Patre erit formaliter Verbum [viz. Filius] sive noscens notitia genita, quod est inconveniens"; *Rep. I-A*, 1.5.2.un., n. 69 (Wolter, 277–8): "Si autem essentia ut est principium quasi materiale [Filii] det esse ad [i.e. 'esse ad' est 'esse divinae essentiae in aliqua persona'], ergo hoc erit vel in prima persona . . . Nec dat 'esse ad' in prima persona, quia secundum idem 'esse ad' istius aliquid est principium materiale generationis et recipit formam; ergo secundum esse istius principii quasi materialis in prima persona recipitur proprietas Filii, et sic filiatio recipitur in Patre et sic Filius substantiae."

[13] Scotus, *Lect.*, 1.5.2.un., n. 84 (*Vat.* 16: 442.15–18): "sicut si superficies sit illud de quo per impressionem est albedo, superficies est illud in quo est albedo,—et per consequens sicut superficies est habens albedinem, ita essentia ut est in prima persona erit habens filiationem."

Now, premises (1)–(4), namely the first half of the argument, look entirely unconvincing. The basic point seems to be that the Son cannot be "from" all three persons, but one might ask: what exactly does it mean for the Son to be *from* all three persons?

Scotus might be thinking that the Son cannot be produced *by* all three persons. And that, of course, would be absurd, for if the Son were produced by all three persons, then he would be produced (at least partly) by himself, and there is no sense in which the Son could explain his own production (and the same goes for the Spirit). But if that is what Scotus is thinking, then premises (1)–(4) should read like this:

(1)   *D* is in all three divine persons.
(2*)   If the Son were "made from" *D*,
       then the Son would be produced
       by all three divine persons.
(3*)   The Son cannot be produced by all three divine persons.
(4)   Therefore, the Son cannot be "made from" *D*.

However, premise (2*) is hardly acceptable, for to say that *A* is made from *B* in no way implies that *A* is produced by *B*. Sculptors make statues *from* clay all the time, but nobody would say that statues are produced *by* their clay.

Consequently, if *D* exists in all three persons, and if the Son is "made from" *D*, then it would not follow that the Son is produced *by* all three persons. On the contrary, all that would follow here is that the Son would have to be "made from" something (namely *D*) that exists in all three persons. Hence, premises (1)–(4) should read like this:

(1)   *D* is in all three divine persons.
(2**)   If the Son were "made from" *D*,
        then the Son would be "made from" something
        that exists in all three divine persons.
(3**)   The Son cannot be "made from" something
        that exists in all three divine persons.
(4)   Therefore, the Son cannot be "made from" *D*.

But why should we accept (3**)? Why *can't* the Son be "made from" something that exists in all three persons? Indeed, suppose I made three successive statues out of the same lump of clay. In that case, it would be true that the same lump of clay exists in all three statues, but nobody would think that just because the same clay exists in a later statue, I could not therefore make my first statue out of that same lump of clay.

Besides, isn't Henry proposing that very thing, namely that the Son is "made from" the same divine essence that the other persons are "made from" too?[14] As far as I can tell, Scotus has provided no reason—at least not within the context of this argument—for why we should accept premise (3**), and it seems to me that Henry would just deny premise (3**).[15]

Nevertheless, the second half of the argument is much stronger. The crucial claim is premise (8), namely that fatherhood and sonship cannot be "imprinted" in the same subject simultaneously. Now, Scotus does not explicitly defend premise (8) here, but presumably the point is that the personal properties are *incompatible* (otherwise they would not distinguish the persons).

After all, Scotus could point out that fatherhood and sonship are irreflexive relations. That is, someone can be the father or son of someone else, but nobody can be the father or son of himself (and the same would apply to active and passive spiration). Thus, Scotus could defend premise (8) simply by appealing to the claim that

---

[14] In the *Lectura*, Scotus says that the divine essence in the Father cannot be the "matter" of the Son, because Henry says so. *Lect.*, 1.5.2.un., n. 84 (*Vat.* 16: 442.4–7): "Si primo modo, igitur ita vere Filius erit genitus de essentia Filii sicut de substantia et essentia Patris; unde et ipsi [viz. Henricus et secii] concedunt quod hoc non potest dici, dicentes quod Filius sit de substantia ut est Patris et non de substantia ut est trium personarum." The reference here is presumably to Henry's *SQO*, 54.3 (*Bad.* II f. 84rF): "Dico autem [Filius generatur] de substantia generantis cum reduplicatione, in quantum scilicet generans est: licet enim eadem sit in tribus, non tamen habet rationem potentiae ut de ea generatur aliquis, nisi secundum quod habet esse in Patre." However, Henry could just say that the Son's "matter" is the divine essence *in the Father* because the other persons have not been produced yet, as it were, but that would not entail that the Son's "matter" cannot be the divine essence *as such*, as I explain in the next note.

[15] I suppose Scotus might be thinking that the Son cannot be made from something in all three persons because that would assume that all three persons already exist. However, to say that sonship is "imprinted" in the divine essence as such does not entail that sonship would be "imprinted" in the divine essence as it *already* exists in all three persons. Indeed, as we shall see in Chapter 11, Scotus himself argues that the Father gets his power to produce the Son from the divine essence as such, but that does not entail that the Father gets his power to produce the Son from the divine essence as it *already* exists in all three persons. So I do not see how Scotus could legitimately press the argument in premises (1)–(4) here, at least not unless he would be willing to subject his own views to it too.

(T26) For any correlative personal properties *F* and *G*,
       F and *G* are incompatible with respect to each other.

And since incompatible properties cannot belong to the same subject, it follows that the divine essence cannot be the subject of fatherhood and sonship at the same time. That would be enough to secure Scotus's conclusion in (9).

Still, one might object that if God's fatherhood and sonship are truly incompatible, then it makes no difference if we construe the divine essence as a lump of matter or a form. Since God's fatherhood and sonship are incompatible, they simply cannot exist in one and the same thing—be it a lump of matter, a form, or anything else. In other words, Scotus's view would be just as susceptible to his own criticism as Henry's.

But Scotus does not seem to think this is a problem. In the *Reportatio*, he writes:

> It is impossible for the numerically same [lump of] matter to remain under the form of the begetter and the begotten [at the same time], whatever sort of thing the begetter or the begotten is, for the same [lump of] matter cannot be simultaneously perfected by two ultimate forms which give complete being to the matter. Nevertheless, the same form can give [a particular kind of] being to many [lumps of] matter simultaneously, or to one [lump of] matter to which it did not give [that particular kind of] being before.[16]

Here Scotus says that a lump of matter cannot have two ultimate substantial forms at the same time, and presumably this is because ultimate substantial forms are incompatible. But the same substantial form can inform different lumps of matter at the same time, or it can come to inform a new lump of matter that it did not inform before.

Scotus goes on to give an example. According to a common medieval theory of nutrition, when humans eat, the food they consume is broken down in the body and eventually converted into organic tissue. That is, the matter in the food loses its food-form, and then it takes on the form of organic tissue. And once it becomes

---

[16] Scotus, *Rep. I–A*, 1.5.2.un., n. 80 (Wolter, 282): "impossibile est eandem materiam numero manere sub forma generantis et geniti, quodcumque sit generans vel genitum, quia non potest eadem materia simul perfici duabus formis ultimis quae dant esse completum materiae; potest tamen eadem forma dare esse pluribus materiis simul, sive uni materiae cui non dabat prius."

organic tissue, it becomes a part of the body, at which point it becomes "informed" by the form of the whole body just like any other part of tissue in the body. So this is an example of how a single form can inform different bits of matter.[17]

Scotus also extrapolates a more hypothetical example in order to illustrate how incompatible divine persons can share the same "form." Suppose, he says, that there is only a heart (we might imagine it sustained by a machine), and a human form exists in it. If the heart then grew other organic parts—say, a hand and a foot—then that form would come to "inform" them too, and again we would have a case where different things share the same form.[18]

---

[17] Scotus, *Rep. I–A*, 1.5.2.un., n. 80 (Wolter, 282): "Patet in augmentatione ubi, corrupta forma alimenti in carnem, forma carnis de novo perficit materiam alimenti, quia caro convertit alimentum in carnem et perficit materiam alimenti ut carnem praeexsistentem in alimento."

[18] In proposing this example, Scotus first asks us to imagine if a heart that is animated by the soul could produce a hand and a foot by sharing its *matter* with it. Then he asks us to imagine it the other way around: where the heart produces a hand and a foot by sharing its *form* rather than its matter. Scotus, *Ord.*, 1.5.2.un., n. 135 (*Vat.* 4: 76.18–77.4): "Aptius videtur exemplum, si ponamus materiam cordis animati posse eandem communicari diversis formis—puta manus et pedis—et hoc virtute activa cordis animati, producentis composita ista ex materia sua communicata et ex formis istis, hic vere esset productio totorum habentium eandem materiam, et esset cum mutatione illius materiae; sed si, ex alia parte, ponamus animam—propter sui illimitationem in ratione actus et formae—posse communicari multis et virtute animae in corde ipsam communicari manui et pedi, productis a corde animato, hic vere esset productio multorum consubstantialium in forma, absque mutatione illius formae." Scotus goes on to explain that this is similar to divine production, *Ord.*, 1.5.2.un., n. 136 (*Vat.* 4: 77.5–16): "In utroque exemplo ponantur producta esse per se subsistentia, non partes eisdem, quia esse partem est imperfectionis. Hoc posito, secundus modus in utroque exemplo, qui est de communicatione formae ipsi producto, perfecte repraesentat productionem in Deo, non primus, qui est de communicatione materiae,—et hoc, adhuc addendo in positione, quod anima in corde et manu et pede non sit forma informans, quia componibilitas includit imperfectionem, sed sit forma totalis qua illa subsistentia sint et animata sint: ita quod intelligitur deitas non communicari quasi-materia, sed relationibus subsistentibus—si personae ponantur relativae—communicatur deitas per modum formae, non informantis sed qua relatio vel relativum subsistens est Deus." See also, *Lect.*, 1.5.2.un., n. 105 (*Vat.* 16: 451.10–21): "Hoc etiam declaratur in exemplo: si aliquid augmentetur in se sine alio adveniente, ut est in rarefactione, ibi forma rei augmentabilis mutatur et recipit novam perfectionem. Sed ponamus quod augmentatio fiat aliquo extra adveniente, isto modo, quod anima habens potentiam et virtutem perficiendi totum corpus organicum tantum perficiat unam partem, ut cor, et quod postea aliae partes corporis addantur, tunc anima—sine ulla mutatione sui—absque hoc quod aliunde perficitur perficit alias partes organicas.—Sic essentia divina, in primo signo naturae est perfectissima; postea, quasi superveniant relationes pullulantes, essentia intimat se eis, dans eis quidquid perfectionis

These examples make it clear that Scotus sees no problem with the numerically same substantial form informing different subjects, so he would also see no reason why the divine essence could not be shared by different persons. Thus, as Scotus sees it, it is Henry's theory that faces the problem of incompatible properties, not his own.

4.4. CONCLUSION

For Scotus then, Henry has divine production all wrong. The divine essence cannot function as a lump of matter from which a divine person is produced. On the contrary, the divine essence must be the formal terminus of divine production: that is, the divine essence must be (or at least play the role of) the substantial form of any divine person who is produced.

After all, Scotus reasons, the divine essence could not be a lump of matter that stands under incompatible personal properties, for nothing can be the subject of incompatible properties. Besides, if a personal property (which is just a relationship) were the formal terminus of divine production, then divine production would amount to a mere change in relationship, and that would not be a genuine instance of begetting.

Still, how does Scotus explain divine production? If the divine essence does not play the role of matter, then what does? If nothing plays the role of matter, then wouldn't the Son be produced without any materials whatsoever? And if that were so, wouldn't the Son be created from nothing? In the next chapter, I will look at how Scotus answers these questions.

habent et quod sint Deus deitate,—et ideo nullo modo habet potentiam passivam ut perficiatur eis"; and *Rep. I–A*, 1.5.2.un., nn. 77–9 (Wolter, 280–1).

5

Scotus on the Son's Production

As Scotus sees it, the divine essence must be the formal terminus of divine production, which is just to say that the divine essence must play the role of the substantial *form* (not the matter) of any produced divine person. Nevertheless, there are plenty of other details that need to be clarified before we can arrive at a complete picture of Scotus's theory. In this chapter, I want to examine what Scotus has to say about these further details.

5.1. BEGETTING DOES NOT REQUIRE ANY MATERIALS

As I explained in section 4.1, Scotus thinks that, formally speaking, change and production are different kinds of processes, for production simply brings something into existence, while change results in a recipient gaining or losing a form. I also pointed out that creatures produce other creatures by effecting a change, for creatures reproduce by causing an already existing lump of matter to acquire a new substantial form.

According to Scotus though, creatures only produce in this way because they are not powerful enough to cause *all* of something to exist. On the contrary, they can only cause *some* of it to exist, namely its form. For Scotus then, creatures are too weak to produce products without using materials.[1]

---

[1] Scotus, *Ordinatio* [= *Ord.*], 1.5.2.un., n. 95 (*Vat.* 4: 61.2–6): "Concomitatur autem mutatio productionem in creaturis propter imperfectionem potentiae productivae, quae non potest dare totale esse termino productionis, sed aliquid eius praesuppositum

God, on the other hand, is infinitely powerful, so he does not need to use any materials to produce things. He is so powerful that he can cause *all* of something—all of its parts, all of its constituents, and everything else in it—to spring into existence out of nothing. And of course, this is just what happens when God creates the universe *ex nihilo*. God does not fashion the world out of pre-existing materials; God causes all of it to come into existence out of nothing.[2]

This provides Scotus with a further reason to claim that change and production are not the same. They coincide in creatures of course, for creatures are too weak to produce without changing pre-existing materials, but change and production need not always coincide in this way, as is clear from the fact that God produces the world without changing any pre-existing materials at all.[3]

Scotus then goes on to argue that when we attempt to map terrestrial begetting onto divine production, we should leave out any imperfections, for we do not want to attribute any imperfections to God. That means we should not say that God produces the Son by using materials. After all, creatures produce things with materials only because they are too weak to do otherwise, but we would not

transmutatur ad aliam partem ipsius et sic producit compositum"; *Lectura* [= *Lect.*], 1.5.2.un., n. 91 (*Vat.* 16: 444.23–28): "generatio in creaturis includit mutationem et productionem. Quia generans est imperfectae virtutis, ideo non solum requirit aliam causam eiusdem generis, sed causam alterius generis causae, et ideo non producit totum compositum, sed praesupponit materiam, et tunc producit formam transmutando materiam."

[2] Scotus, *Ord.*, 1.5.2.un., n. 96 (*Vat.* 4: 61.8–13): "Hoc etiam apparet in creatione, ubi propter perfectionem potentiae productivae ponentis primo in esse totum, vere est ratio productionis, in quantum per eam terminus productus accipit esse,—sed non est ibi ratio mutationis, in quantum mutatio dicit aliquid substratum 'aliter nunc se habere quam prius', ex VI *Physicorum* [234b5–7, 10–13]. In creatione enim non est aliquid substratum"; *Lect.*, 1.5.2.un., n. 91 (*Vat.* 16: 445.6–12): "ex quo patet quod ratio productionis separabilis est a ratione mutationis—amota imperfectione agentis—sine contradictione, nam productio est qua res capit esse. Nunc autem accidit rei quae producitur—et quae esse capit per productionem—quod mutetur, sicut patet in creatione, ubi vere producitur totum sine mutatione praecedente; unde ubi est perfecta virtus activa, ibi potest res capere totum esse sine mutatione."

[3] Scotus, *Lect.*, 1.5.2.un., n. 91 (*Vat.* 16: 445.12–18): "Productio igitur separabilis est a mutatione . . . tum quia agens perfectae virtutis potest agere, et ibi erit tunc productio, sed non mutatio; unde in creatione, quia producitur aliquid a perfecto producente, est productio et non generatio [ex materia]"; *Ord.*, 1.5.2.un., nn. 94–5 (*Vat.* 4: 60.16–61.7): "Generatio in creatura duo dicit, mutationem et productionem, et istorum formales rationes aliae sunt et sine contradictione separabiles ad invicem . . . Ergo sine contradictione [productio et mutatio] possunt separari, et realiter separantur comparando ad potentiam productivam perfectem."

want to say that God is weak, for that would imply that he is imperfect.[4]

As Scotus sees it, the only aspects of terrestrial begetting that we can transfer over to divine production are those that do not imply any imperfections, and that, he thinks, only includes the primary and formal termini of production. Thus, a divine production results in a *product* (the primary terminus of that production), and it results in that product having a *form* (the formal terminus of that production).[5]

The upshot here is that Scotus thinks begetting can occur without any materials. As he puts it in the *Reportatio*:

> Insofar as it implies production, begetting as such does not require matter or quasi-matter, and where it happens without matter, begetting is said to be perfect and without any imperfection. Therefore, this is how it has to be ascribed to God, for in no way can begetting be conceived without imperfection if it is understood to presuppose matter.[6]

Thus, Scotus thinks we can say that divine production is like terrestrial begetting, even though it occurs without any pre-existing materials. So, for instance, when the Father begets the Son, he (i) produces

[4] Scotus, *Ord.*, 1.5.2.un., n. 97 (*Vat.* 4: 61.14–62.7): "Ad propositum. Cum in divinis nihil ponendum sit imperfectionis, sed totum perfectionis, et mutatio de ratione sui dicit imperfectionem, quia potentialitatem, et hoc in mutabili,—et concomitanter etiam dicit imperfectionem potentiae activae in mutante, quia talis requirit necessario causam concausantem ad hoc ut producat (non autem fit ibi aliqua imperfectio, nec qualis est potentiae passivae, nec etiam aliqua imperfectio potentiae activae, sed summa perfectio),—nullo modo ponetur ibi generatio sub ratione mutationis nec quasi-mutationis . . . Et ideo generatio ut est in divinis, est sine materia,—et ideo generationis ut est in divinis non assignabitur materia nec quasi-materia."
[5] Scotus, *Ord.*, 1.5.2.un., n. 97 (*Vat.* 4: 62.3–10): "sed tantum generatio ut est productio, in quantum scilicet aliquid per eam capit esse, ponetur in divinis . . . et ideo generationis ut est in divinis non assignabitur materia nec quasi-materia, sed tantum terminus: et hoc vel totalis sicut primus, id est adaequatus—qui scilicet primo producitur in esse—vel terminus formalis, secundum quem terminus primus formalis accipit esse." Also, *Lect.*, 1.5.2.un., n. 92 (*Vat.* 16: 445.19–25): "Auferendo igitur illud quod est imperfectionis in generatione (scilicet praesuppositio materiae, quae requiritur propter imperfectionem agentis), transfertur generatio ad divina. Et ideo generatio tantum transfertur ad divina prout includit productionem, et non mutationem,—et ideo nullo modo in divinis est subiectum aut materia nec quasi-materia, cum ibi non sit mutatio nec quasi-mutatio."
[6] Scotus, *Reportatio I–A* [= *Rep. I–A*], 1.5.2.un., n. 74 (Wolter, 279): "generatio ut importat productionem, quae ut sic non requirit materiam nec quasi materiam et ut sic dicit perfectionem sine imperfectione; ergo ut sic habet attribui Deo. Sed nullo modo concipitur sine imperfectione ut intelligitur praesupponere materiam."

the Son, for the Son is the primary terminus of that production, and (ii) he shares his form (namely the divine essence) with the Son, for the divine essence is the formal terminus of that production. But the primary and formal termini of begetting are all we need in order to say that the Son is begotten. We do not need to postulate any "materials" in divine production.

5.2. THE SON IS NOT CREATED FROM NOTHING

But what of the creation problem? As I explained in section 3.1, Henry argues that if the Son were produced without any materials, he would be created. Scotus, however, argues that the Son is produced without any materials whatsoever, so wouldn't it follow for Scotus that the Son is created *ex nihilo*?

According to Scotus, the answer is no. Scotus agrees that when material substances beget other material substances, the reason those begotten substances are not created is that they are made from pre-existing materials. But he points out that it is not the *matter* that is relevant here; it is the fact that it *pre-exists*. That is, a product does not need to be made from pre-existing materials in order to be uncreated, it just needs to be produced with a pre-existing constituent, and that can be a lump of matter, it can be a form, or it can be any other sort of constituent that is not produced by the production that brings the product in question into existence.

Likewise in the divine case. Although the Father does not produce the Son with any *materials*, the Father still shares the divine essence with the Son, so the Son is produced with at least one "pre-existing ingredient," so to speak, and that is the divine essence. Thus, the Son is not created from nothing, and the same goes for the Spirit. As Scotus puts it:

> The reason that a begotten creature is not [produced] from nothing is that something in it (such as matter) pre-exists. Therefore . . . if the form of something were to pre-exist and the matter were newly added to it so that it were informed by that pre-existent form, that very product would not be [produced] from nothing, for something in it pre-existed [the production] . . . Therefore, if someone [like Henry] were to say that [the Son] is not [produced] from nothing 'because his essence existed in the Father prior in the order of origin', and if [he said that] the essence is

the matter, so to speak, in the Son's begetting, then how much more would it be the case that the Son is not [produced] from nothing if the [divine] essence that 'exists in the Father prior in origin' is a form, as it were, that is shared with the Son?[7]

Now, talk here about "pre-existing ingredients" is not very precise, for as I mentioned in the Introduction, production in God is eternal. That is, there are no temporal "before" or "after" moments to speak of, so nothing in God can pre-exist anything else in God, temporally speaking. Instead then, we should talk about this in terms of produced and unproduced constituents. As I put it in section 3.2:

(T15) For any x, y, and F,
      F is an unproduced constituent of y =$_{df}$ iff
      (i) x produces y by a production P,
      (ii) F is a constituent of y, and
      (iii) x does not produce F by P.

(T16) For any x, y, and F,
      F is a produced constituent of y =$_{df}$ iff
      (i) x produces y by a production P,
      (ii) F is a constituent of y, and
      (iii) x produces F by P.

With these definitions at hand, we can restate Scotus's point more accurately: something is created from nothing if *all* of its constituents are produced constituents, while something is not created if *at least*

---

[7] Scotus, *Ord.*, 1.5.2.un., n. 103 (*Vat.* 4: 64.3–13): "quia 'creatura genita' non est de nihilo, quia aliquid eius praeexsistit, ut materia. Ergo . . . si forma alicuius praeexsisteret et materia de novo adveniret et informaretur illa forma iam praeexsistente, ipsum productum non esset de nihilo, quia aliquid eius praeexstitisset . . . Ergo si Filius non diceretur esse de nihilo 'quia essentia eius secundum ordinem originis praefuit in Patre', et hoc si illa essentia esset quasi-materia generationis Filii, multo magis nec Filius erit de nihilo si illa essentia 'prius origine exsistens in Patre' sit quasi-forma communicata Filio." See also *Lect.*, 1.5.2.un., n. 96 (*Vat.* 16: 447.9–21): "dico quod Filius non est de nihilo, licet non sit de substantia Patris quasi de materia,—quia Filius est de substantia Patris sicut de principio consubstantiali-formali originanti et originato, et hoc salvat verissime Filium non esse de nihilo, et verius quam si Filius generaretur quasi ex materia. Exemplum in creaturis: si ignis generaret ignem ita quod non praesupponeret materiam—nec praeexsisteret materia—sed produceret materiam et communicaret formam, verius esset ignis tunc non de nihilo quam modo quando praesupponit materiam, et eo verius quo forma est verius ens quam materia. Sic Filius non est de nihilo, quia est de substantia Patris ut de termino formali, quia Pater communicat totum ut terminus; et ideo Filius, licet non sit ex materia nec praesupponat aliquid in ratione materiae, non tamen est de nihilo."

one of its constituents is an unproduced constituent. Thus, Scotus would not see T3 as an accurate definition for creation, namely:

(T3) For any x and y,
  if x produces y,
  x creates y from nothing iff
  x produces y without any materials m.

Instead, Scotus would define creation like this:

(T27) For any x and y,
  x creates y from nothing $=_{df}$ iff
  (i) x produces y by a production P, and
  (ii) for any constituent F of y,
  F is a produced constituent of y.

In the Son's case, the divine essence is an unproduced constituent of the Son, for when the Father produces the Son, he does not produce the divine essence in the Son. Rather, the Father simply shares the divine essence with the Son. As Henry already pointed out (see section 3.2):

(T18) For any divine persons x and y,
  if x produces y by a production P,
  the divine essence D in y
  is an unproduced constituent of y.

Consequently, Scotus reasons that the Son cannot be created from nothing, for he includes at least one unproduced constituent, namely the divine essence, and by T27, that is enough to show that the Son is not created from nothing. Unlike Henry then, Scotus rejects T3 and accepts T5:

(T5) For any divine persons x and y,
  if x produces y,
  x cannot produce y with any materials m.

Nevertheless, although Scotus admits that the Son is produced without any materials, Scotus solves the creation problem by insisting that the Son is not created *ex nihilo* for the simple reason that he includes one unproduced constituent: namely, the divine essence itself.

5.3. THE SON IS BEGOTTEN FROM
THE FATHER'S SUBSTANCE

As I have already noted, the Nicene Creed says that "the Son is begotten from the substance of the Father," and as we have seen, Henry argues that we must interpret this to mean that the Father's "substance" (namely, the divine essence) plays the role of matter, for otherwise the Son would be created from nothing. Scotus, however, argues that there is no "matter" in the Godhead, so how does Scotus understand the Nicene Creed's statement that "the Son is begotten from the substance of the Father"?

According to Scotus, there are two key terms in this Creedal statement, and they should be interpreted as follows. First, the term "from" indicates that the Son comes "from" the Father in the way that any product comes from its producer. Second, Scotus says that the phrase "the substance of" indicates that the Father and the Son are "consubstantial," i.e. that they share the numerically same substantial form. Thus, as Scotus sees it, the Creedal statement can be restated more perspicuously like this: the Father produces the Son such that the Father and Son share the numerically same form.

However, Scotus is careful to point out that the Son must be *both* (i) produced by the Father, *and* (ii) consubstantial with the Father. After all, if we *only* said that the Son comes "from" the Father in the way that any product comes from its producer, then we could just as easily say that every creature is "from the substance of the Father" too, for every creature is produced by the Father (and the Son and Spirit). Similarly, if we *only* said that the Father and the Son share the same form, then we could just as easily say that the Father comes "from the substance of the Son," which is clearly absurd, for the Father produces the Son, not vice versa.[8] As Scotus explains in the *Ordinatio*:

---

[8] Scotus, *Lect.*, 1.5.2.un., n. 93 (*Vat.* 16: 446.1–12): "dico quod vere Filius generatur et est de substantia Patris. Nam doctor tenens priorem opinonem [viz. Henricus], dicit quod Magister concedit quod Filius sit de substantia Patris secundum causalitatem originis,—et certe, si [Magister] hoc diceret, non sufficienter diceret [intellectus huius sermonis 'Filius est de substantia Patris'], quia sic creatura est de substantia Patris secundum causalitatem originis. Unde nec [Magister] dicit solam causam originantem, nec solam consubstantialitatem, quia sic posset dici quod Pater esset de Filio, sed praepositio 'de' in proposito notat originationem et consubstantialitatem, sicut unus antiquus doctor dicit; unde notat in proposito consubstantialitatem cum origine, et sic nec est creatura de Patre nec Pater de Filio."

The word 'from' here does not indicate an effecting or originating cause alone, for if it did, creatures would be from the substance of God. Nor does it indicate consubstantiality alone, for then the Father would be from the substance of the Son. Rather, it indicates origination and consubstantiality at the same time. That is, insofar as the term 'substance' is combined with the preposition 'from', it indicates consubstantiality, such that the Son has the same substance and quasi-form as the Father, from whom he is originated. And insofar as the term 'substance' is combined with 'of the Father', it indicates the [Son's] originating principle. Thus, the whole statement 'the Son is from the substance of the Father' has this sense: the Son is originated from the Father such that he is consubstantial with him.[9]

On Scotus's view then, the Father produces the Son, and in doing so, he causes the Son to share the same divine essence as a form. And that is all that the Nicene Creed's statement means.

5.4. THE CONSTITUTION OF THE DIVINE PERSONS

As we have seen, Henry believes that when the Father produces the Son, the divine essence plays the role of a lump of matter, and the Son's sonship plays the role of a substantial form. Hence, on Henry's view, the Son is constituted by the divine essence and sonship analogous to the way that a begotten organism is constituted by a lump of matter and a substantial form.

But as we have also seen, Scotus entirely rejects Henry's matter-form analogy, and that might lead one to wonder: how does Scotus think the divine essence and sonship are joined together in the Son? If they are not joined together in the manner of matter and form, then how exactly *are* they joined together? The answer to this requires

---

[9] Scotus, *Ord.*, 1.5.2.un., n. 99 (*Vat.* 4: 62.15–63.4): "Ubi per ly 'de' non notatur tantum efficientia vel originatio, quia si tantum efficientia, tunc creaturae essent de substantia Dei,—nec notatur per illud 'de' tantum consubstantialitas, quia tunc Pater esset de substantia Filii,—sed notatur simul originatio et consubstantialitas: ut scilicet in casuali huius praepositionis 'de' notetur consubstantialitas, sic quod Filius habet eandem substantiam et quasi-formam cum Patre, de quo est originaliter,—et per illud quod in genitivo construitur cum isto casuali, notetur principium originans; ita quod totalis intellectus huius sermonis 'Filius est de substantia Patris' est iste: Filius est originatus a Patre ut consubstantialis ei."

some discussion of the various ways that Scotus thinks some *A* and *B* can be joined or united together.[10]

First, Scotus recognizes that any number of items can be put together to make up an aggregate or heap.[11] The two crumpled pieces of paper I just threw into the corner are united in this way, for together they make up a single pile of trash. Nevertheless, the papers in that pile are united only very loosely, for I can easily kick them apart in a fit of frustration, and a solid blast of air could scatter them just as well.

But there are other cases where some *A* and *B* might be joined together a little more tightly. For instance, we all have a variety of characteristics that come and go throughout our lives.[12] If I go to the beach, I might acquire a new tan, in which case my new tan would be joined to me in a tighter way than the pieces of paper in the corner are joined together in a pile. (For one thing, the wind cannot blow off my tan.) But still, any tan I get will eventually fade and disappear altogether, so it will not be joined to me in any permanent sort of way.

Beyond that, Scotus maintains that there are cases where some *A* and *B* can be joined together even more tightly. For example, Scotus would say that I am composed of a body and a soul—my body being the material part of me that would survive my death (though it would eventually decay), and my soul being the part of me that is responsible for my sensing, thinking, and willing. However, my body and soul are joined together even more tightly than a tan could ever be joined to me. Indeed, although tans come and go, my body and soul will stick together, as it were, until the very moment of my death.[13]

Nevertheless, Scotus would point out here that my body and soul can survive being separated from each other. After all, when I die, my

---

[10] Scotus explicitly details a number of ways that some *A* and *B* can be joined or united together, e.g., in *Ord.*, 1.2.2.1–4, n. 403 (*Vat.* 2: 356.7–8): "Vel, ut propriissime, dicatur: sicut possumus invenire in unitate multos gradus."

[11] In fact, Scotus maintains that aggregates or heaps can be organized or unorganized (or, as Scotus puts it, ordered or unordered). *Ord.*, 1.2.2.1–4, n. 403 (*Vat.* 2: 356.8): "primo [gradu unitatis], minima est aggregationis; in secundo gradu est unitas ordinis, quae aliquid addit supra aggregationem."

[12] Scotus, *Ord.*, 1.2.2.1–4, n. 403 (*Vat.* 2: 356.10–11): "in tertio [gradu unitatis] est unitas per accidens, ubi ultra ordinem est informatio, licet accidentalis, unius ab altero eorum quae sunt sic unum."

[13] Scotus, *Ord.*, 1.2.2.1–4, n. 403 (*Vat.* 2: 356.11–13): "in quarto [gradu unitatis] est per se unitas compositi ex principiis essentialibus per se actu [e.g. forma] et per se potentia [e.g. materia]."

body will remain for a time (while it decays). Similarly, Scotus would say that my soul will survive too, for like most Christians, he believes that our souls survive our deaths and eventually end up in heaven. So Scotus would say that even though my body and soul are joined together even more tightly than I would be joined to a new tan, the unification of my soul and body is not *entirely* permanent, for each can survive separation.

Scotus also recognizes cases where some *A* and *B* can be united even more tightly—so tightly, in fact, that they cannot survive separation (at least, not without God's intervention).[14] For example, Scotus maintains that my soul can be divided into at least two "parts" or "faculties." On the one hand, there is the animal part of me (i.e. the part that is responsible for sensing the outside world), and on the other hand, there is the rational part of me (i.e. the part that is responsible for thinking and willing).

But, says Scotus, these two "parts" or "faculties" cannot be separated. As Scotus sees it, if the rational part of me were destroyed, the animal part would be too. They are, after all, essential aspects of one and the same soul (my human soul). Thus, one could say that the animal and rational parts of my soul are joined together even more tightly than my soul and body are, for although my soul and body can survive separation, the animal and rational parts of my soul cannot.

It is important to notice that in these sorts of cases, *A* and *B* can still have different defining characteristics. For example, the animal and rational parts of my soul are defined rather differently: the animal part of me is defined by my ability to sense the outside world, whereas the rational part of me is defined by my thinking and willing. So even though the animal and the rational parts of me

---

[14] In such cases (where *A* and *B* cannot be separated), Scotus often says that *A* and *B* are "really the same." See, for instance, the texts that Cross cites in *Duns Scotus* (Oxford: Oxford University Press, 1999), page 212, note 14, namely *Quod.*, 3, n. 15 (*Wad.* 12: 82; *AW*, 73–4 (para. 3.46)): "Universaliter enim quod convenit alicui sic, quod omnimoda contradictio sit illud esse sine hoc, hoc est idem realiter illi: et per oppositum, ubi non est omnimoda contradictio, non oportet esse omnino"; and *Ord.*, 2.1.4–5, n. 200 (*Vat.* 7: 101.8–9): "nihil est idem realiter alicui, sine quo potest esse realiter absque contradictione" (see also nn. 201–4 (*Vat.* 7: 102.3–103.16)). The background for these claims is likely a comment by Aristotle in *Topics*, 7.1, 152b34–35 (*Iunt.*, 1, part 3: 114vL): "Amplius, si potest alterum sine altero esse, non enim erit idem ad idem."

are joined together very tightly, they still retain their own defining characteristics.[15]

To use Scotus's terminology, whenever some *A* and *B* have their own defining characteristics (or, in cases where *A* and *B* are not strictly definable, would have if they were definable), then *A* and *B* are "formally distinct."[16] Thus, to take the animal and rational parts of my soul again, Scotus would say that even though they are joined together so tightly that they cannot survive separation, they are still "formally distinct."[17]

All of that being said, Scotus thinks we can go even further. If we restrict our attention to cases where *A* and *B* are joined together in this very tight way—that is, when *A* and *B* cannot survive separation but still have their own defining characteristics—we can still distinguish between two different sorts of cases.

First, Scotus thinks there are cases where one of *A* or *B* implies some kind of potentiality with respect to the other. For example, if we consider the animal part of me all by itself, in abstraction, we can see that there is a sense in which it has the potential to join with the rational part of me in order to constitute my human soul. After all, there are animals roaming the planet who do not have rational

---

[15] As Scotus explains, when some *A* and *B* are "really the same" or "identical" (i.e. are very tightly united), *A* and *B* need not be *formally* the same, which is to say that *A* and *B* can still have their own defining characteristics. *Ord.*, 1.2.2.1–4, n. 403 (*Vat.* 2: 356.13–357.1): "in quinto [gradu unitatis] est unitas simplicitatis, quae est vere identitas (quidquid enim est ibi, est realiter idem cuilibet, et non tantum est unum illi unitate unionis, sicut in aliis modis)—ita, adhuc ultra, non omnis identitas est formalis. Voco autem identitatem formalem, ubi illud quod dicitur sic idem, includit illud cui sic est idem, in ratione sua formali quiditativa et per se primo modo."

[16] Scotus, *Ord.*, 1.8.1.4, n. 193 (*Vat.* 4: 261.14–262.5): "quia 'includere formaliter' est includere aliquid in ratione sua essentiali, ita quod si definitio includentis assignaretur, inclusum esset definitio vel pars definitionis; sicut autem definitio bonitatis in communi non habet in se sapientiam, ita nec infinita [bonitas] infinitam [sapientiam]: est igitur aliqua non-identitas formalis sapientiae et bonitatis, in quantum earum essent distinctae definitiones, si essent definibiles."

[17] There is a good deal of literature on Scotus's formal distinction. See, for example, Maurice Grajewski, *The Formal Distinction of Duns Scotus* (Washington, D.C.: The Catholic University of America Press, 1944); Hester Gelber, "Logic and the Trinity: A Clash of Values in Scholastic Thought, 1300–1335" (PhD dissertation, University of Wisconsin, 1974), 71–102; Marilyn McCord Adams, "Ockham on Identity and Distinction," *Franciscan Studies* 36 (1976): 25–43; and Richard Cross, "Scotus's Parisian Teaching on Divine Simplicity," in *Duns Scotus à Paris: Actes du colloque de Paris, septembre 2–4, 2002*, ed. Olivier Boulnois et al. (Turnhout: Brepols (Textes et Etudes du Moyen Age, 26), 2004), 519–62.

powers like I do, just as there are animals roaming the planet who do (namely, other humans).[18]

Second, Scotus believes there are certain cases where there is no potentiality at all amongst *A* and *B*, and this occurs when at least one of *A* or *B* is intensively infinite. To explain what he means by "intensively infinite," Scotus asks us to imagine a body of mass extended infinitely in all directions, and then he asks us to imagine all of that mass collapsed into a single point. Something that is "intensively infinite" is infinite in an analogous way: it is infinite by *intension* rather than by *extension*.[19]

Now, if one of *A* or *B* is intensively infinite, then Scotus claims that there cannot be any potentiality between the two at all. The reason, presumably, is that potentiality implies a lack of something (e.g. although I have the potential to become a very skilled mathematician,

---

[18] Scotus, *Ord.*, 1.8.1.3, n. 106 (*Vat.* 4: 201.11–202.4): "Aliquando, quando non sunt ibi res et res (sicut in accidentibus), saltem in una re est aliqua propria realitas a qua sumitur genus [e.g. animalitas] et alia realitas a qua sumitur differentia [e.g. rationalitas]; dicatur prima *a* et secunda *b*: *a* secundum se est potentiale ad *b*, ita quod praecise intelligendo *a* et praecise intelligendo *b*, *a* ut intelligitur in primo instanti naturae—in quo praecise est ipsum—ipsum est perfectibile per *b* (sicut si res esset alia), sed quod non perficitur realiter per *b*, hoc est propter identitatem *a* et *b* ad aliquod totum, cui realiter primo sunt eadem, quod quidem totum primo producitur et in ipso toto ambae istae realitates producuntur; si tamen altera istarum sine altera produceretur, vere esset potentialis ad eam et vere esset imperfecta sine illa."

[19] Scotus, *Quod.*, 5, nn. 2–3 (*Wad.* 12: 118; *AW*, 109–10 (para. 5.6–8)): "Ex hoc ad propositum conmutemus rationem infiniti in potentia, in quantitate, in rationem infiniti in actu, in quantitate, si posset ibi esse in actu. Si enim nunc necessario semper cresceret quantitas infiniti per acceptionem partis post partem, sic et imaginaremur omnes partes acceptibiles esse simul acceptas vel simul remanere, haberemus infinitam quantitatem in actu, quia tanta esset in actu, quanta esset in potentia. Et omnes illae partes, quae in infinita successione essent reductae in actum et haberent esse post alias, tunc simul essent in actu conceptae, illud infinitum in actum vere esset totum ... Ex hoc ultra. Si in entibus intelligamus aliquid infinitum in entitate [viz. in intensione] in actu, illud debet intelligi proportionabiliter quantitati imaginatae infinitae in actu, sic ut ens illud dicatur infinitum quod non potest ab aliquo in entitate excedi ... quia licet totum infinitum actu in quantitate nulla parte sui, nec etiam parte quantitatis talis, careret, tamen quaelibet pars esset extra aliam, et sic totum esset ex imperfectis; sed ens infinitum in entitate [viz. in intensione] sic nihil entitatis habet extra ... Sic enim totum est quod nullam habet partem extrinsecam ... Sic ergo ex ratione infiniti ... applicando secundum imaginationem ad infinitatem actualem in quantitate, si esset possibilis: ulterius applicando ad infinitatem actualem in entitate [viz. in intensione], ubi est possibilis, habemus aliqualem intellectum qualiter concendendum est ens infinitum intensive." See also Cross, *Duns Scotus on God*, 91–8, and the references cited there.

I lack that skill at present). But infinity, on the other hand, cannot lack anything, for just as the set of all real numbers includes every real number, so too must an intensively infinite being be everything it could possibly be. Thus, as Scotus sees it, if at least one of A or B is intensively infinite, then there cannot be any potentiality between them at all.[20]

In cases like these, i.e. when at least one of A or B is intensively infinite, Scotus says that A and B are "perfectly identical."[21] Unfortunately, this label can be somewhat misleading, for these days, when we say that some A and B are *identical*, we normally mean that A and B are just the exact same thing. But Scotus does not have that sort of strict identity in mind when he talks about "perfect identity." To see this, consider the following two points.

First, when A and B are strictly identical, they have the very same properties. For example, since Cicero and Tully are the very same person, anything true of the one must ultimately be true of the other. But this does not apply to the case at hand, for as we have seen, Scotus believes that even when A and B are united together so tightly

[20] To make this point, Scotus explains that (as I will indicate in a moment) the divine essence is intensively infinite, and for that reason, there cannot be any potentiality in God in the way that there is potentiality between my animality and rationality. *Ord.*, 1.8.1.3, n. 103 (*Vat.* 4: 200.5–10): "quia genus [e.g. animalitas] sumitur ab aliqua realitate quae secundum se est potentialis ad realitatem a qua accipitur differentia [e.g. rationalitas]; nullum infinitum est potentiale ad aliquid, ut patet ex dictis in quaestione praecedente. Probatio ista stat in compositione speciei et potentialite generis, sed utraque removetur a Deo, propter infinitatem"; *Ord.*, 1.8.1.3, n. 107 (*Vat.* 4: 202.5–11): "Ista composito realitatum—potentialis et actualis—minima est, quae sufficit ad rationem generis et differentiae et ista non stat cum hoc quod quaelibet realitas in aliquo sit infinita: realitas enim si esset de se infinita, quantum-cumque praecise sumpta, non esset in potentia ad aliquam realitatem; ergo cum in Deo quaecumque realitas essentialis sit formaliter infinita, nulla est a qua formaliter posset accipi ratio generis."

[21] One minor technicality needs to be mentioned here. I say "when *at least* one of A or B is intensively infinite" because Scotus recognizes cases not only where *one* of A and B are infinite, but also cases where *both* are (e.g. God's goodness and wisdom are both intensively infinite, whereas the divine essence is intensively infinite but the Son's sonship is not). When both of A and B are infinite, Scotus calls this "mutual perfect identity"; and when one of A and B is infinite, Scotus calls this "adequate perfect identity." For the distinction between "mutual" and "adequate" perfect identity, see *Ord.*, 1.8.1.4, nn. 215–16 (*Vat.* 4: 272–4). For the claim that the divine essence is infinite but personal properties like sonship are not, see note 7 in section 12.1 below.

that they cannot be separated, they still retain their own defining characteristics.[22]

Second, strict identity is transitive: if *A* is identical to *B* and *B* is identical to *C*, then *A* is identical to *C* as well. But Scotus does not think this applies to the case at hand either. If *A* is directly united to *B*, and *B* is directly united to *C*, it does not follow that *A* is directly united to *C* as well. On the contrary, *A* is united to *C* only through *B* as an intermediary.[23]

This makes it clear that Scotus does not think of perfect identity as a kind of strict identity. Instead, he thinks of it as a very tight kind of unification. So when Scotus says some *A* and *B* are "perfectly identical," he means that *A* and *B* are joined together in the tightest possible way, without any semblance of potentiality.

Of course, this sort of bond only occurs in the Godhead, for as Scotus sees it, the only entity that is intensively infinite is the divine essence (and, derivatively, its proper attributes like power and goodness). So far as Scotus is concerned then, anything that is joined to the divine essence is going to be joined to the divine essence in the tightest possible way, and there cannot be any potentiality involved in that bond.[24]

---

[22] This is especially clear in the divine case, for although Scotus admits that sonship (say) and the divine essence are "perfectly identical," each retains their formal characteristics. *Ord.*, 1.26.un., n. 31 (*Vat.* 6: 10.4–10): "licet relatio [e.g. filiatio] maneat sic quod non est formaliter essentia, tamen relatio—propter infinitatem essentiae— transit in eam secundum perfectam identitatem ad eam. Manet ergo formaliter relatio, quia ratio eius secundum quam est formaliter, non est ratio essentiae,—et transit propter perfectam identitatem ad essentiam, licet non in identitatem formalem."

[23] The fact that transitivity does not apply to "perfect identity" is again clear in the divine case. For although Scotus believes that fatherhood and sonship are really distinct from each other, he also believes (as we shall see in a moment) that fatherhood and sonship are each "perfectly identical" with the divine essence. Consequently, Scotus points out that if "perfect identity" did imply transitivity, then the Father and Son would be identical to each other, and Scotus denies that. *Ord.*, 1.2.2.1–4, n. 398 (*Vat.* 2: 354.9–355.2): "distinctio divinorum suppositorum est realis; ergo cum non possit idem eodem formaliter, quod est aliquid sui, convenire realiter tantum, sic quod non ex illo distingui, et differre realiter tantum, sic quod non illo convenire (quia si est omnino idem re, quare hoc est tantum principium identitatis et non-distinctionis et idem tantum principium distinctiones et non-identitatis?), concluditur aliqua differentia vel distinctio essentiae in qua supposita conveniunt ab illis rationibus quibus supposita distinguuntur."

[24] Scotus, *Ord.*, 1.5.2.un., n. 117 (*Vat.* 4: 69.6–13): "Qualiter autem stat quod ratio relationis [e.g. filiationis] in re non sit formaliter eadem rationi [divinae] essentiae et tamen in eodem concurrentes non constituunt compositum,—hoc ideo est, quia illa ratio est perfecte eadem illi: propter infinitatem enim unius rationis, quidquid potest

This provides Scotus with another reason to reject Henry's matter-form analogy. According to Scotus, the Son's sonship cannot be joined to the divine essence in the way that a form is joined to matter, for part of the reason that a form can be joined to a lump of matter in the first place is that the latter has the *potential* to combine with the former. But for Scotus, that simply cannot happen in the Godhead, for the divine essence is infinite, and infinity excludes potentiality altogether.[25]

In fact, Scotus believes that the divine essence and the Son's sonship are both forms, or at least both play the role of forms. In particular, the divine essence is like a substantial form (which provides its possessor with its kind-nature), and sonship is like a distinguishing form (which provides its possessor with its unique individuality by distinguishing it from others).[26] As Scotus himself

esse cum ea, est perfecte idem sibi. Perfectio ergo identitatis excludit omnem compositionem et quasi-compositionem [potentialitatis et actualitatis], quae identitas est propter infinitatem,—et tamen infinitas non tollit formales rationes quin haec formaliter non sit illa."

[25] Scotus, *Ord.*, 1.2.2.1–4, n. 400 (*Vat.* 2: 355.10–13): "in una [divina] persona non est aliqua differentia rerum [potentialis et actualis], propter simplicitatem divinam [i.e. propter infinitatem divinam]; . . . quia nihil est ibi in potentia quod non est in actu"; *Ord.*, 1.5.2.un., n. 118 (*Vat.* 4: 69.14–16): "Non est ergo ex istis [viz. divina essentia et filiatione] quasi-compositum. Et ideo nihil est ex eis tamquam compositum ex actu et potentia, sed est unum simplicissimum ex istis"; ibid., n. 125 (*Vat.* 4: 72.8–11): "Ultra hoc, prior responsio dat modum 'in'—qui est relationis [e.g. filiationis] in fundamento [i.e. divina essentia]—qui non reducitur ad esse formae in materia nisi ubi fundamentum est limitatum, in tantum quod non habet perfecte identice in se ipsam relationem"; ibid., n. 119 (*Vat.* 4: 71.1–3): "Et quod additur quod 'unum oportet esse in alio', concedo ut relatio [sicut filiatio] est in fundamento sive radice [i.e. divina essentia], sed hoc non est ut actus in potentia sed ut identice continentur in pelago infinito"; ibid., n. 120 (*Vat.* 4: 71.4–7): "potest dici quod omnes istae sunt verae, 'deitas est in Patre, paternitas est in Patre', 'Pater est in deitate sive natura divina, paternitas est in deitate', et tamen nullum 'in' est ibi ut actus in potentia."

[26] Scotus, *Ord.*, 1.5.2.un., n. 127 (*Vat.* 4: 72.16–19): "Concedo relationem [e.g. paternitatem vel filiationem] esse actum personalem [personae], non actum quidditativum [personae],—quia personaliter distinguit et non quidditative. Essentia [divina] autem est actus quidditativus [personae] et quidditative distinguens." That Scotus sees the personal properties as individual forms, or at least as playing the role of individual forms, is clear from the following. *Lect.*, 1.7.un., n. 58 (*Vat.* 16: 494.3–4): "[personae divinae] non assimilantur in proprietatibus relativis, quae correspondent proprietatibus individualibus in creaturis"; ibid., n. 59 (*Vat.* 16: 494.14–15): "proprietates personales [personarum divinarum] sint diversae, quae correspondent differentiis individualibus in creaturis"; *Ord.*, 1.7.1, n. 59 (*Vat.* 4: 132.10–13): "Ita hic, in proposito, per relationes [i.e. paternitas et filiatio] distinctas specie, vel quasi-genere . . . possunt aliqua [divinae personae] distingui personaliter tantum, in eadem specie sive in eadem natura." For more on this, see my "Are the Father and Son Different in

says of the Father (and we can assume that a similar story can be told about the Son and Spirit):

> It is true that deity [i.e. the divine essence] is in the Father as a [substantial form which contributes a] kind-nature to a person who has the sort of existence that corresponds to that kind-nature . . . but this is not because deity is the sort of form that 'informs' [some material aspect of] that person . . . It is also true that fatherhood is in the Father as the personal [i.e. distinguishing] form of that person,—but again not because it 'informs' [some material aspect of] that person. For it is just as true of a form that provides [a person with] a kind-nature as it is true of a form that provides [a person with its] individuality . . . that although it is a form in that person, it does not 'inform [some material aspect of] that person. For here [i.e. in creatures], a form is just a part, as it were, [of that creature, the matter being the other part,] but there [in God], it is, as it were, one formal nature [i.e. a form] that formally joins with another to constitute one simple person who has within himself many formal natures.[27]

So contra Henry, Scotus believes that when it comes to the Father, neither the divine essence nor fatherhood plays the role of matter, nor does either play the role of a form that "informs" some material aspect of the Father. On the contrary, both are like non-informing forms which, nevertheless, are bound together in the tightest possible way, without any semblance of potentiality. And the same goes for the Son and Spirit as well.

For Scotus then, we simply should not be thinking about the divine essence and a personal property as a composite of matter and form. Rather, we should be thinking of them as two tightly joined forms, one of which provides the person in question with their divine nature, and the other of which distinguishes that person from the others.

Kind? Scotus and Ockham on Different Kinds of Things, Univocal and Equivocal Production, and Subordination in the Trinity," *Vivarium* 48 (2010): 312–14.

[27] Scotus, *Ord.*, 1.5.2.un., nn. 121–22 (*Vat.* 4: 71.8–17): "Nam prima [viz. 'deitas est in Patre', cf. n. 120] est vera ut natura est in supposito, habente 'esse' quiditativum ea . . . sed non propter hoc est forma informans suppositum . . . Secunda [viz. 'paternitas est in Patre', cf. n. 120] est vera ut forma hypostatica est in hypostasi,—sed nec informat ipsam. Tam enim quiditas quam forma hypostatica . . . licet sit forma suppositi, non tamen est forma informans, sed ibi [viz. in creaturis] quasi pars, hic [viz. in divinis] autem quasi una ratio formalis concurrens cum alia, formaliter, ad idem simplex sed habens in se plures rationes formales."

5.5. CONCLUSION

According to Scotus, divine production is a very un-Aristotelian sort of production. For instance, the Son is not fashioned out of any materials, and neither the divine essence nor sonship "informs" the Son in the way that a statue shape informs a lump of clay. On the contrary, the divine essence and sonship are like pure forms, as it were, that combine by "perfect identity" (i.e. the tightest kind of unification) to constitute the Son. Thus, when the Father begets the Son, he simply brings the Son into existence without any materials, but in so doing, the Father shares the divine essence with the Son, and for that reason, the Son is not created from nothing.

6

Ockham against Scotus

As Ockham sees it, everybody agrees on the bare essentials of divine production, so for him, this debate really boils down to a disagreement about how to best describe divine production in the most intelligible way. He writes:

> On this question, everyone agrees, as it were, about the reality [of divine production], but they disagree about the way to speak about it. For everyone proposes that (i) the divine essence is common to the three persons, that (ii) the Father shares the divine essence with the Son and the Holy Spirit, that (iii) the persons are constituted from their personal properties and the divine essence itself, and that (iv) it is precisely a person [not the divine essence] that produces [another person] and is produced [by another person]. But as for whether or not the divine essence itself should be called the 'subject' or 'matter' or 'quasi-matter' of [divine] begetting, some disagree, saying that the divine essence is the quasi-matter of this begetting.[1]

According to Ockham then, he and all of his contemporaries agree on the following claims (which were already noted in section 1.4):

1. The divine essence is shared by all three persons (T8).
2. The Father shares the divine essence with the Son and Spirit (which is derived from T8).

---

[1] Ockham, *Ordinatio* [= *Ord.*], 1.5.2 (*OTh* 3: 48.14–22): "In ista quaestione omnes quasi concordant in re, sed in modo loquendi discordant. Ponunt enim omnes quod essentia divina est communis tribus suppositis, et quod communicatur Filio et Spiritui Sancto a Patre, et quod istae personae constituuntur ex proprietatibus et ipsa divina essentia, et quod suppositum praecise producit et producitur. Sed an ipsa essentia divina debeat dici subiectum vel materia vel quasi-materia istius generationis, in hoc discordant aliqui et dicunt quod essentia divina est quasi-materia in ista generatione."

3. Each divine person is constituted by the divine essence and a unique personal property (T9).
4. In divine production, it is the persons who produce each other, not the divine essence (T11).

As Ockham sees it, these are the basic claims that any theologically adequate account of divine production will affirm. I say "theologically adequate" because as I pointed out in section 1.4, the above claims were canonized by the Fourth Lateran Council of 1215, and so for Ockham and his contemporaries, these claims are part of the minimal theological requirements for any adequate theory of divine production.

However, Ockham recognizes that over and above affirming these claims, a scholastic theologian might also make further claims in an attempt to provide a philosophical theory that explains divine production more fully. Of course, this can naturally lead to the development of *competing* philosophical theories, in which case Ockham would say that so long as those theories retain the above mentioned claims, they should be evaluated on their theoretical merits (e.g. their coherence or intelligibility, their simplicity, and so forth).

As far as Ockham is concerned, Henry and Scotus are doing just that when they provide competing theories about whether or not the divine essence should be construed as a lump of matter. For although both Henry and Scotus agree on the above-mentioned claims, each goes on to further provide a different philosophical theory in their respective attempts to explain divine production more fully, and Ockham wants to evaluate those theories accordingly.

So which theory does Ockham think is best? The short answer is that Ockham agrees with Scotus, or at least for the most part. He writes:

> Along with one Doctor [viz. Scotus] who explains this conclusion more subtly [than others], I say to this question that the Son is from the substance of the Father, not as if he were from [a lump of] matter or quasi-matter, but rather as from something consubstantial to him, and thus the Son is from the substance of the Father, that is, from the Father who is consubstantial with the Son. Further, [I agree with this Doctor that] the Son is not [created] from nothing, though not because he is [produced] from some presupposed matter, but rather because he is from the Father, in whom the Son's substance [also] exists. The Subtle Doctor [viz. Scotus] sees this view [clearly], as well as the [correct] way

of putting it (which he expressly wishes to consider), and I hold his opinion and his way of putting it, [at least] with respect to his principle conclusion.[2]

Ockham makes it clear here that he agrees with Scotus that the Son and Spirit are not produced with materials, and he agrees that the Son and Spirit are not created, for the divine essence is an unproduced constituent in the Son and Spirit. Like Scotus then, Ockham solves the creation problem by insisting that the Son and Spirit are produced without materials—

(T5) For any divine persons x and y,
    if x produces y,
    x cannot produce y with any materials m.

—and rejecting Henry's claim that products are created *ex nihilo* if they are produced without any materials:

(T3) For any x and y,
    if x produces y,
    x creates y from nothing iff
    x produces y without any materials m.

On the contrary, for Ockham (following Scotus), all a product needs to be uncreated is at least one unproduced constituent, and that can be a form rather than something material.

Despite agreeing on these points, however, Ockham disagrees with Scotus on other points. For our purposes here, the most important disagreement is this: while Scotus maintains that the divine essence is the *formal terminus* of divine production, Ockham says it is not. In this chapter, I want to discuss Ockham's criticisms of Scotus on this point in detail.

---

[2] Ockham, *Ord.*, 1.5.2 (*OTh* 3: 56.2–11): "Ideo dico ad quaestionem, cum uno Doctore qui subtilius istam conclusionem declaravit, quod Filius est de substantia Patris, non sicut de materia nec quasi-materia, sed sicut de aliquo quod est sibi consubstantiale, et ita est de Patris substantia, hoc est de Patre qui est Filio consubstantialis. Et ita non est Filius de nihilo, non quia sit de aliqua materia praesupposita, sed quia est de Patre in quo est substantia Filii. Istam positionem et modum ponendi qui vult expresse videre, videat Doctorem Subtilem, cuius opinionem et modum ponendi teneo quantum ad conclusionem principalem."

6.1. THE FORMAL TERMINUS OF PRODUCTION

As I explained in section 4.1, Scotus believes that the formal terminus of a production is the form of the product:

(T24) For any x, y, and F,
       F is the formal terminus of a production $P =_{df}$ iff
       (i) x produces y by P, and
       (ii) F is the (ultimate) substantial form of y.

However, this might suggest that the formal terminus is so-called because it is a *form*. Similarly, it might suggest that we should call the *matter* of a product the "material terminus." But to this, Ockham says the following:

> I respond that there is equivocation concerning the term 'formal'. In one way, 'formal' is concrete for the form itself... But people do not commonly speak this way when they say that this or that [entity in the product] is the formal terminus [of the production]. In another way, the formal terminus [of a production] is said to be that which primarily and in itself acquires all of its being through such a production. In this way, matter can be the formal terminus [of a production, e.g. when God creates a lump of matter].[3]

In this passage, Ockham explains that when medieval philosophers talk about the "formal terminus" of a production, they are usually referring to the product or a constituent of the product that comes to exist through that production, and that need not be a form. It could be any producible constituent, even a lump of matter (e.g. if God were to create a lump of matter all by itself).[4]

The idea here is that the word "formal" does not always pick out a form. For instance, if I were to think about a lump of material (or

---

[3] Ockham, *Ord.*, 1.5.3 (*OTh* 3: 71.11–18): "respondeo quod aequivocatio est de 'formali'. Quia 'formale' uno modo est concretum ipsius formae... Et sic non loquuntur communiter utentes isto vocabulo quando dicunt quod hoc vel illud est terminus formalis. Alio modo dicitur terminus formalis illud quod primo et secundum se totum habet esse tali productione. Et isto modo materia potest esse terminus formalis."

[4] Perhaps Ockham is following Peter Aureol here, who claims in *Sent.*, 1.5.17, n. 73 (ed. Buytaert, 2: 787.4–10): "Ratio enim formalis termini in hoc consistit, quod capit quod sit et sua realitas accipit quod realitas sit per productionem, sicut ratio subiecti in hoc consistit quod recipit realitatem illam. Hoc autem patet in omni productione; nam si albedo non acciperet entitatem per dealbationem, non esset formalis terminus dealbationis, nec forma ignis ignitionis; et sic de omni formali termino."

even a composite), it would be the "formal object" of my thought even though I would not be thinking of a form, for the "formal object" of thought is so-called not because it is a form, but rather simply because it is *thought about*.[5] Likewise, the "formal terminus" of a production is so-called not because it is a form, but rather simply because it is *produced* through that production. For Ockham, coming to exist through a production is precisely what makes something the "terminus" of that production.[6]

Note, however, that in terrestrial begetting—e.g. cases where one living organism begets another by introducing a substantial form into a lump of matter—it turns out that the form is the formal terminus of that production. For in such cases, the matter does not come to exist through that production, but the form does. So why doesn't Ockham just agree that the formal terminus is the form of the product?

The reason is that Ockham thinks it is logically possible for the matter to be produced too, for God could always produce the matter but not the form. As he puts it:

I say that although in creatures [lumps of] matter are presupposed by the action and production of natural causes, when it comes to God's action, matter is no more presupposed than a form. For why can't God create [a lump of] matter under a pre-existing natural form, just as he creates a substantial form in a pre-existing [lump of] matter?[7]

---

[5] Ockham, *Ord.*, 1.5.3 (*OTh* 3: 71.21–26): "Sicut si materia praecise intelligatur aliquo actu, non dicimus quod materia est obiectum materiale, sed dicimus quod materia est obiectum formale. Similiter, si aliquod totum intelligatur, et ratio terminandi illam intellectionem non sit plus forma quam materia, adhuc diceremus quod est obiectum formale et non materiale."

[6] Ockham, *Ord.*, 1.5.3 (*OTh* 3: 70.22–23): "dico quod terminus formalis productionis est illud quod capit esse simpliciter per illam productionem."

[7] Ockham, *Ord.*, 1.5.2 (*OTh* 3: 62.20–63.4): "dico quod quamvis in creaturis in actione et productione causarum naturalium materia praesupponatur, tamen quantum ad actionem Dei non plus praesupponitur materia quam forma. Quin sicut Deus creat formam substantialem in materia praeexistente ita posset creare materiam sub forma naturali praeexsistente?" One might object that if God created a lump of matter under a pre-existing form, a new substance would not be produced. After all, as I explained in section 2.1, the identity of a substance is determined by the presence of its individual substantial form. Thus, if the substantial form already existed, then the substance would exist already too, and so if God were to create a new lump of matter under that form, he would not produce a new substance; God would simply cause an already existing substance to be newly embodied. But that need not concern us, for the relevant point that Ockham is making here is just that it is logically possible for the matter to be produced rather than the form.

Hence, it is at least logically possible that the matter is produced but the form is not, and since Ockham believes the formal terminus of a production comes to exist through that production, it is at least logically possible that the formal terminus be the matter instead of the form. Ockham writes:

> From this, it follows that something is not called the 'formal terminus' [of a production] because it is the form [of the product]. For if God were to create [a lump of] matter that existed all by itself [without a form], that [lump of] matter would be the formal terminus [of the production], but it would not be a form. Similarly, if God were to create [a lump of] matter under a pre-existing form, the matter would be a formal terminus [of that production], not the form.[8]

In short, what matters when we talk about something as a formal terminus of production is not whether it is a form or a lump of matter. What matters is whether or not it is produced.

However, we need to be careful here. What about the production itself? Would that count as a formal terminus? Consider the following. If the Father did not produce the Son, then there would be no "production" to speak of, so surely there is a sense in which the Father brings about the production itself. But if that were right, wouldn't the production itself count as a formal terminus too?

Ockham admits that there is a sense in which the producer brings about the production itself, but as Ockham sees it, to say that a producer produces the production is a very improper way of speaking. Properly speaking, productions are not products, they are how products come about.[9] Thus, the formal terminus of a production cannot be totally identical to the production itself. Whatever we point

---

[8] Ockham, *Ord.*, 1.5.3 (*OTh* 3: 71.4–9): "Et ex isto sequitur quod non dicitur aliquid terminus formalis quia est forma. Nam si Deus crearet ipsam materiam per se exsistentem, illa materia esset terminus formalis, et tamen non esset forma. Similiter, si Deus crearet materiam sub forma praeexsistente, forma non esset terminus formalis sed ipsa materia."

[9] Strictly speaking, Ockham uses the word "communicates" rather than "produces," but I take it that the point is the same. Ockham, *Ord.*, 1.5.3 (*OTh* 3: 70.10–11, 17–21): "Secundo, dico quod 'communicari per productionem' accipitur multipliciter . . . Aliter accipitur largissime pro omni illo quod quocumque modo non habet esse sine illa productione. Et isto modo tam productum quam productio quam quidlibet quod est in producto communicatur. Sed iste est impropriissimus modus loquendi."

to as the formal terminus of a production, we had better be sure it is not just the production itself:

> I say that [to be] a formal terminus of a production requires some non-identity with the production itself when the production is a true thing— that is, [when the production] is not formally the same [as the formal terminus].[10]

The reason Ockham gives for this is that one and the same thing cannot be the terminus of itself.[11] He does not explain this in more detail, but he might be thinking that starting points are (at least logically) prior to ending points. And since it makes no sense to talk about something as being prior or posterior to itself, so also would it make no sense to talk about something as the terminus or end point of itself.[12]

Alternatively, Ockham might be trying to avoid an infinite regress here. If we said that productions themselves were produced, then we would have the following situation: if x were to produce a production P, then x would have to produce P by a further production P_1, and x would then have to produce P_1 by a further production P_2, and so on ad infinitum. In order to avoid this infinite regress, Ockham would want to say that productions themselves are not produced.

Either way, Ockham is clear that the formal terminus of a production cannot be the production itself. Consequently, the formal terminus must be (i) produced, and (ii) it cannot be the production itself.

---

[10] Ockham, *Ord.*, 1.5.3 (*OTh* 3: 80.23–81.1): "dico quod ad terminum formalem requiritur aliqua non-identitas ad ipsam productionem quando productio est vera res, hoc est, quod non sit idem formaliter."

[11] Ockham, *Ord.*, 1.5.3 (*OTh* 3: 72.13–14): "Secundum [viz. quod productio non est formalis terminus] ostendo, quia nihil unum et idem potest esse terminus sui ipsius."

[12] Ockham, *Ord.*, 1.5.3 (*OTh* 3: 68.15–17): "Praeterea, idem non est elicitivum alicuius productionis et terminus formalis eiusdem, quia idem non est prius et posterius se ipso." Ockham goes on to apply this to the divine case: if the divine essence is the power source for the Son's production (as Scotus says it is, as we shall see in Chapter 11), then it cannot also be the terminus of the Son's production. *Ord.*, 1.5.3 (*OTh* 3: 68.17–20): "Sed, secundum istos [viz. Scotus], principium elicitivum est prius origine, terminus autem formalis est posterior origine, maxime secundum eos. Sed essentia, secundum istos, est principium elicitivum generationis, igitur non est terminus formalis eiusdem."

Thus, Ockham rejects Scotus's T24 and defines the formal terminus of a production like this:[13]

> (T28) For any x and y,
> y is the formal terminus of a production $P =_{df}$ iff
>   (i) x produces y by P, and
>   (ii) y is not the same as P in every way.

Ockham also talks about the "total terminus" of production. He does not give a clear description of what he means by the "total terminus," except for the following obscure statement:

> Just as the nature of the total terminus of a production is not to have being totally except through that production, so also the nature of the formal terminus [of a production] is not to have being formally except through that production . . . Therefore, every terminus, whether it is the total or formal terminus [of some production], has the being that belongs to it through that production.[14]

As far as I can tell, this just means that the "total terminus" of a production is the *total product*. And, I think, the reason Ockham would want to distinguish between the total and formal terminus of a production is that sometimes total products include constituents that are also produced. If so, then like formal termini, total termini come to exist through a production, and presumably they cannot be identical to the production that brought them about either. However, a formal terminus might be a constituent of a larger whole product produced by the same production, whereas a total terminus will never be a constituent of a larger whole product produced by the same production.

If I am right about this, then the total terminus of a production will always be a formal terminus of that same production. After all, the total product comes to exist through its production, and it is not identical to the production itself, so it would satisfy all the requisite conditions in T28 for being a formal terminus. Thus, every total

---

[13] Ockham, *Ord.*, 1.5.3 (*OTh* 3: 73.18–20): "illud potest dici terminus formalis alicuius productionis quod simpliciter habet esse per productionem et non est formaliter ipsa productio."

[14] Ockham, *Ord.*, 1.5.3 (*OTh* 3: 68.4–13): "sicut de ratione termini totalis alicuius productionis est non habere esse totale nisi per productionem, ita de ratione termini formalis est non habere esse formale nisi per illam productionem . . . Igitur omnis terminus, sive totalis sive formalis, habet esse sibi conveniens per productionem."

product (the total terminus) will be a formal terminus of its production as well.

But not every formal terminus will be a total terminus. For example, when Isaac begets Jacob, Jacob's human form is a formal terminus of Jacob's production, for it comes to exist through Jacob's production, and it is not identical to Jacob's production. But it is not the total terminus, for the total product is Jacob himself. Thus, when the formal terminus is a constituent of a larger whole product produced by the same production, it will not be the total terminus of that production. And that, I take it, is the point of the following statement by Ockham:

> Whence, when the formal terminus and the total terminus [of some production] are distinguished, the formal terminus is something [e.g. a constituent] that belongs to the total terminus, and it comes to exist unqualifiedly through the production [of the total terminus].[15]

Given that, let me run through two different sorts of cases to help make this clear. Consider the following.

1. If God were to create a lump of matter all by itself (without any forms), it would be both the formal and the total terminus of production, for it would be the total product, and every total terminus is a formal terminus. Further, there would be no other formal termini, for nothing else is produced. Similarly, if God were to create a form all by itself, that form would be the total and the formal terminus of that production, and there would be no other formal termini.

2. When one living organism begets another by causing a pre-existing lump of matter to acquire a new substantial form, the produced offspring would be the total terminus of production, and like every total terminus, it would be a formal terminus too. However, its substantial form would be a formal terminus, but not a total terminus of that production. Its matter, in turn, would not be a terminus of the production at all, for it would not come to exist through that production.

---

[15] Ockham, *Ord.*, 1.5.3 (*OTh* 3: 70.23–71.4): "Unde quando terminus formalis et terminus totalis distinguuntur, terminus formalis est aliquid ipsius termini totalis, capiens simpliciter esse per illam productionem."

With all that said, let me define the total terminus of production like this:

(T29) For any *x* and *y*,
        y is the total terminus of a production *P* =$_{df}$ iff
        (i) *x* produces *y* by *P*,
        (ii) *y* is not the same as *P* in every way, and
        (iii) *y* is not a constituent *F* of some *z*, where
        x produces *z* by *P*, and *z* is not the same as *P* in every way.

In brief, Ockham believes that the formal terminus of a production is anything that comes to exist through that production which is not entirely the same as the production itself. This includes the whole product (the "total terminus," as Ockham calls it), or any other constituent that comes to exist in the product as part of the productive process. So whether or not the formal terminus of a production is a *form* is irrelevant. All that matters is whether or not it is produced.

6.2. THE TERMINUS OF DIVINE PRODUCTION

Having explained how he understands the formal and total terminus of production, Ockham then turns to divine production. When the Father produces the Son (for instance), what is the terminus there?

Obviously, the Son is the total terminus of his production, for he is the total product. That also means that the Son is a formal terminus of his production too, for as I explained in the last section, every total terminus is a formal terminus of that same production. However, the Son is constituted by the divine essence and his unique personal property of sonship, so are either of those a formal terminus as well?

Ockham says no. He first points out that the divine essence cannot be the formal terminus because it is not produced, and anything that is not produced through a particular production is just not a terminus of that production.[16] Ockham therefore rejects Scotus's claim that the divine essence is the formal terminus of production—

---

[16] Ockham, *Ord.*, 1.5.3 (*OTh* 3: 72.10–12): "Primum patet per argumenta facta contra priorem opinoinem [viz. opinionem Scoti quod essentia divina est formalis terminus productionis], quia terminus formalis est ille qui simpliciter habet esse per productionem; sed essentia non est huiusmodi. Igitur etc."; *Ord.*, 1.5.3 (*OTh* 3: 69.10–14): "Praeterea, si essentia sit terminus formalis generationis, aut hoc est quia

(T25) For any divine persons x and y,
    if x produces y by a production P,
    the divine essence D is the formal terminus of P.

—and instead, he agrees with Henry's claim that the divine essence is not the terminus of divine production at all:

(T23) For any divine persons x and y,
    if x produces y by a production P,
    the divine essence D is not the terminus of P in any sense.

What about the Son's unique personal property of sonship? Does it count as the formal terminus of the Son's production? On the face of it, one might think that Ockham would say yes. After all, there would be no sonship if the Son were not produced, so it would seem that the Son's sonship comes to exist through the Son's production.

But Ockham denies this. According to him, the Son's sonship just is the Son's production. Ockham defends this claim elsewhere,[17] and I will say a little more about this in section 13.2 later, but here we can think of it like this: "sonship" is just an abstract label for *being produced by a father*, so the Son's sonship is nothing more than his production itself. Consequently, the Son's sonship cannot be the formal terminus of his production, for as I explained in the last section, Ockham maintains that no production is the formal terminus of that production.[18]

The only terminus of the Son's production, then, is the Son himself, for the divine essence and sonship both fail to satisfy the requisite conditions for being termini of the Son's production. On Ockham's

---

simpliciter habet esse per productionem, aut quia habet esse in producto per productionem. Non propter primum, quia essentia, cum sit in Patre, non habet esse simpliciter per quamcumque productionem."

[17] Ockham, *Ord.*, 1.7.1 (*OTh* 3: 119.15–25).

[18] Ockham, *Ord.*, 1.5.3 (*OTh* 3: 72.13–16): "Secundum ostendo, quia nihil unum et idem potest esse terminus sui ipsius; sed ipsa productio [Filii] est relatio [viz. filiatio] realiter et formaliter, sicut post patebit; ergo relatio non potest esse terminus formalis ipsius productionis"; *Ord.*, 1.5.3 (*OTh* 3: 80.23–81.4): "Ad secundum dico quod ad terminum formalem requiritur aliqua non-identitas ad ipsam productionem quando productio est vera res, hoc est, quod non sit idem formaliter. Nunc autem in proposito, generatio et filiatio sunt idem formaliter, et ideo filiatio non est terminus formalis generationis, quamvis extensive loquendo se ipso capiat esse."

view, there is just one terminus in divine production, and that is simply the produced person.[19] As Ockham puts it:

> [The major premise:] That which can be called the 'formal terminus' of some production is that which comes to exist unqualifiedly through that production and which is not formally [the same] as the production itself. [The minor premise:] But the [produced] person [viz. the Son] comes to exist unqualifiedly through [his] being begotten, and he is not formally [the same as] the begetting itself. Therefore, he can be called the formal terminus of his begetting—though not by distinguishing [him] from the total terminus [of his generation, for in the Son's case, the 'formal terminus' and the 'total terminus' are the same, namely the Son himself]. The major premise is evident, and maximally so when nothing else can satisfy those conditions. So also is the minor premise true, for only the [produced] person [viz. the Son] satisfies those conditions. For although the [divine] essence is not formally [the same as] the begetting itself, it does not come to exist unqualifiedly through that begetting. Similarly, although the [Son's unique] relation [of sonship] in some way does come to exist through [the Son's] being begotten (like how the same thing is its own self), still that relation is not distinct in any way from the begetting [itself]. Therefore, etc.[20]

Now, Scotus does not believe that the divine essence is produced, but he is still willing to call it the formal terminus of the Son's production. Is Ockham's disagreement with Scotus here just a verbal

---

[19] Ockham, *Ord.*, 1.5.3 (*OTh* 3: 72.5–9): "Ex istis respondeo ad quaestionem. Primo, quod essentia non est terminus formalis generationis; secundo, quod nec relatio est terminus formalis; tertio, quod ipsa persona potest dici terminus formalis, non tamen distinguendo terminum formalem contra terminum totalem"; *Ord.*, 1.5.3 (*OTh* 3: 81.5–10): "Ad tertium dico quod persona est terminus formalis, non quidem distinguendo contra terminum totalem, quia ibi non distinguitur terminus formalis a totali. Utrum autem debeat proprie vocari terminus formalis vel terminus totalis vel neutro modo, est magis difficultas vocalis quam realis, ideo non est illi insistendum"; *Ord.*, 1.5.3 (*OTh* 3: 83.12–14): "Ad argumentum principale patet quod persona est terminus et formalis et totalis, eo modo quo est ibi terminus totalis et formalis."

[20] Ockham, *Ord.*, 1.5.3 (*OTh* 3: 73.18–74.3): "quia illud potest dici terminus formalis alicuius productionis quod simpliciter habet esse per productionem et non est formaliter ipsa productio. Sed persona habet simpliciter esse per generationem et non est formaliter ipsa generatio. Igitur potest dici terminus formalis ipsius, non tamen distinguendo contra terminum totalem. Maior est manifesta, maxime quando nihil aliud est quod habeat illas condiciones. Et ita est minor vera, quia sola persona habet istas condiciones. Essentia enim quamvis non sit formaliter ipsa generatio, non tamen habet esse simpliciter per generationem. Similiter relatio [viz. filiatio] quamvis habeat aliquo modo esse per generationem, sicut idem est se ipso, tamen nullo modo distinguitur a generatione, igitur etc."

disagreement, a mere quibble over what we should *call* the divine essence in the Son?

I do not think so. As I understand it, Ockham believes that production is, at bottom, all about *producing* things, so the "terminus" of a production has got to be produced. That is just what it means for something to be the terminus of a *production*. Consequently, if something is not produced, then it makes no sense to call it the "terminus" of production.

Indeed, if I gave you a piece of candy, nobody would say that your having my scrumptious piece of candy is the terminus of a "production." We might say it is the terminus of an act of giving, but not of an act of production.[21] Likewise, since the divine essence is not produced in the Son, it cannot be a terminus of production either. Instead, Ockham thinks we should just say that the divine essence is *shared* with the Son.

This last point about sharing requires some comment. Medieval authors like to talk about how things are "shared" or "communicated" through production. For instance, when Isaac begets Jacob, Isaac communicates a human form to Jacob. But Ockham points out that there are different ways that things can be "shared" or "communicated" through production. He writes:

> I say that 'to be shared [or communicated] through production' is taken in many ways. First, most strictly, and in this way, something is shared [through production] when, existing in the begetter, it [also] comes to exist in the begotten through the production [of that begotten thing]. In this way, the [divine] essence is shared with the Son just as much as the act of producing the Spirit is. Second, ['to be shared or communicated through production' can be taken] broadly, and in this way whatever exists in the product through the production [of that product] and is

---

[21] Or, to put it more abstractly, it is the terminus of a particular sort of *relationship*, and the terminus of that relationship is determined by the sort of relationship it is, as Ockham says in the following quotation from *Ord.*, 1.5.3 (*OTh* 3: 81.12–21): "Hoc patet, quia illud dicitur terminus alicuius respectus respectu cuius aliud denominatur ab illo respectu. Sed pater vere dicitur generans in habitudine ad filium, quia pater vere dicitur generans filium, sicut dominus vere dicitur dominus servi et simile simili simile. Igitur sicut servus est terminus illius respectus, scilicet dominii, ita Filius vere dicetur terminus illius generationis. Praeterea, illud quod vere refertur, vere habet terminum terminantem illum respectum; sed Pater vere refertur ad Filium; ergo Filius vere terminat relationem." From these comments, I think it is fair to extrapolate the following point on Ockham's behalf: if the relationship in question is a *production* relationship, then surely the terminus of that relationship is *produced*.

not the same in every way with the production and the product is communicated [to the product through the production]. In this way, [a lump of] matter is communicated [to the product through the production] just as much as a form is.[22]

Here Ockham explains that in a loose way, a medieval author can say that a producer communicates, e.g. a lump of matter or a substantial form to a product, but that really just means that the producer causes it to become a constituent of the product (irrespective of whether it is produced in the product or not). Strictly speaking though, one can only say that a producer *shares* something with a product if the shared item exists in the producer, and then *also* comes to exist in the product through the production. So let me define sharing like this:

(T30) For any *x*, *y*, and *F*
  x shares *F* with *y* by a production *P* =$_{df}$ iff
  (i) *x* produces *y* by *P*,
  (ii) *F* is a constituent of *x*, and
  (iii) *x* causes *F* to also be a constituent of *y* by *P*.

And of course, as Ockham notes in the above-quoted passage, this is precisely how the Father shares the divine essence with the Son. The divine essence exists in the Father, and by producing the Son, the Father causes the numerically same divine essence to also come to exist in the Son.

Ockham also points out that the Father shares lots of things with the Son through production (e.g. his act of producing the Spirit), but those things are not the "formal termini" of production. And from that, Ockham infers that sharing and producing must have different termini:

To be shared through some production and to be the formal terminus of that production are different. This is clear because by begetting [the Son], [the Father] shares his act of producing the Spirit with the Son. For whatever the Son has, he has from the Father through being begotten by the Father, and therefore the act of producing the Spirit

---

[22] Ockham, *Ord.*, 1.5.3 (*OTh* 3: 70.10–17): "dico quod 'communicari per productionem' accipitur multipliciter. Primo strictissime, et sic illud communicatur quod habens esse in generante capit esse in genito per productionem. Et isto modo tam essentia quam spiratio activa communicatur Filio. Aliter accipitur large, et sic omne quod habet esse in producto per ipsam productionem et non est idem omnibus modis cum productione et producto communicatur. Et isto modo tam materia quam forma communicatur."

belongs to the Son through his being begotten by the Father. By consequence, the [Father] shares [his act of producing the Spirit] with the Son through [the Son's] generation, but nevertheless, the act of producing the Spirit is not the formal terminus of [the Son's] production.[23]

Given this distinction between sharing and producing, we can see why Ockham would not want to call the divine essence the "formal terminus" of production. The divine essence is shared, not produced, so if anything, it is the terminus of an act of sharing, not an act of production.

In the end then, Ockham rejects Scotus's claim that the divine essence is the formal terminus of divine production. However, Scotus's criticisms of Henry are based on this claim, but since Ockham rejects this claim, Ockham must attack Henry in a way different from Scotus. As we shall see in the next chapter, that is exactly what Ockham does.

---

[23] Ockham, *Ord.*, 1.5.3 (*OTh* 3: 70.2–9): "quod aliud est communicari per aliquam productionem et esse terminum formalem illius productionis. Patet, quia spiratio activa comunicatur Filio per generationem. Quia quidquid habet Filius, habet a Patre et nascendo habet a Patre; igitur spirationem activam nascendo habet a Patre; et per consequens communicatur sibi per generationem. Et tamen spiratio activa non est terminus formalis illius productionis."

7

Ockham against Henry

As I pointed out at the beginning of the last chapter, Ockham sides with Scotus against Henry's view that the divine essence plays the role of matter in divine production. But Ockham critiques Henry with a strategy different from Scotus. For if, says Ockham, the divine essence is supposed to play the role of matter, then Henry must mean this in a literal way or a figurative way. That is, Henry must think either that the divine essence *really is* a lump of matter, or he must think that it is only *like* a lump of matter.[1] As we shall see in this chapter, Ockham believes that Henry and his followers have no good reason to sustain either option.

7.1. THE DIVINE ESSENCE IS NOT A LITERAL LUMP OF MATTER

As for the first of the two options I just mentioned—that the divine essence is literally a lump of matter—Ockham offers a number of reasons why this cannot be true, and two of those are worth mentioning.

First, Ockham points out that one of the defining characteristics of lumps of matter is that they have the potential to acquire substantial forms.[2] For Ockham, part of what this means is that lumps of matter

---

[1] Ockham, *Ordinatio* [= *Ord.*], 1.5.2 (*OTh* 3: 53.6–8): "Ideo arguo contra praedictam opinionem [Henrici]. Quaero: aut essentia divina dicetur proprie materia, aut per similitudinem tantum et non per proprietatem."

[2] Ockham, *Ord.*, 1.5.2 (*OTh* 3: 53.8–11): "Non primo modo [i.e. essentia non dicetur proprie materia], quia materia ita dicitur praecise de materia quae vere est

and substantial forms must be really distinct. Indeed, so far as Ockham is concerned, the fact that forms can be gained and lost entails that they are extrinsic to the lumps of matter that gain and lose them. The divine essence, however, cannot be really distinct from the personal properties it combines with in order to constitute the persons, for as I explained in section 1.4, the divine essence is really the same as everything in the Godhead. Thus, the divine essence cannot literally be a really distinct lump of matter because it is really the same as the personal properties.[3]

Ockham's second reason for saying that the divine essence is not literally a lump of matter runs as follows:

> In this way then, the divine essence is not said to literally be [a lump of] matter, for it could just as easily be said to literally be a donkey or a cow. This is clear because whenever something common is divided into inferiors, each of which is always denied of the other, then nothing contained under one of them can be said to truly and literally be anything contained under the other. But 'being' is first divided into 'created being' and 'uncreated being', and it is always the case that no created being is uncreated, and conversely, that no uncreated being is a created being. Therefore, nothing contained under 'created being' is said to literally be an uncreated being. But 'created being' is divided into 'substance' and 'accident', and 'substance' is further divided into 'matter', 'form', and 'composite'. Therefore, neither matter, form, nor a composite [of both] is said to literally be an uncreated being.[4]

in potentia ad formam aliquam differentem sicut forma dicitur praecise de altera parte perficiente materiam differentem."

[3] Ockham, *Ord.*, 1.5.2 (*OTh* 3: 61.18–62.1, 62.5–9): "dico quod potentia et actus non possunt competere nisi rebus realiter distinctis. Et ideo sicut in Deo, secundum omnes, non est ponenda nec compositio nec quasi-compositio, ideo eodem modo non est ponendum ibi quod aliquid sit potentia vel actus respectu alterius, et hoc propter identitatem realem essentiae [divinae] et relationis [e.g. filiationis] in divinis . . . dico quod quaecumque concurrunt ad constitutionem alicuius et distinguuntur realiter, oportet quod unum sit potentia et aliud actus, nisi sint partes integrales. Sed relatio et essentia sunt una res [quia sunt perfecte eaedem], et ideo neutrum est potentia respectu alterius."

[4] Ockham, *Ord.*, 1.5.2 (*OTh* 3: 54.3–54.15): "Sic igitur essentia divina non dicitur proprie materia, quia eadem facilitate diceretur proprie asinus et proprie bos. Hoc patet quia quando aliquod commune dividitur in sua inferiora quorum utrumque universaliter negatur ab alio, nullum contentum sub quocumque illorum potest vere et proprie verificari de reliquo contento. Sed ens primo dividitur in ens creatum et in ens increatum. Et universaliter nullum ens creatum est increatum, et e converso nullum ens increatum est ens creatum. Ergo nullum contentum sub ente creato dicitur proprie de ente increato. Sed ens creatum dividitur in substantiam et accidens, et ultra

According to Ockham here, the category of "being" is divided into two mutually exclusive subcategories: created being and uncreated being. But since this division is mutually exclusive, nothing that belongs on the one side can also belong on the other. Lumps of matter, of course, belong on the side of "created being," so they cannot belong on the side of "uncreated being."

7.2. THE DIVINE ESSENCE IS NOT LIKE A LUMP OF MATTER

Since the divine essence cannot literally be a lump of matter, one might think that Henry must mean it is only *like* a lump of matter. But as I said above, Ockham does not believe Henry and his followers have any good reason to sustain this either.

As Ockham sees it, we can only say one thing is like another if the two have something in common by which we can compare them in the first place.[5] For instance, if Socrates had nothing in common with Beulah the cow (and for the sake of argument, let us ignore the fact that both are animals), we would have no reason to say "Socrates is like Beulah." But if, say, Socrates had the unfortunate and socially embarrassing habit of chewing his cud, just like Beulah, then we could say "Socrates is like Beulah" insofar as both chew their cuds.

Similarly, if Henry wants to say "the divine essence is like a lump of matter," then Henry can only say this if God and lumps of matter have something in common by which they can be compared. Thus, Henry needs to identify precisely what it is that God and lumps of matter have in common, for that is the only way Henry could justify such a comparison.

Some of Henry's followers seemed to realize this, for they try to do just that. Ockham considers one of these attempts, namely that of Robert Cowton. Robert was a supporter of Henry's theory and a near

---

substantia in materiam et formam et compositum. Igitur nec materia nec forma proprie dicitur de ente increato nec etiam compositum."

[5] Ockham, *Ord.*, 1.5.2 (*OTh* 3: 54.16–19): "Si dicatur quod materia dicitur tantum per similitudinem, non per proprietatem, hoc non potest esse nisi propter aliquas condiciones communes Deo et materiae et aliis, vel propter condiciones proprias Deo et materiae."

contemporary of Ockham's at Oxford.[6] According to Robert, lumps of matter have some features that are perfect, and some that are imperfect.[7] As for the imperfect features, Robert claims there are three.[8]

(1) When one living organism begets another,
   the producer and the product have *different* lumps of matter:
   there is one lump of matter in the producer,
   and another in the product.

(2) A lump of matter has the *potential*
   to acquire really distinct forms.

(3) Living organisms beget their offspring
   through a *change*.

In addition to these three imperfections, Robert thinks there are also three perfections of note:[9]

(4) When one living organism begets another,
   the lumps of matter in the producer and the product
   are the *same in kind*, for both are lumps of matter.

(5) A lump of matter combines with something else
   (i.e. a substantial form) in order to constitute
   a *unified object*, e.g. a living organism
   (though Robert notes that it is an imperfection that
   this unification comes about through composition).

---

[6] For more about Robert's life and works, see Andrew Little, *The Greyfriars in Oxford* (Oxford: Clarendon Press, 1892), 222–3. For more about Robert's theological thought in general, see Hermann Theissing, *Glaube und Theologie bei Robert Cowton, OFM* (Münster: Aschendorffsche Verlagsbuchhandlung, 1970).

[7] Ockham, *Ord.*, 1.5.2 (*OTh* 3: 49.11–13), quoting Robert Cowton, *Sent.*, 1.5.1 (cod. Oxon., Merton 93, f. 88va-vb): "Ista opinio ab aliquibus declaratur sic: «Circa materiam istorum generabilium et corruptibilium est invenire aliqua perfectionis sed plura imperfectionis»."

[8] Ockham, *Ord.*, 1.5.2 (*OTh* 3: 49.13–50.2), quoting Robert, ibid.: "«Primum imperfectionis est quod materia est alia secundum essentiam in generante et genito; secundum, quod est in potentia ante actum quantum est ex se ad formam realiter differentem; tertium, quod per realem transmutationem vadit de potentia ad actum»."

[9] Ockham, *Ord.*, 1.5.2 (*OTh* 3: 50.2–7), quoting Robert, ibid.: "«Sed perfectionis est quod materia est eiusdem rationis in generante et genito; secundum, quod cum termino formali constituit per se unum,—licet sit imperfectionis quod cum termino formali realiter componit—; tertium, quod materia est illud de quo constitutum generatur, ne sit de nihilo»."

(6) Lumps of matter explain why naturally begotten
organisms are *not created ex nihilo*.

Having identified these imperfections and perfections, Robert then
claims that the divine essence shares perfections (4)–(6) with lumps
of matter, but not the imperfections (1)–(3).

As for (1), Robert points out that the Father and Son do not have
distinct "lumps of matter." On the contrary, they share the very same
divine essence. With respect to (2), Robert admits that the divine
essence has no potentiality, and so the potentiality in matter does not
transfer over to divine production. And as for (3), Robert claims that
there is no change in divine production. This clearly follows from (2):
if the divine essence has no potentiality, it cannot go from a potential
state to an actual state, and so of course there cannot be any change in
divine production.

But as I said, Robert maintains that the divine essence does have
the three perfections (4)–(6) in common with lumps of matter. As for
(4), the "lump of matter" in the Father and the Son (i.e. the divine
essence) is the same in kind, just as lumps of matter in living organisms are the same in kind. With respect to (5), the divine essence
"combines," so to speak, with a personal property to constitute a
unified divine person, just as lumps of matter combine with substantial forms to constitute unified organisms. And as for (6), the divine
essence explains why the Son is not created *ex nihilo*, just as lumps of
matter explain why naturally begotten organisms are not created
from nothing. As Robert himself puts it:

> Therefore, by ignoring all these imperfections—namely the diversity of
> matter in the begetter and the begotten, matter's potential for diverse
> forms, and the change by which it goes from potentiality to a really
> different actuality—and by considering matter only insofar as it is
> common to the begetter and the begotten, and insofar as it is that
> from which something is not [created] from nothing, and insofar as
> along with something [else] it formally constitutes a complete produced
> person, it is said that in this way matter should be postulated in God [so
> that the Son] is not [produced] from nothing or from some alien
> substance.[10]

[10] Ockham, *Ord.*, 1.5.2 (*OTh* 3: 50.8–19), quoting Robert, ibid.: "«Circumscribendo
igitur omnes istas imperfectiones, scilicet diversitatem materiae in generante et genito,
et potentialitatem ipsius ad diversas formas, et transmutationem per quam vadit de
potentia ad actum realiter differentem, considerando solam materiam ut est

Thus, one could see Robert as attempting to identify precisely what the divine essence has in common with lumps of matter, and that commonality is what licenses saying that the divine essence is like matter.

Nevertheless, Ockham is not convinced. He points out that commonality sometimes extends to other things too, in which case we have no reason to compare any two of those things over any other two. To use my example of Socrates and Beulah again, Socrates and cows are not the only animals who chew cuds. Camels, llamas, giraffes, and other animals do too. Consequently, if the only reason that we can say "Socrates is like Beulah" is that Socrates and Beulah both chew their cuds, then we would have just as much reason to say "Socrates is like a camel" or "Socrates is like a llama."

Likewise in the divine case. If Henry and his followers identify something that not just the divine essence and lumps of matter have in common, but rather something that the divine essence and lumps of matter also have in common with *other things*, then we would have no more reason to say "the divine essence is like a lump of matter" than we would to say that the divine essence is like something else.[11]

As Ockham sees it, this is precisely the problem with Robert's view, for Robert has identified features that the divine essence has in common not just with lumps of matter, but also with forms. Consider Robert's (4)–(6) again. First, (4) states that the lumps of matter in a begetter and the begotten are the same in kind, but this is true of forms too, for children have the same kinds of forms as their parents. Second, (5) states that a lump of matter combines with a form to constitute an internally unified object, but of course, this is also true of forms. Finally, (6) states that lumps of matter explain why products are not created *ex nihilo*, but as we have seen, Ockham insists that it is logically possible for the form rather than the matter to be the "pre-

communis gignenti et genito, et ut est de quo est aliquid ne sit de nihilo, et ut cum aliquo formali constituit suppositum perfectum productum, dicitur quod sic materia ponenda est in divinis ne sit de nihilo vel de substantia aliena»."

[11] Ockham, *Ord.*, 1.5.2 (*OTh* 3: 54.16–21): "Si dicatur quod materia dicitur tantum per similitudinem, non per proprietatem, hoc non potest esse nisi propter aliquas condiciones communes Deo et materiae et aliis, vel propter condiciones proprias Deo et materiae. Non propter primum, quia tunc ita diceretur quod essentia divina esset asinus vel lapis, quae omnia dicuntur de Deo per similitudinem, non per proprietatem."

existing ingredient," so to speak, that can also explain why a product is not created from nothing.[12]

But since the divine essence has these features in common with forms too, then as far as Ockham is concerned, Robert has no more reason to say that the divine essence is like a lump of matter than he does to say it is like a form. And the implication is this: if Henry and his followers want to claim that the divine essence is like a lump of matter rather than a form, they are at least going to have to identify something that is common *only* to the divine essence and lumps of matter.

Robert may recognize this too, for he tries to argue that the divine essence is *more* like matter than a form. Ockham recites three of Robert's arguments for this conclusion, but the first of them is the most illuminating. Robert argues as follows:

> That which is in itself constitutive of a produced person and is pre-supposed by that generation corresponds more to the matter in natural begetting than a substantial form. But the [divine] essence has all of the being that is proper to it in the Father prior in origin than it does in the Son. Therefore, sonship has more of the character of the formal terminus [of production] than the [divine] essence.[13]

Ockham is not convinced by this argument either. In response, he writes:

---

[12] Ockham, *Ord.*, 1.5.2 (*OTh* 3: 55.7–16): "Praeterea, nihil perfectionis competit ipsi materiae quin illud idem competat formae. Patet inductive, quia illa forma est eiusdem rationis in generante et genito sicut materia. Similiter, ita cum aliquo constituit unum sicut materia. Similiter, ita potest forma esse illud de quo constitutum producitur ne sit de nihilo sicut materia. Probatio istius: si anima intellectiva praecederet materiam, et Deus crearet materiam sub anima intellectiva, illud totum non esset de nihilo quia tunc crearetur, quod falsum est, cum aliquid ipsius praesupponatur. Igitur, est de forma, ne sit de nihilo." See also *Ord.*, 1.5.2 (*OTh* 3: 54.25–55.7): "Probatio assumpti: quia una condicio formae in generatione univoca est quod forma est eiusdem rationis in generante et genito, licet imperfectionis sit quod numeretur in eis. Haec autem condicio competit divinae essentiae, quia est eiusdem rationis innumerata in Patre et Filio. Et similiter perfectionis est in forma quod cum aliquo constituit unum, licet sit imperfectionis quod componit. Ergo illud attribuitur divinae essentiae quod perfectionis est, removendo illud quod est imperfectionis."

[13] Ockham, *Ord.*, 1.5.2 (*OTh* 3: 51.1–6), quoting Robert, ibid.: "«illud quod est per se constitutivum suppositi producti et praesupponitur ipsi generationi, magis convenit cum materia in generatione naturali quam cum forma substantiali. Sed essentia habet totum esse sibi proprium in Patre prius origine quam sit in Filio. Igitur filiatio magis habet rationem termini formalis quam essentia»."

I say that [the claim] that 'the [divine] essence has all of the being that is proper to it [in the Father] prior in origin than it does in the Son' can be understood in two ways. Either it [means that the divine essence] is totally in the Father, who is prior in origin to the Son, and in this way, it should be conceded. But it does not follow from this that [the divine essence] is more [like] matter than form. Alternatively, [the aforementioned claim] can be understood like this: the [divine] essence itself is prior in origin to the Son [as a producer is to its product], and this I say is unqualifiedly false, for then the Son would be from the [divine] essence and he would be produced from the [divine] essence, which is unqualifiedly false. Nevertheless, this [second kind of] priority, if it were there [in God], would mean nothing for [the claim] that [the divine essence] is [like a lump of] matter.[14]

As Ockham explains here, Robert says that the divine essence is "prior in origin" to the Son, but Robert could mean two things by this. Either he means that the divine essence is totally in the Father too, in which case the divine essence is just an unproduced constituent in the Son (which is true); or Robert means that the divine essence itself produces the Son (which is false). But either way, Ockham thinks this has no bearing on whether the divine essence is more like a lump of matter than it is like a form.

Indeed, as we have seen, Ockham insists that it is logically possible for forms to be unproduced constituents just like lumps of matter, so just being an unproduced constituent is not enough to make the divine essence more like a lump of matter than a form. Additionally, nobody thinks the divine essence actually produces the Son (see T11 in section 1.4). But even if that were an option, it would give us no reason to say that the divine essence is more like a lump of matter than a form. If anything, it would make the divine essence more like a substance, for substances are normally producers, and lumps of matter are not.

Besides, even if Henry and his followers could identify something common only to the divine essence and lumps of matter, Ockham

---

[14] Ockham, *Ord.*, 1.5.2 (*OTh* 3: 64.12–21): "dico quod [divinam] essentiam habere esse totum sibi proprium prius origine quam sit in Filio potest intelligi dupliciter. Vel quod sit in Patre tota, qui est prior origine Filio, et sic est concedendum. Sed ex hoc non sequitur quod sit plus materia quam forma. Aliter potest intelligi quod ipsamet essentia sit prior origine Filio, et hoc dico esse simpliciter falsum, quia tunc Filius esset ab essentia et produceretur ab essentia, quod est simpliciter falsum. Tamen illa prioritas, si esset ibi, nihil faceret ad hoc quod esset materia."

thinks it is still easy enough to point to other features that are common only to the divine essence and forms.[15] For instance, unlike lumps of matter, forms are the constituents that make composite substances the kinds of things they are, and that includes giving them powers to do certain things (I will say more about this in Part II). Lumps of matter do not function in this way at all, so why shouldn't Henry and his followers use this as a reason to say that the divine essence is more like a form than matter?[16] Ockham summarizes this whole argument concisely when he writes:

> If it is said that [God is a lump of] matter not literally but rather only by some likeness, this can only be because there are some features that are common to God, [lumps of] matter, and other things, or because there are features that are unique to God and [lumps of] matter. Not the first, because then it could be said that the divine essence is a donkey or a stone, for all things are said of God by some likeness and not literally. Not the second, because just as some properties belong to God and [lumps of] matter uniquely (according to them [viz. Henry and his followers]), so also do other properties belong uniquely to God and forms. Consequently, the divine essence could be called a form just as much as [a lump of] matter.[17]

What is illuminating about all of this is that it highlights the precise point of comparison that Henry draws between the divine essence and lumps of matter. For Henry and his followers, it seems to boil

---

[15] Ockham, *Ord.*, 1.5.2 (*OTh* 3: 54.16–25): "Si dicatur quod materia dicitur tantum per similitudinem, non per proprietatem, hoc non potest esse nisi propter aliquas condiciones communes Deo et materiae et aliis, vel propter condiciones proprias Deo et materiae ... Nec propter secundum, quia sicut aliquae proprietates conveniunt Deo et materiae praecise, secundum eos, ita aliquae conveniunt praecise Deo et formae, et ita per consequens essentia divina diceretur forma sicut materia."

[16] Ockham, *Ord.*, 1.5.2 (*OTh* 3: 55.16–20): "Similiter, perfectionis est facere constitutum esse in actu; sed hoc verius competit formae quam materiae. Similiter, perfectionis est esse principium agendi; sed hoc vel praecise competit formae vel verius sibi quam materiae; igitur verius poterit dici quod essentia divina sit forma Filii quam materia."

[17] Ockham, *Ord.*, 1.5.2 (*OTh* 3: 54.16–25): "Si dicatur quod materia dicitur tantum per similitudinem, non per proprietatem, hoc non potest esse nisi propter aliquas condiciones communes Deo et materiae et aliis, vel propter condiciones proprias Deo et materiae. Non propter primum, quia tunc ita diceretur quod essentia divina esset asinus vel lapis, quae omnia dicuntur de Deo per similitudinem, non per proprietatem. Nec propter secundum, quia sicut aliquae proprietates conveniunt Deo et materiae praecise, secundum eos, ita aliquae conveniunt praecise Deo et formae, et ita per consequens essentia divina diceretur forma sicut materia."

down to this: like lumps of matter in terrestrial begetting, the divine essence is an *unproduced constituent* of the Son. And it is this that ultimately justifies Henry's theory that the divine essence plays the role of matter in divine production.

But as we have seen, Ockham believes that it is at least logically possible for forms to be unproduced constituents too. So just because the divine essence is an unproduced constituent in the Son gives Henry and his followers no good reason to say that the divine essence is more like a lump of matter than a form.

7.3. CONCLUSION

Like Scotus, Ockham believes that producers can produce products without materials, but this does not mean that such products are created *ex nihilo*. On the contrary, a product only needs one unproduced constituent to be uncreated, and that can be a form just as much as it can be something material. Scotus and Ockham, then, are united against Henry on this question.

Nevertheless, Ockham is far more agnostic about this issue than either Henry or Scotus. As I explained at the beginning of the last chapter, Ockham thinks everybody agrees about the "bare essentials" of divine production, so as he sees it, the issue is really about how to best characterize divine production.

Of course, Ockham thinks that Scotus's theory is the most intelligible way to characterize divine production, but Ockham admits that there is no good way to *disprove* Henry's theory. Scotus makes a valiant attempt, but Ockham thinks his fundamental premise—that the divine essence must be the formal terminus of divine production—is false, and that means Scotus's criticism just does not work against Henry's theory.

Similarly, one could attempt to disprove Henry's theory by pointing to the imperfections of matter, but Henry and his followers (in a somewhat ad hoc way) claim that those imperfections are simply not there in God, and so far as Ockham is concerned, this just goes to show that Henry and his followers are simply picking and choosing which aspects of "matter" they want to apply to God. As Ockham himself puts it:

This opinion [of Henry and his followers] is difficult to disprove, because it consists more in an abusive way of speaking than in [an abusive way of understanding] reality. For it cannot be disproved [as Scotus tries to do] by asserting that the [divine] essence is the formal terminus of [divine] begetting, for...the [divine] essence is not the formal terminus of divine begetting. Nor can it easily be disproved by asserting that material causality is said to be imperfect...for they said—by an abuse of words—that the material cause [in divine production, namely the divine essence]...is not said to be imperfect. Whence, speaking metaphorically, they said that the material cause [in divine production] is said to be perfect unqualifiedly, and so it should be postulated with respect to the Son because he is not [created] from nothing...Many other arguments against the aforesaid [opinion] are [even] less valid, because those arguments accept many things that are just plain false.[18]

With that, we have reached the end of Part I. Thus far, I have discussed what Henry, Scotus, and Ockham think is involved when a divine person is *produced*. In Part II, I will look at what these authors think it takes for a divine person to be a *producer*.

---

[18] Ockham, *Ord.*, 1.5.2 (*OTh* 3: 52.9–53.5): "Istam opinionem, quia magis consistit in abusivo modo loquendi quam in re, difficile est improbare. Non enim potest improbari per hoc quod essentia est terminus formalis generationis quia...essentia non est terminus formalis generationis divinae. Nec potest faciliter improbari per hoc quod...causalitas materialis non dicit perfectionem, quia dicerent—abutendo vocabulo—quod causa materialis...non dicit aliquid imperfectionis. Unde dicerent sic, metaphorice loquendo, quod causa materialis dicit perfectionem simpliciter et ponenda est respectu Filii quia non est de nihilo...Multa alia argumenta contra praedicta minus valent, quia multa eorum accipiunt simpliciter falsa."

Part II

How a Divine Person is a Producer

8

Action and Producers

In Part I, we saw that Henry, Scotus, and Ockham take inspiration from an Aristotelian model of production when they discuss how a divine person is *produced*. Here in Part II, I want to look at the way these same authors explain how a divine person is a *producer*. As we shall see, they take inspiration from Aristotelian philosophy on this front too, though in this case, the model focuses on action and power, for it seeks to explain not only how action comes about, but also how things get the power to bring about action. In this chapter, I want to provide a brief outline of this Aristotelian approach to action and power. This model is designed to explain action amongst creatures, so my discussion here is accordingly restricted to the domain of creatures. We will see in later chapters how Henry, Scotus, and Ockham each apply this model to the Godhead.

8.1. ACTION

According to the Aristotelian model of change I discussed in section 2.1, a change occurs when a capable recipient gains or loses a form. However, changes need something to bring them about, for recipients are passive with respect to the process of change. Indeed, recipients are called "recipients" precisely because changes happen *to them*. Thus, a change needs something to cause it to happen. That is, it needs an agent.

But that is not all. A change also needs the right kind of agent, namely one that is capable of causing the change in question. After all, not every agent can bring about just any change whatever. I, for one, simply do not have the ability or know-how to bake a fancy wedding cake, so I could not do so even if all the ingredients were laid out before me.

In this sense, agents must be "capable" just like recipients. As I pointed out in section 2.1, recipients are only capable of undergoing certain types of changes. Pots of water, for example, can be heated, but angels or disembodied souls cannot. So any given type of change can only happen to those recipients that have the capacity to undergo that type of change. Likewise for agents: only those with the ability to bring about that type of change can do so.

Consequently, since agents only have the ability to bring about certain types of changes, and since recipients likewise only have the capacity to undergo certain types of changes, it follows that any given change can occur only if the right kind of agent is matched up with the right kind of recipient. A change requires both a capable recipient and a capable agent.

Of course, before a change can occur, capable agents and recipients have to be in the right circumstances. For medieval Aristotelians, this means first that the recipient must be near enough for the agent to act on it, and second, that there cannot be any obstacles standing in the way. But provided that a capable agent and a capable recipient are near enough and there are no obstacles, the agent can cause the recipient to undergo the change in question.

Consider, for example, flames and pots of water: flames are capable of heating other things, and pots of water are capable of being heated. However, a flame cannot heat a pot of water from all the way across the room, nor can it heat a pot of water through a heat shield. A flame can only heat a pot of water if the pot is near enough and there are no obstacles standing in the way. Hence, action requires a capable agent, a capable recipient, and the right circumstances.

Now, it is important to note that in this context, action occurs, properly speaking, only when agents act *upon* recipients. As an analogue, we might compare agents to surgeons, for surgeons always operate upon patients. So also on this model: agents always act upon a susceptible recipient. Consequently, whenever an agent performs an action, a corresponding recipient undergoes that same action, similar to the way that when a surgeon performs a surgery, there is a patient who undergoes that very same surgery.

However, the surgery analogy only goes so far. When a surgeon perform a surgery, she first brings about certain changes in herself—e.g. she moves her arm, that moves the scalpel, and so on—and those changes in turn bring about the relevant change in the patient. But that much does not apply to the Aristotelian model of action we are considering here. On the contrary, according to this model, the agent undergoes no change itself. Rather, the only change that happens occurs in the recipient.

More precisely, there is *one change* for any given action, and it always happens to the recipient alone. The "doing" and the "undergoing" refer to that same change, but in different respects. The "doing" refers to the change with respect to the agent who causes it, and the "undergoing" refers to that very same change with respect to the recipient who undergoes it. Still, there is just one change on this model, and it occurs only in the recipient.

To modern ears, this idea might sound strange, but let me try to motivate it in the following way. If we try to come up with a theory of action purely on the basis of what we can observe, then there are many cases where it appears that the change happens only in the recipient. For instance, when a flame heats a pot of water, there is clearly an observable change in the water, but—and here is the bit to notice—nothing at all appears to happen to the flame. The flame just sits there, flickering and doing its thing, as it were, while the water gets hotter and hotter. The flame is clearly causing the water to get warmer, but it seems to be doing so by exercising its causal powers "invisibly," so to speak.

Of course, when an agent acts on a recipient, a *causal relationship* develops that was not there before the agent started acting on the recipient. But on the model we are considering here, that is the only major difference between an inactive agent and an active one. Strictly speaking, when an agent acts on a recipient, all that "happens to it" is that it enters into this causal relationship with the recipient, whereas the recipient alone undergoes the change on which that causal relationship is based.

What I have described thus far is a model for what we might call "transient" activity, i.e. the sort of activity that occurs when an agent's activity is directed outside itself and onto something else. And as I mentioned a moment ago, there are plenty of cases where this sort of thing happens. When flames heat pots of water, when the sun makes Socrates tan, and so on—all of these are clear cases where an agent acts on a recipient. Similarly, there are plenty of cases where agents act on a part of themselves (like when I raise my arm and scratch my head), and those sorts of activities count as "transient" activity too, for the part that undergoes the change is distinct from the part that causes the change.

But there are other cases where an agent does not seem to act on a recipient at all. For instance, when I ponder the great mysteries of the universe, it might seem as if I am not acting on anything. After all, I am just sitting there, staring up into the stars. Similarly, when I decide that later in the day I will go to the park instead of going to class, it might seem as if I am not acting on anything there either. Instead, I am just choosing to take a certain course of action later in the day.

These sorts of activity are what we might call "immanent" activity, i.e. activity that remains within the agent rather than extending outside the agent. And indeed, medieval Aristotelians think that the two paradigm cases of "immanent" activity are thinking and willing, like in the two examples I just mentioned.

I should note, however, that willing is a unique kind of activity because it happens voluntarily, and this highlights the Aristotelian distinction between natural and voluntary changes. A change is natural if it is the type of change that an agent brings about whenever, wherever, and to the fullest extent that it can. In other words, natural changes happen "automatically," so to speak, whenever a capable agent and recipient are in the right circumstances. For instance, flames heat naturally because they heat whatever they can, to the fullest possible extent, and at every opportunity. Similarly, certain involuntary acts of thought are natural in the same way. When I see a tree, for example, I cannot help but become aware of that tree.

Voluntary changes, on the other hand, are not like this, for voluntary changes only come about if the agent chooses to bring them about. Thus, even if a capable agent and recipient are in the right circumstances, a voluntary change need not occur, for it requires an extra step, namely that the agent chooses to bring it about.

Nevertheless, even in cases of thinking and willing, the model of "transient" action can be applied in an extended sense. For when I think and will, one could say that my mind or soul counts as a recipient in some sense because it comes to have various thoughts and volitions it did not have before.

According to this Aristotelian model then, action occurs when an agent causes a change in a recipient. But in order for that to happen, the agent must have the ability to bring about the change in question, the recipient must likewise be capable of undergoing the change, and the two must be near enough and there cannot be any obstacles.

There is, however, just one change, and it happens in the recipient. The agent undergoes no change itself, save for entering into a causal relationship with the recipient undergoing the change.

8.2. POWER

Still, one might wonder: what makes an agent or recipient "capable"? On this model, capability is parsed out in terms of powers. That is, "to be capable" means "to have the power" to do or undergo the activity in question. Thus, an agent is capable of doing something when it has the power to do such a thing, and a recipient is capable of undergoing something when it likewise has the power to have such a thing done to it.

Note that there are two basic kinds of powers at work here: active ones and passive ones, i.e. powers to do something, and powers to undergo something. Consequently, agents and recipients are matched up for action only when they have appropriately corresponding active and passive powers. For as I explained already, if an agent has the (active) power to perform a specific activity, it cannot act on just anything whatever. On the contrary, it can only act on a recipient that has the corresponding (passive) power to have such a thing done to it.

But where do agents and recipients get their powers? After all, certain sorts of things only have certain powers, while other sorts of things have entirely different powers. What explains why a thing has the powers it has? To help answer these sorts of questions, medieval Aristotelians often distinguish between what they call the *quod* and the *quo*. In Latin, *quod* means "that which" and *quo* means "that by which," so the *quod* is the thing that has the feature in question, and the *quo* is that in virtue of which it has that feature.

Now, for writers like Henry, Scotus, and Ockham, things typically have the features they have because they have certain constituents. For instance, all these authors would say that Socrates's human nature is a concrete individualized constituent in Socrates, and Socrates has human features precisely because he has that constituent. In terms of the *quod/quo* distinction, Socrates is the *quod*, for he is the thing that has human features, but his human nature is the *quo*, for it is that in virtue of which Socrates has human features.

This applies to powers too. That is, things have the powers they have—be they active powers or passive powers—because they have certain constituents. The idea here is that certain kinds of constituents bring certain kinds of powers along with them, and so anything with a power-providing constituent of kind *K* will have *K*-type powers.

For example, Henry, Scotus, and Ockham believe that heat is a concrete constituent that exists in things, and anything that is hot has the power to heat other things. Hence, heat is the sort of constituent that gives its possessors heating power. There are plenty of other examples as well: human souls give their possessors the power to think and love, lumps of matter make their possessors perishable, and so on. But whatever the power, it ultimately derives from some constituent in its possessor.

I will refer to such a power-providing constituent as the "power source" (or more simply the "source") of its possessor's activity. After all, power-providing constituents ultimately explain why things have the powers they have, and that in turn explains why they can do or undergo the things they can do or undergo. In terms of the *quod/quo* distinction, the thing that has the power is the *quod*, but the constituent that serves as the source of its power is the *quo*, for it is that in virtue of which that thing has the power in question.

8.3. WHAT IS THE SOURCE OF DIVINE PRODUCTION?

With all that said, let me turn now to the central question that will occupy us throughout the rest of Part II: what does it take for a divine person to be the *producer* of another divine person? According to the Aristotelian model I discussed in the last two sections, it would seem that one condition a divine person must satisfy in order to be a producer is that it must have a power source for productive activity—that is, it must have some constituent that provides it with the power to produce another divine person.

But if that is so, what exactly would that power source be? Scholastic authors could (and did) offer a variety of answers to this question. For example, they could say it is the divine essence itself, or even some particular aspect of the divine essence. Alternatively, they could say it is a particular relationship (like fatherhood), or that it is the divine essence in combination with such a relationship. They could even say that there simply is no such thing as a "source" or "power" for internal divine production.[1]

In the following chapters, I will examine the respective views that Henry, Scotus, and Ockham each take on this issue. As we shall see, their discussions are focused on identifying the source of the *Father's* reproductive activity, for that was the traditional way to approach this topic at the time. Nevertheless, what these authors say about the Father's power source applies to any divine person who produces another, so the Father is just a "test case" for their more general theories about how any divine person is the producer of another.

---

[1] Peter Aureol provides a convenient list of the options in *Sent.*, 1.7.19. See especially nn. 8–45 (ed. Buytaert, 2: 839.2–847.23). Peter himself argues that there is no such thing as a "source" or "power" for internal divine production. For instance, in n. 53 (ed. Buytaert, 2: 849.6–850.21), he writes: "potentia generandi non nominat aliquod principium productivum in divinis. Unde omnes istae opiniones [ad oppositum] supponunt id quo est impossibile, et idcirco nihil probabile dicitur convenienter. Impossibile namque est quod sit aliquod formale principium elicitivum generationis vel spirationis divinae. Quod quidem potest multipliciter declarari. Ubi enim productiones non sunt elicitae, vanum est quaerere productivam potentiam aut principium producendi. Sed in divinis generare et spirare non sunt productiones elicitae . . . Ergo vanum est quaerere productivam potentiam vel principium producendi respectu istarum productionum, sive relationem sive essentiam vel aliud quodcumque" (I will discuss Peter's arguments for the claim that internal divine productions are not "elicited" in section 14.3 below). Walter Chatton also follows Peter here, though in a qualified sense. See, for instance, *Reportatio super Sententias*, ed. Joseph Wey and Girard Etzkorn (Toronto: Pontifical Institute of Medieval Studies, 2002), 1.5.1, n. 63 (1: 402.7–12): "De facto tamen non est actus [generationis] elicitus, nec essentia de facto elicit . . . Et hoc probant argumenta Doctoris Petri potius quam prima opinio"; also 1.7.un., n. 40 (1: 437.6–8): "Dico igitur quod de facto essentia non est principium elicitivum generationis activae, hoc enim implicaret distinctionem de facto in re inter ea, cuius oppositum probavi."

9

Henry of Ghent on Powers

As I explained in the last chapter, the question that concerns me here in Part II is this: given that one divine person produces another, is there anything in the producer that we might label as a productive *power*? That is, does the Father (for instance) have the power to produce a Son, and if so, what exactly is the source of that power?

Of course, answering this question involves saying something about what a power is in general, but it also involves saying something about how, not to mention whether, there can be any "power" within God for internal production in the first place. For as I mentioned at the end of the last chapter, some scholastic philosophers thought there simply is no such thing as a power to produce divine persons in God. In this chapter, I want to look at Henry of Ghent's ontology of powers, and why he thinks powers can exist in God.

9.1. HENRY'S ONTOLOGY OF POWERS

According to Henry, a power is defined with reference to the activity for which it is a power. To help clarify this idea, one could point out that we do not normally speak about power without reference to some activity. For instance, we do not say that "Jane has power" without specifying (or at least implying) what Jane has the power *for*. So powers are always directed at specific activities, and as Henry sees it, that means they must be defined with respect to those activities.[1]

---

[1] Henry of Ghent, *Quod.*, 3.14 (*Bad.* I, f. 68rY): "Potentia enim non definitur nisi ex relatione ad actum"; ibid., (*Bad.* I f. 70rB): "Potentia enim id quod est dicitur ex

However, Henry does not think this need to "reference activity" is merely part of the way that we describe or conceptualize powers. On the contrary, he believes it captures the very nature of a power. For on Henry's view, a power is, in fact, just such a relationship with the activity in question. As Henry himself puts it:

> Concerning the nature of a power (in as much as it is a power), it is spoken of with reference to activity, so it is not some absolute thing, but rather just this relatedness [to the activity in question] that is based on something absolute.[2]

Here, Henry states his ontology of powers rather clearly: a power is a *relationship*, not just some absolute (i.e. non-relational) thing, and in particular it consists in a relationship with the activity for which it is a power. Thus, an active power consists in a certain relationship with the activity an agent performs, and a passive power consists in a certain relationship with the activity a recipient undergoes. But either way, the nature of the power consists in a relationship with the activity in question.[3]

This is not to say that absolute things play no role in powers, for Henry maintains that all real relationships are ultimately based on the absolute make-up of the related things.[4] That is, relationships are always based on the absolute features, parts, or constituents of the things that are related.[5] For instance, the fact that a 2kg block of ice is

relatione ad actum, quae ex obiectis sumit species"; SQO, 35.8 (*Opera*, 28: 78.57): "potentia significat 'ad aliquid' [viz. ad actum], et a ratione respectus imponitur."

[2] Henry, SQO, 35.2 (*Opera*, 28: 15.62–64): "de ratione potentiae in quantum potentia, est quod dicatur ad actum, ita quod nihil absolutum sit, sed solus respectus fundatus in re super aliquo absoluto."

[3] Henry, SQO, 35.2 (*Opera*, 28: 15.64–16.74): "Quod autem convenit alicui ex ratione naturae et essentiae suae, convenit et omni contento sub eo, in quantum habet in se huiusmodi naturam. Potentiae ergo passivae in quantum potentia est, convenit quod de ratione sua dicatur ad actum, et hoc secundum modum et rationem qua convenit ei quod sit potentia; ita quod, sicut sub ratione potentiae simpliciter differt ratio potentiae passivae a potentia activa, sic diversimode convenit dici ad actum et ei, et potentiae activae; et cum potentiae activae in quantum activa est, convenit dici ad actum, ipsum agendo, et potentiae passivae convenit dici ad actum, ipsum recipiendo, ut potentia passiva dicatur esse in aliquo ex eo quod est susceptivum alicuius actus."

[4] In what follows, I will only provide a brief sketch of Henry's theory of relations, but for a more detailed account, see Mark Henninger, *Relations: Medieval Theories 1250–1325* (Oxford: Clarendon Press, 1989), 40–58.

[5] Henry, *Quod.*, 15.5 (*Opera*, 20: 26.73–74): "res super quam fundatur praedicamentum relationis in quantum huiusmodi omnino absoluta est absque ordine ad

twice the size of a 1kg block is based on the fact that each block has a certain mass, and the fact that the chairs in my kitchen are similar in color is based on the fact that they are all white.[6]

Nevertheless, Henry does not believe that a real relationship consists simply in two things being constituted in the right sort of way. For if that were the case, thinks Henry, then the only connection between them would be something we draw in our minds. But real relationships are *real*, so there must be some aspect of "relatedness" that exists outside the mind.[7]

However, Henry does not think this real aspect of relatedness can be a distinct thing in its own right.[8] After all, if it were a distinct thing, then it would have to be related to its basis by some further aspect of relatedness, and if that relatedness were also a distinct thing, it too would have to be related by yet another relatedness, and so on ad infinitum. But that is absurd, so Henry concludes that the aspect of relatedness we are seeking cannot be a distinct thing in its own right.[9]

aliud"; *Quod.*, 9.3 (*Opera*, 13: 59.63–64): "cum in relationibus realibus non est fundatus nisi in re."

[6] As Henry explains in *Quod.*, 9.3 (*Opera*, 13: 72.45–73.49), two things are not related unless they both have the right sorts of constituents: "sed non se ipso duo est subduplum ad quattuor nec quattuor duplum ad duo, sicut neque se ipso album unum est ad aliud album sine aliquo coalbo. Ipsa enim subiecta neque secundum se nec ut subsunt fundamentis relationum, non sunt ex se aut per se ad—sed solummodo ipsa habitudine qua partipiant—, nisi per coexistens."

[7] In *Quod.*, 9.3, Henry considers the opinion that relationships only exist in the mind, but he rejects this, citing Simplicius in support (*Opera*, 13: 49.70–50.96): "aliqui, ut Stoici, ponebant quod relatio praeter suum fundamentum non est aliquid in entibus existens a natura in rebus extra anima, sed in anima tantum, ut quod similitudo nihil aliud sit quam conceptus mentis ex collatione habita circa duas qualitates conformes, puta circa duo alba...Quod [Simplicius] statim improbat [quod relationem esse in anima tantum]...Simpliciter ergo concedendum est quod relatio sive habitudo praeter suum fundamentum sit aliquid in rebus extra animam, et non solum nomen aut conceptus mentis."

[8] And indeed, Henry claims that no aspect of relatedness could exist all by itself (i.e. without a basis) in *SQO*, 32.5 (*Opera*, 27: 88.49–50): "Respectus enim separatus in se non existit. Esse ergo ad aliquid ex se non potest poni in esse."

[9] Henry, *SQO*, 32.5 (*Opera*, 27: 94.33–95.40): "Et ipsa relatio quae est [e.g.] duplum aut simile, non est res aliqua alia ab illa super quam fundatur, sed solum respectus ipsius quantitatis et subiecti eius, quo formaliter utrumque eorum vel alterum refertur ad aliud. Aliter enim super illam rem primo fundaretur ille respectus, et ipsa, aut subiectum eius aut utrumque, primo per illum respectum referretur ad aliud. Et tunc eadem ratione ille respectus adhuc esset res alia, quae respectu illo referretur ad aliud, aut subiectum eius aut utrumque. Et esset similiter ire in infinitum, ut patet inspicienti."

Instead, says Henry, it is just a special "way of existing" for the absolute basis in question.[10] In particular, it is a way of existing which "looks outwards at" (*respicit*, in Latin), and so points towards, something else. And in virtue of this outward-looking characteristic (*respectus*), the absolute basis becomes a "pointing thing," so to speak.[11] Hence, on Henry's view, some *x* is really related to some *y* because it really has something in it that points towards *y*.[12]

The same goes for powers: they too are based on the absolute features, parts, or constituents that make up the things which have those powers (e.g. the heat in a flame, the muscles in my arm, and so on), but the basis for a power must also "look outwards at," and so genuinely point towards, its corresponding activity.[13] Thus, like any

---

[10] Henry, *Quod.*, 7.1–2 (*Opera*, 11: 23.53–55): "circumscripta realitate fundamenti, nihil manet de realitate in praedicamento relationis, sed solummodo praecisa ratio seu intentio qua intelligitur modus essendi ad aliud"; *Quod.*, 9.3 (*Opera*, 13: 59.61–62): "Sic igitur patet quod, circumscripta re fundamenti, relatio, sive in Deo sive in creaturis, non est nisi modus quidam essendi ad aliud"; ibid., (*Opera*, 13: 55.55–57): "habitudinem, quae circumscripta realitate fundamenti ut in se et per se consideratur, purus modus essendi ad aliud est"; *SQO*, 32.5 (*Opera*, 28: 91.43–45): "respectus nihil addit rei illi, supra quam immediate fundatur, sed solum subiectum suum dicit ad aliud esse quantum est de formali suo significato, quod non est nisi esse ad aliud."

[11] Henry, *Quod.*, 9.3 (*Opera*, 13: 55.52–55): "habitudinem, quae nuda est secundum se et non nisi modus quidam [essendi ad aliud], ipsum fundamentum, in quantum fundatur in ipso, characterizat, communicans ei per hoc quodam modo realitatem suam"; ibid., (*Opera*, 13: 54.20–22): "Et quibus duobus, scilicet ex modo [essendi ad aliud] et realitate quam [respectus] habet per characterizationem a fundamento, integratur, et in eisdem consistit hypostasis relationis"; ibid., (*Opera*, 13: 70.77–79): "in praedicamento enim relationis relatio ex ordine ad id cuius est [viz. fundatum], habet realitatem, et ex ordine ad id ad quod est [viz. relatum], habet rationem modi [essendi ad aliud] tantum."

[12] Henry, *SQO*, 32.5 (*Opera*, 27: 87.26–28): "Sequitur de aliis septem [praedicamentorum relationis], quorum ratio est ad aliud referre suum subiectum, quae scilicet significant rem cuius esse est in aliquo in respectu ad aliud"; ibid., (*Opera*, 27: 87.35–40): "Est ergo . . . ratio illorum septem praedicamentorum significare rem cuius esse est in aliquo in respectu ad aliud. In quo non est eis proprium quod significant rem aliquam: hoc enim est omnibus aliis praedicamentis commune. Neque quod significant rem cui convenit esse in alio: hoc enim convenit omnibus accidentibus. Sed solum eis est proprium quod esse in respectu ad aliud significant."

[13] Henry, *SQO*, 35.4 (*Opera*, 28: 37.76–77): "Et quia omnis potentia, in quantum potentia, fundatur in aliquo ut respectus ad aliud." And more generally, Henry maintains that being a source implies a relationship with that for which it is the source, ibid., (*Opera*, 28: 37.67–69): "quia principium ut principium non dicitur secundum substantiam, sed solum secundum relationem, et relationem importat ad aliud, ut ad principiatum."

other relationship, a power includes two constituents: (i) an absolute basis, *and* (ii) an outward-looking characteristic.[14]

In fact, Henry says we can even think about a power as if it were composed of a lump of matter and a form, where the absolute basis plays the role of the matter, and its outward-looking characteristic plays the role of the form:[15]

> A power is signified as a certain property that 'looks outwards' at something else, and it includes in its significate an [absolute] essence insofar as it has the character of that property. Thus, its significate is composed, so to speak, of two things: the subsistent [absolute] thing, which is signified as if it were matter, and the [relative] property, which is signified as if it were a form.[16]

In short, when Henry says that some x has a power for some activity A, he means that x has something in it which points towards A, where the "pointing thing" in x is some absolute feature, part, or constituent of x which has an aspect of relatedness R that "looks outwards" at A.[17]

---

[14] That a power requires this "relatedness" in addition to the basis is especially clear in the following passage from Henry, *Quod.*, 3.14 (*Bad.* I f. 81rF): "Sicut caliditas separata si esset calefactiva in se, non esset nisi qualitas per essentiam, et non esset potentia quaedam nisi ex . . . respectu ad actum calidi: ita quod iret in actum quandocumque approximaretur calefactibili, et cessaret ab actu absente calefactibili." The implication here is this: without any sort of relationship with an act of heating, a free-floating bit of heat would just be heat (a quality), and so in order for it to be classified as a power, it would need a relationship with an act of heating (which will only exist when it actually heats something).

[15] Actually, Henry suggests that we can think of any categorical entity like this. *SQO*, 32.5 (*Opera*, 27: 81.57–60): "Intentio ergo praedicamenti constituitur ex re naturae subiecta, quae est res praedicamenti, quasi materiale in ipso, et modo quo esse ei convenit . . . quae est ratio praedicamenti circa rem ipsam, quasi formale in ipso."

[16] Henry, *SQO*, 35.8 (*Opera*, 28: 78.66–70): "Potentia vero significat ut proprietas ad aliquid respiciens, quod in suo significato includit essentiam sub ratione illius proprietatis, ut suum significatum sit quasi compositum ex duobus, scilicet ex ipso subsistenti, quod significat quasi materialiter, et illa proprietate, quam significat quasi formaliter."

[17] For further discussion on Henry's theory of powers, as well as Aquinas's and Scotus's, see Richard Cross, "Accidents, Substantial Forms, and Causal Powers in the Late Thirteenth Century: Some Reflections on the Axiom '*actiones sunt suppositorum*'," in *Compléments de substance: Etudes sur les propriétés accidentelles offertes à Alain de Libera* (Paris: Vrin, 2008): 133–46.

9.2. POWERS CAN EXIST IN THE GODHEAD

Can any of this apply to the Godhead? Henry's theory of powers
might lead one to think that there simply cannot be any power for
internal activity within the Godhead. For according to the Aristotelian model of action I discussed in section 8.1, activity (at least in the
earthly realm) always results in a change, but since there is no change
in God, there simply cannot be any sort of activity that would bring
about a change in God. And if there is no activity in God, then there
cannot be any relationships with that activity either. So wouldn't
Henry have to admit from the start that there simply cannot be any
"power" for activity within the Godhead?[18]

According to Henry, the answer is no, for as he sees it, the Father
really does beget a Son. There must, then, be some sense in which the
Father really engages in the activity of begetting, and there must be
some sense in which the Son really is begotten. Consequently, there
must be divine powers for these activities as well, for it would be
absurd to say that there are activities without corresponding
powers.[19] But how could this be, given that there is no change in God?

To explain this, Henry claims there are two ways that *potentia* and
actus can be related. In some cases, they really differ (or at least they
are more than just conceptually different), and those cases involve

---

[18] As Henry puts it on behalf of the objector in *SQO*, 35.2 (*Opera*, 28: 13.14–20):
"Philosophus dicit, V° et IX° *Metaphysicae*: «*Potentia passiva est in ipso passo
principium transmutationis ab alio secundum quod est aliud*» . . . Sed Deus omnino
ab alio transmutari non potest, quia ipse omnino est immutabilis. Ergo in ipso nullo
modo potest esse principium transmutationis ab alio, cuius est potentia passiva."
[19] Henry, *SQO*, 35.2 (*Opera*, 28: 16.91–93, 16.97–17.00): "immo talem potentiam
passivam necesse habemus in ipso [viz. Deo] ponere . . . respectu actus ut agere qui est
operari . . . cum secundum actum ut agere, immo potius ut fieri, dicitur generari et
spirari, necesse est quod in Deo sit potentia passiva ad posse generari et spirari"; ibid.,
(*Opera*, 28: 19.60–68): "Quod autem . . . passionis necesse est ponere in Deo, manifeste ex hoc apparet, quod in Deo necesse est ponere actionem [e.g. generare] . . . Nunc
autem non est ponere actionem sine passione sibi respondente, quia correlativa sunt.
Sicut igitur omni actioni, qualiscumque sit, respondet potentia activa, sic omni
passioni, qualiscumque sit, respondet potentia passiva. Sicut enim, ut dictum est
supra, nulla actio provenit ex eo quod non habet potentiam ad illam"; *SQO*, 35.1
(*Opera*, 28: 8.95–00): "Et ideo absolute dicendum quod in Deo est potentia, quod
claret nobis ex hoc quod multa agit. Non enim agit, nisi quod potens est agere. Nam
quod non potest agere, impossibile est agere, et quod impossibile est agere, necesse est
non agere. Et similiter de intelligere et intelligi, generare et generari, et de ceteris
huiusmodi [in Deo]."

some sort of a change from *potentia* to *actus*. But there are other cases where the *potentia* and *actus* differ only conceptually, namely where the *potentia* is "permanently fixed" to the *actus*. In those cases, there is no change from *potentia* to *actus*.[20]

Of course, there is no *potentia* within God in the first sense, for change is simply not possible in God.[21] But Henry insists that there is *potentia* within God in the second sense, for as I mentioned a moment ago, Henry believes that the Son really is begotten, so there must be some sense in which the Son is capable of being produced, even if this does not involve change.[22]

It is difficult to interpret what Henry means here, but one plausible option is that Henry is drawing a distinction between temporary activities that bring about changes, and eternal activities that do not. Examples of the first sort are readily available. For instance, when the flame on my stove heats a pot of water, the water undergoes a real change: first it was cold, and now it is hot.

But imagine a scenario where the flame eternally heats the water such that the water always has the maximum amount of heat it can receive from the flame (and let us also suppose that the water does not evaporate). In this scenario, there would be no change from cold to hot, for the water would always be as hot as it could be. Nevertheless, the flame would still be engaged in activity, for it would always be causing the water to be maximally hot.

In the first case, distinct states of affairs correspond to the water's merely being "capable of" and "actually" being hot, for first the water

---

[20] Henry, *SQO*, 35.2 (*Opera*, 28: 16.77–86): "Sed hoc modo se habere per potentiam ad actum contingit intelligi dupliciter. Uno modo, ut potentia et actus circa idem differunt, vel secundum rem vel secundum intentionem, et non sola ratione, quemadmodum contingit in creaturis ubi materia est in potentia passiva ad formam, et vadit ad ipsam per transmutationem et motum; et similiter genus est in potentia ad differentiam, et vadit ad ipsam per compositionem secundum actum et motum rationis. Alio modo, ut potentia et actus differant sola ratione, et nulla transmutatione omnino intelligitur transitus in re a potentia in actum, immo nec omnino transitus, sed fixa permanentia perfectionis potentiae per actum."

[21] Henry, *SQO*, 35.2 (*Opera*, 28: 16.87–88): "Loquendo de potentia passiva primo modo [viz. ut potentia et actus circa idem differunt], illam omnino removemus a Deo, quia non est nisi in mobili et transmutabili."

[22] Henry, *SQO*, 35.2 (*Opera*, 28: 16.91–17.00): "Secundo modo [viz. ut potentia et actus different sola ratione] non removemus potentiam passivam a Deo, immo talem potentiam passivam necesse habemus in ipso habere ... Similiter, cum secundum actum ut agere, immo potius ut fieri, dicitur generari et spirari, necesse est quod in Deo sit potentia passiva ad posse generari et spirari."

is cold, and then it is hot. But in the second case, the only difference between these states of affairs is in our conceptualization, for the water is always hot. And if that is right, then Henry's point would be this: even though a power consists in a relationship with activity, it does not matter if that activity results in a change. It could, after all, be an eternal activity that involves no temporal change from *not-F* to *F*.[23]

Indeed, Henry goes on to argue that doing or undergoing activity need not involve any change at all. According to Henry, doing or undergoing something consists in a relationship with the activity that is done or undergone, much like a power. Hence, Jane never just "does" or "undergoes." She always does or undergoes some specific activity. So on Henry's view, doings and undergoings essentially involve reference to activity, much like powers.[24]

Now, in the earthly realm, Henry agrees that these "doing" and "undergoing" relationships are typically based on change. Thus, the fact that an earthly agent *does* something is based on the fact that it causes a change in a recipient, and the fact that the recipient *undergoes* something is based on the fact that this very same change happens to it.[25]

---

[23] Henry, *SQO*, 35.4 (*Opera*, 28: 38.83–89): "Ad secundum, quod «Deus non est principium transmutationis», dicendum quod illa definitio potentiae activae non est generalis ad quamlibet potentiam activam, sed solum ad illam quae est agentis in subiectam materiam, quae est in potentia passiva ad alicuius transmutationis susceptionem. Non enim est proprie transmutatio nisi circa aliquod subiectum praeexsistens a termino in terminum variatio, per abiectionem scilicet unius et acquisitionem alterius"; *SQO*, 36.2 (*Opera*, 28: 96.52–59): "Oportet ergo distinguere de potentia, dicendo quod est quaedam potentia, quae de se nata est, esse sine actu et tempore praecedere actum, et est alia potentia, quae non est nata esse nisi simul cum actu et idem cum ipso. Quod considerandum est hoc modo. Quoniam potentia aut dicit aptitudinem solam in subiecto ad actum, aut aptitudinem cum privatione actus, qua potentia contrarietatem habet ad actum, potentia primo modo est illa quae sequitur ad necessarium et non est nisi cum actu, immo ipse actus." Cf. also *SQO*, 35.2 (*Opera*, 28: 22.16–27).

[24] Henry, *SQO*, 35.2 (*Opera*, 28: 17.2–5): "passio secundum propriam rationem qua praedicamentum est, non dicit nisi quemdam respectum ad actum, ut in quo recipitur transmutatio illata ab agente, et fundatur super motum . . . quam agit agens in passum."

[25] Henry, *SQO*, 32.5 (*Opera*, 27: 96.91–95): "Circa distinctionem igitur actionis et passionis sciendum, quod ambo accidentales respectus dicunt in creaturis, quia fundatur in motu, et hoc [motu] uno et eodem numero, et distinguuntur secundum solos respectus qui sunt esse ab alio et in alium. Et secundum hoc ab illo uno [motu] duo diversimode denominantur: hic quidem agens, ille vero patiens"; ibid., (*Opera*, 27:

However, the particular basis of a relationship is not always essential to that relationship. Two things can be similar in lots of ways— they can be similar in color, shape, and so on—but none of these bases are essential to similarity. (There must be *some* basis, but it need not be any particular one.) As Henry sees it, this is true for "doing" and "undergoing" relationships as well: change is not essential to them any more than color is essential to similarity.[26]

But of course, there is more to a relationship than its basis. As I explained above, there is also some sort of relatedness, and *that*, says Henry, can transfer over to the Godhead. Thus, although the changes that are involved in earthly doings and undergoings do not occur in God, the sheer relatedness which constitutes doing or undergoing does.[27]

In this way, Henry maintains that there are genuine doings and undergoings within the Godhead that do not involve any change, and consequently, there are powers for these activities as well. For example, the Father really begets the Son, so he has the (active) power to perform that activity. Likewise, the Son really is begotten, so he has the (passive) power to undergo that activity as well.[28]

97.12–14): "agens in creaturis denominatur secundum motum quem causat in passum, passum vero secundum motum quem habet in se."

[26] Henry, *SQO*, 35.2 (*Opera*, 28: 17.6–15): "transmutatio non pertinet ad naturam passionis . . . ut, ponendo quod passio non sit nisi respectus fundatus in motu, motus non est plus de essentia et natura passionis quam albedo de essentia similitudinis fundatae super ipsam—, nullo modo passio ut est praedicamentum potest esse in aliquo nisi in quo sit motus sicut neque similitudo nisi in eo in quo est albedo, vel aliquid huiusmodi super quod fundatur."

[27] Henry, *SQO*, 35.2 (*Opera*, 28: 17.15–16, 20–21, 18.34–36): "Passio enim praedicamentum necessario duo dicit: et respectum, et ipsum in motu fundatum . . . Hoc secundo modo loquendo de passione, determinatum est supra quod passionis praedicamentum nullo modo in Deo cadit . . . Si autem consideremus passionem praecise quantum ad rationem respectus, hoc modo dictum est supra quod ratio praedicamenti passionis cadit in Deo"; *SQO*, 32.5 (*Opera*, 27: 97.99 1, 7 9): "Unde, si huiusmodi duo praedicamenta [viz. actio et passio] ad divina transferuntur, non manent nisi secundum communem rationem puri respectus, secundum quem etiam denominatur agens omne in quantum agens est . . . Et sicut actio manet in Deo secundum rationem sui respectus, similiter et passio, absoluta omni ratione motus et pluralitatis distantis ab actu"; *SQO*, 35.4 (*Opera*, 28: 31.21–23): "Dicendum ad hoc, quod sicut potentia simpliciter cognoscitur inesse Deo ex respectu ad actum simpliciter qui reperitur in Deo, et potentia passiva ex respectu ad actum ad quem est, sic potentia activa cognoscenda est inesse Deo ex respectu ad actum ad quem est."

[28] Henry, *SQO*, 32.5 (*Opera*, 27: 97.9–11, 16–19): "Ut, sicut in Deo generatio activa sive generare dicitur vera actio propter verum respectum actionis, sic generato passiva

For Henry then, powers can exist in God precisely because they are relationships. For like all relationships, a power is constituted by (i) an absolute basis, and (ii) some aspect of relatedness that points towards the activity in question. And although the bases for earthly activities and their corresponding powers do not transfer over to the Godhead, the relatedness in which activities and powers consist do.

sive generari dicitur vera passio propter verum respectum passionis . . . Si tamen passio nominet purum respectum, non fundatum super motum . . . nihil absurdum esset intelligenti dicere quod generari est pati, sicut generare est agere"; SQO, 35.2 (*Opera*, 28: 18.40–43): "Et sic generari dicitur passio, quemadmodum generare actio, et posse generari potentia passiva, sicut posse generare potentia activa, et hoc sine omni transmutatione"; ibid., (*Opera*, 28: 20.71–76): "Nec debet absurdum videri, quod nomen passionis et potentiae passivae, sane intelligendo, ponantur in Deo, quia non omnis passio et potentia passiva dicuntur modo motus, secundum quod usitata sunt ista vocabula. Immo, passio, ut ex ratione sui praedicamenti dicit purum respectum ad agens in quantum huiusmodi, rationem motus non importat etiam in creaturis, licet in eis fundatur super motum."

10

Henry of Ghent on Powers in the Godhead

Although powers and activities typically involve some sort of change here in the earthly realm, Henry argues that they do not necessarily have to involve change, and for that reason, they can exist in the Godhead. Nevertheless, powers and activities must be based on *something*, even when it comes to God. The question, then, is this: if there is no change in the Godhead, then what exactly *is* the basis for divine activities and powers, and how exactly is it related to those activities and powers? As we shall see, Henry provides a distinctive answer to these questions, and it is an answer which again provokes a vigorous response from Scotus and Ockham.

10.1. THE BASIS FOR DIVINE ACTIVITY AND POWER

In the *Summa*, 39.4, Henry asks, "is the divine essence the basis for performing all divine activity?"[1] Given what we have already seen about Henry's theory of powers, it is clear that this question amounts to the following: is the divine essence the absolute entity on which divine "power" and "doing" relationships are based, or is something else the basis for these relationships?

In response, Henry begins by pointing out that there are only two sorts of constituents in the Godhead: there is one absolute thing (the divine essence), and then there are the various relationships (like fatherhood or sonship) that are based on the divine essence. But since Henry understands a relationship to ultimately be constituted

---

[1] Henry of Ghent, *SQO*, 39.4 (*Opera*, 28: 193.2–3): "Utrum divina essentia sit in Deo ratio agendi omnem divinam actionem."

by some absolute thing in combination with some aspect of relatedness, all of the relationships in God should ultimately be understood
as being constituted by the divine essence plus some aspect of relatedness.

It follows, then, that the two most fundamental sorts of ingredients
in the Godhead are these: (i) an *absolute thing* (the divine essence),
and (ii) various aspects of *relatedness*.[2] Hence:

(T31) For any constituent F in God,
         F is either
         (i) the divine essence x,
         (ii) some aspect of relatedness R, or
         (iii) something y which is constituted by x and R.

Consequently, whatever the basis for divine activity is, it must be (i)
the divine essence itself, (ii) some relative aspect in God, or (iii) some
combination of both, for those are the only options.

Right away, Henry rules out (ii) by arguing in accordance with
Aristotle's *Physics* 5.2, that since relationships hold *between* the
source and the result of activity, they cannot be the *source* of activity.[3]
In other words, activity issues *from* a source, and it is directed *towards*
a result, so the relatedness that is involved in activity is neither the
"source" nor the "result," but rather the "from-ness" or "towards-
ness." Thus, no activity can arise from any aspect of relatedness:[4]

---

[2] Henry, *SQO*, 39.4 (*Opera*, 28: 196.81–85): "Dicendum ad hoc, quod, secundum
supra determinata, in Deo super ipsam puram essentiam deitatis nihil additur, neque
secundum rem, neque secundum veridicam intelligendi rationem, nisi ratio respectus,
sive in attributis substantialibus, sive in rationibus perfectionum aut idearum, sive in
ipsis motionibus et proprietatibus personarum."

[3] Henry, *SQO*, 39.4 (*Opera*, 28: 196.85–88): "De natura autem respectus secundum
quod est respectus, clarum est secundum Philosophum, V *Physicorum*, quod nec
potest habere per se rationem principii aut termini actionis." See Aristotle, *Physics*,
5.2, 225b10–13 (*AL*, 7, 1.2: 196.16–22; *Iunt.*, 4: f. 215rC-D): "Secundum substantiam
autem non est motus propter nullum substantie contrariorum inesse. Neque iam ad
aliquid; contingit enim altero mutante verum esse alterum nichil mutans, quare
secundum accidens motus horum est. Neque agentis et patientis, neque omnis quod
movetur aut moventis, quia non est motus motus neque generationis generatio neque
omnino mutatio mutationis."

[4] Note though, that Henry thinks the "result" of activity can be either the act itself,
something other than the act that remains in the agent, or something other than the
act that exists outside the agent. See, for instance, Henry, *SQO*, 39.4 (*Opera*, 28:
200.81–90): "Qui in universo [actiones] sunt in triplici genere: quidam qui est actus,
qui est operatio; quidam autem, qui est actio; quidem vero, qui est factio . . . differunt
in hoc, quod operatio dicitur quando non est aliquid ab ipso actu proveniens

(T32) For any activity *A*,
    A cannot be based on any aspect of relatedness *R*.

Presumably, this rules out option (iii) as well, namely that the basis for divine activity is something constituted by both the divine essence (an absolute thing) and some aspect of relatedness. For as we saw in section 9.1, on Henry's view, an absolute thing together with some aspect of relatedness just is a relationship, but since relationships are always based on the *absolute* constituents of the things that are related, surely that disqualifies relationships from serving as bases.

As for option (i), the divine essence itself, Henry argues that here we have the answer we are seeking: the divine essence must be the basis for all divine activity. After all, Henry says, the basis for any activity must be something positive and real. That is, it must be some absolute feature, part, or constituent of the agent in question. But since the only absolute entity in the Godhead is the divine essence, the divine essence must therefore be the basis for all divine activity.[5]

Now, this is not to say that the divine essence is the thing that performs internal divine actions. On the contrary, Henry is clear: the divine essence does not *do* anything. Rather, the divine essence is that "through which" the divine persons act, which is just to say that the divine essence is the basis for the power of the persons. Thus, according to Henry, divine activities are performed only by the persons, not the divine essence.[6]

---

tamquam finis eius, sed ipse est finis . . . Actio vero dicitur, quando aliquid ab ipso actu est proveniens quod manet in agente . . . Factio vero dicitur, quando aliquid ab ipso tamquam finis eius procedit ab ipso extra agentem."

[5] Henry, *SQO*, 39.4 (*Opera*, 28: 196.91–197.97): "Quod autem est tale principium in re, necesse est quod sit aliquid positivum reale . . . Quare cum, ut dictum est, praeter respectus in Deo nihil est reale positivum nisi pura substantia, quae est deitas, sive ipsa divina essentia, in Deo igitur ponendum est, quod ratio agendi elicitive divinas actiones, quaecumque sint illae, non sit nisi ipsa pura divina essentia."

[6] Henry, *SQO*, 39.4 (*Opera*, 28: 197.97–1). "ita quod, licet nulla actio omnino attribuatur essentiae divinae velut principio agenti, sicut determinatum est in praecedenti quaestione, omnis tamen divina actio attribuitur ei ut principio elicitivo, et quo agens principale, scilicet suppositum unum vel duo vel tria, simul agunt omnes actiones divinas." See also *SQO*, 39.3 (*Opera*, 28: 186.82–91): "ideo dicendum simpliciter, quod in divinis nulla actio potest aut debet attribui illi quod se habet ut alicuius et sicut existens in alio, sed solum «illi» quod se habet ut cuius est aliquid; hoc autem est solum suppositum. Cetera enim omnia divina se habent ut aliquid suppositi seu aliquid existens in supposito, ut sunt ipsa divina essentia, relativa proprietas, et universaliter omnia essentialia attributa, veluti sunt potentia, sapientia et cetera huiusmodi. Ideo dicendum simpliciter, quod nulli talium proprie loquendo debet

By Henry's reckoning then, the divine essence is the sole basis for all divine activities, even though it is not the agent of those activities. And indeed, the divine essence *must* be the sole basis, for every relationship is based on some absolute feature, part, or constituent of the thing in question, and the only absolute entity in the Godhead is the divine essence.[7]

10.2. ONE BASIS FOR MANY DIVINE ACTIVITIES AND POWERS

Still, Henry recognizes that the divine persons perform lots of different activities.[8] For instance, they create the world, they save humans from damnation, and some of them even produce other divine persons. However, Henry believes that uniform activity issues from a uniform source. Consequently, any diversity (i.e. difference in kind) at the level of activity must arise from some sort of corresponding diversity at the level of the source:[9]

(T33) If there is any diversity at the level of activity,
    then there must be some diversity
    at the level of the source for that activity.

So if we observe a single kind of activity issuing from an agent, then we can assume that there is a single power source for that activity in the agent. But if we observe different kinds of activities coming from a single agent, then we must assume that there are different sources for those activities—or at least there must be different aspects or parts of a single source, each of which could give rise to a different type of activity. So also in the Godhead: since the divine persons perform different sorts of activities, there must be *some* diversity at the level of

attribui actio aliqua ut agenti, et ita quod divina essentia nullam agat actionem, sed suppositum omnes."

[7] Henry, *SQO*, 39.4 (*Opera*, 28: 198.37–39): "ratio propria essentiae Dei, secundum quod essentia est mere et absolute, est fundamentum omnium aliarum, tamquam illarum quae important respectus fundatos in ipsa essentia."

[8] Henry, *SQO*, 39.4 (*Opera*, 28: 197.2): "Sed quia huiusmodi actiones divinae differentes sunt inter se."

[9] Henry, *SQO*, 39.4 (*Opera*, 28: 197.2–3): "et non est differentia in actionibus nisi ex differentia ex parte principii elicitivi."

the source to explain this—or at least there must be different aspects or quasi-parts of that source, each of which could give rise to a different type of activity.

But where could this diversity come from? For Henry, the divine essence is entirely simple, and no differences can be found within it. That is, the divine essence is intrinsically uniform, so in and of itself, it is *indifferent*, as it were, to the various activities that are based on it. Consequently, says Henry, it must be "determined" to each activity by something other than itself.

But according to T31, the only other entities in God besides the divine essence are various aspects of relatedness. Thus, the divine essence must be "determined" to each activity by some relative aspect. And in particular, it must be "determined" to each activity by the aspect of relatedness that points towards that activity, for powers are constituted by their relationships with their corresponding activities.[10]

---

[10] Henry, *SQO*, 39.4 (*Opera*, 28: 197.18–20): "ut penes differentiam ipsorum, ipsi essentiae determinarentur actus differentes, cum secundum se nullum omnino determinat, et ideo nullum determinate eliceret nisi ab aliquo sibi determinaretur"; ibid., (*Opera*, 28: 197.4–10): "divina autem essentia, sub ratione qua est essentia, nullam rationem differentiae in se habet, quod autem nullam differentiam ex se omnino potest in se habere, si in se aliquam habeat, oportet quod hoc sit ab aliquo sibi supervenienti, essentiae autem divinae nihil potest supervenire nisi ratio respectus, essentia ergo, ut sit ratio differentium actionum, oportet eam in se differre, saltem secundum rationes diversorum respectuum"; *SQO*, 36.2 (*Opera*, 28: 95.32–35): "Unde, sicut potentia simpliciter dicitur esse in Deo ex relatione divinae essentiae ad actum simpliciter qui ei competit, sic ad determinatum actum dicenda est potentia determinata esse in Deo"; *SQO*, 39.5 (*Opera*, 28: 210.29–211.34): "Sed est intelligendum quod, sicut essentia, in quantum se habet ut principium elicitivum istorum actuum, cum ex se sit omnino absoluta, necesse est eam aliquo respectu comparari ad actum, et determinari ipsum actum ipsi, ut, licet per se actum eliciat, tamen sub ratione alicuius respectus quoad actum eliciendum comparetur et determinetur sibi actus." Note that Henry believes the human soul is "determined" to its various sentient and mental activities in exactly the same way, namely by its relationships with those activities. *Quod.*, 3.14 (*Bad.* I f. 67rS): "Aut etiam accidet ei quod fiat agens in actu, quia indiget ut determinetur aliquo quo fiat in eo potentia ad eliciendum actionem determinatam circa determinatum obiectum. Sicut contingit in actionibus animae intellectivis vel sensitivis ad quas non habet anima ex nuda essentia sua aliquas potentias determinatas nisi aliquo alio determinetur quo respiciat determinatum obiectum et determinatam actionem. Ita quod eius substantia quae una est secundum rem, secundum diversa esse, et secundum diversas determinationes, sortitur rationes diversarum potentiarum intellectivarum et sensitivarum, cum in radice nihil sit potentia in eadem nisi eius simplex substantia, quae in se considerata, essentia sive substantia est et forma animati, considerata vero secundum diversa esse per diversas determinationes et operationes ad diversas actiones, et ad diversa obiecta, dicitur potentiae diversae quae non ponunt super essentiam eius nisi solum respectum ad diversos actus specie."

Indeed, Henry goes on to explain that if we consider the divine essence all by itself in terms of what it is, it is just an absolute substance. More precisely, taken in itself, the divine essence is just an absolute constituent that exists in all three divine persons and makes each of them a divine being.[11] Hence, the divine essence *as such* is not related to any activity except the activity of "being divine." Therefore it is not, in and of itself, the source or power for, say, reproduction, because as we have seen, Henry maintains that a power must be related to the activity it empowers.[12]

In order for the divine essence to qualify as the source or power for a specific activity, it must satisfy two requirements. First, it must be an *absolute* thing that can serve as the relevant sort of basis, and second, it must be *related* (or as Henry puts it, "determined") to the activity for which it is a power. Of course, the divine essence satisfies both of these requirements for every divine activity: it is the one and only absolute constituent in the Godhead that can serve as the basis for any relationship, but it is also related to every divine activity precisely because it is that on which each of those activities are based.[13]

So when we consider the divine essence *plus* some aspect of relatedness which points towards the activity in question, the divine

---

[11] Henry, *SQO*, 39.4 (*Opera*, 28: 198.39–42): "quae [viz. divina essentia] non est nisi unica forma realis absoluta existens in divinis suppositis, cui ex se ipsa primo et per se non convenit nisi actus qui est esse, qui in ipsa communicatur suppositis."

[12] Henry, *SQO*, 39.4 (*Opera*, 28: 197.13–17): "cum secundum se [viz. divina essentia], absque ratione omnis respectus penitus absolutum 'quid est', et nullo modo respicit actum eliciendum; nunc autem nullo modo posset esse ratio agendi ipsum, actum nisi aliquo modo ipsum respiceret, et ad ipsum aliquo modo ordinaretur"; *SQO*, 35.4 (*Opera*, 28: 37.61–69): "Et iterum, si illud principium secundum rem sit ipsa substantia, quia Deus agit per suam essentiam, tamen non est substantia sub ratione qua est substantia, sed solum sub ratione qua est potentia, et hoc propter eandem rationem: quia substantia de ratione substantiae quid absolutum dicit, et nullo modo ut ad aliud se habens. Et ita non importat de se sola rationem principii eliciti actus determinati, quia principium ut principium non dicitur secundum substantiam, sed solum secundum relationem, et relationem importat ad aliud, ut ad principiatum."

[13] Henry, *SQO*, 39.4 (*Opera*, 28: 198.24–27): "Et sic ad agendum actum aliquem a persona divina ut a principali agente, duplex ratio qua agit eum, requiritur: una ut qua ipsam elicit, alia ut qua eliciens actum respicit, et determinatur sibi actus"; ibid., (*Opera*, 28: 198.27–31): "Primo modo [viz. ut qua ipsam elicit] dico, ut iam dictum est, quod sola divina essentia secundum rationem essentiae est ratio agendi omnes divinas actiones, scilicet in eliciendo ipsas. Secundo vero modo [viz. ut qua elicens actum respicit, et determinatur sibi actus] dico, quod respectus fundati in divina essentia sunt ratio agendi a Deo divinas actiones, scilicet in determinando ipsas ut eliciantur."

essence qualifies as the source or power for that specific activity.[14] For Henry then, there is one divine essence that has many aspects of relatedness which point towards many activities. And since each of those relative aspects gives the divine essence the characteristic of being a power for that specific activity,[15]the divine essence qualifies as *many* powers, even though it is just *one* thing in and of itself.[16]

Nevertheless, Henry points out that the divine persons elicit all their activities directly through the divine essence and not through any aspect of relatedness, even though those relative aspects relate the

[14] Henry, *SQO*, 39.4 (*Opera*, 28: 198.42–199.47): "Illum autem actum [viz. actum divinae essentiae qui est esse et qui communicatur suppositis], tamquam primum quem respicit et sibi determinat, ex ratione sibi propria et absoluta secundum rectam rationem nostram intelligendi, sequuntur omnes alii actus tamquam secundi, quos respicit, et qui sibi determinantur, ut dictum est, ex rationibus respectuum potentialium, qui in ea fundatur"; *SQO*, 35.6 (*Opera*, 28: 45.61–65): "Sciendum ergo, cum potentia sit quasi medium in Deo inter essentiam et actum ad quem est, secundum quod supra dictum est, potentia ergo in Deo tam activa quam passiva potest considerari respectu divinae essentiae, ut scilicet in ipsa fundatur, vel respectu actus, ut ad quem terminatur."

[15] Indeed, Henry often talks about how the divine essence takes on the "character" (*ratio*) of the various aspects of relatedness for which it is the basis. E.g., *SQO*, 35.7 (*Opera*, 28: 73.81–84): "quoniam id ipsum quod in Deo habet rationem absoluti ut essentia est, habet rationem respectus ut potentia est, et id ipsum quod absolutum est et essentia in se, intrat in rationem potentiae, assumendo in se ipsa rationem respectus ad actum"; *Quod.*, 3.3 (*Bad.* I f. 50rI): "Dicendum ad hoc quod esse quod est Deus sive divina essentia, radix est et fundamentum omnium eorum quae sunt in divinis, et ab ipsa originantur, et ad ipsam reducuntur. Unde divina essentia est radix et origo omnium divinarum actionum et productionum. Et omnis actio, et omne productum in Deo vel ei attributum realiter non est nisi ipsa divina essentia, et esse purum simplicissimum, licet secundum aliam et aliam rationem aliquando dicitur potentia, aliquando relatio, aliquando proprietas personalis, aliquando persona, aliquando actio vel operatio, et sic de caeteris. Ita quod quicquid nominatur vel concipitur in divinis, licet propter aliam rationem quam sit ratio substantiae, alio modo significatur et concipitur, semper tamen ipsam divinam essentiam includit, et est ipsa, sub alia tamen et alia ratione quam sit ratio essentiae vel substantiae. Quod enim in Deo est potentia, hoc est essentia sub ratione potentiae, et similiter quod est relatio, est ipsa essentia sub ratione respectus, et caetera huiusmodi."

[16] Henry, *SQO*, 39.4 (*Opera*, 28: 198.32–35): "ita videlicet, quod unica est ratio omnis eliciens, scilicet ipsa divina essentia sub sua ratione absoluta qua essentia est, plures vero sunt rationes determinantes secundum pluralitatem actuum, scilicet ipsi respectus diversi"; *SQO*, 35.3 (*Opera*, 28: 26.47–50): "Unde, cum ratio respectus importatus nomine potentiae sit ad actum, idcirco potentia passiva debet distingui et diversificari ex diversitate actuum ad quos sunt, et cognoscenda est diversitas et definitio passivarum potentiarum"; *SQO*, 35.5 (*Opera*, 28: 39.19–40.22): "Dicendum ad hoc secundum supra dicta de definitione et diversitate potentiarum passivarum ex respectu ad actus ad quos sunt, quod distinctio et diversitas potentiarum activarum consimiliter debet sumi ex respectu ad actus ad quos sunt."

divine essence to the activities it empowers. In other words, these aspects of relatedness are not distinct bases in and of themselves (by T32). Rather, they simply relate the divine essence to the activities in question.[17]

To support this claim, Henry argues that if this were not the case, then we would end up with an infinite regress, and this is true for the basis of *any* power. Consider, for instance, a lump of matter. Matter has the capacity to receive substantial forms, but what is the basis for this capacity? If it were something other than the matter itself, then the matter would have to be capable of receiving that *other* thing, and if that capacity were based on still a third thing, the matter would have to be capable of receiving that as well. And so on, ad infinitum. Thus, the matter itself must be the basis for its capacity to receive forms.[18]

Similarly, the divine essence itself must be the immediate basis for all of its relationships, just as a lump of matter is the immediate basis for its receptivity. Thus, the divine essence "stands under" and "supports," so to speak, the various aspects of relatedness that are based on it. Those relative aspects, then, are not distinct bases in and of

---

[17] Henry, *SQO*, 39.4 (*Opera*, 28: 199.47–53): "Cum autem sibi determinati sunt actus, se ipsa ut essentia est, immediate est ratio eliciendi eos, ut, quemadmodum materia nullum ordinem habet ad formam et ad pati in recipiendo aliquid in se nisi per rationem potentiae passivae, in nuda tamen substantia sua formas recipit, sic divina essentia nullum ordinem habet ad actum qui est agere simpliciter nisi per rationem potentiae activae, pura tamen substantia sua est ratio eliciendi omnium actuum"; *SQO*, 39.2 (*Opera*, 28: 182.74–76): "Dicendum ergo quod divina essentia secundum aliam rationem est id quo procedit divina actio ut ratio agendi, et forma qua agit suppositum, ut infra dicetur."

[18] Henry, *SQO*, 39.4 (*Opera*, 28: 199.53–57): "Ita quod, sicut potentia receptiva sive passiva in materia non est aliquid re absoluta aliud ab ipsa essentia materiae, quia si sic, materia ex se esset in potentia ad illud, et si potentia illa esset similiter aliud, esset abire in infinitum, quod est incoveniens, et ideo necesse est stare in primo"; cf. *Quod.*, 3.14 (*Bad.* I f. 66Vr-rR): "Potentia vero passiva primo et per se invenitur in prima materia, in qua sua potentia passiva ita est pura quod est ipsa essentia materiae sub sola ratione respectus ad formam, qui nullam rem apponit, neque compositionem aliquam in re, quia si in aliqua re absoluta differret potentia ab essentia materiae, esset accidens et forma in materia, cuius proculdubio materia esset receptiva, et in potentia ad eam, et de illa potentia esset eadem quaestio. Et procederet in infinitum, nisi pura essentia materiae assumpto quodam respectu esset ipsa sua potentia passiva, non aliquod accidens eius. Aliter enim materia non esset potentia per se, sed per aliquid sui."

themselves. Rather, they simply give the divine essence the characteristic of being a power for each of the activities that are based on it.[19]

10.3. THE POWER TO PRODUCE ANOTHER DIVINE PERSON

With all that said, we can now turn to the original question: what is
the Father's reproductive power? By now, Henry's answer should be
obvious. As we have seen, Henry maintains that the power for any
activity A is constituted by two ingredients: (i) some absolute feature,
part, or constituent F in the agent or recipient, and (ii) an aspect of
relatedness R that points towards A, and which is based on F. But
since the divine essence is the only absolute entity in the Godhead, the
divine essence is the basis for the Father's reproductive power, and
the aspect of relatedness that points towards the Father's act of
reproduction is precisely what gives the divine essence the characteristic of being the source or power for reproduction.[20] In short, the
Father's reproductive power is the divine essence *plus* the aspect of
relatedness that points towards his act of producing the Son, just as
any power is some absolute basis plus the aspect of relatedness that
points towards the activity in question.

To sum up, Henry believes that a power essentially consists in a
relationship with the activity for which it is a power. In the Godhead
though, all relationships are based on the divine essence, but since the
divine essence is intrinsically indifferent to the various activities that
are based on it, it must be "determined" to each specific activity by its
relationship with that activity. Thus, the divine essence only counts as

---

[19] Henry, *SQO*, 39.4 (*Opera*, 28: 199.57–70): "quod potentia receptiva materiae
non est aliquid re absoluta aliud ab ipsa essentia materiae, sed solum respectus
fundatus in ipsa essentia materiae, quae ex se et secundum suam substantiam subintrat rationem respectus . . . consimiliter potentia activa, in ipsa divina essentia fun-
data, non est aliud re absoluta, aliud ab ipsa essentia, et hoc consimili ratione, sed est
solum respectus fundatus in ipsa divina essentia, quae ex se secundum suam essentiam subintrat rationem respectus."

[20] Henry, *SQO*, 39.4 (*Opera*, 28: 201.19–24): "Idem similiter patet in actu qui est
agere sive actio proprie dicta. Actum enim generandi filium elicit divina essentia, ut
habet esse in Patre sub ratione respectus importati nomine potentiae generandi
activae; non quod ille respectus eliciat actum generandi, sed ipsum in Patre elicit
ipsa essentia pura, ut per respectum illum in Patre sibi talis actus est determinatus."

the power for one type of activity rather than another insofar as it is related to the one rather than the other. Likewise for divine production: the Father's power to reproduce is the divine essence insofar as it is related to the Father's act of producing the Son, and similarly, the Father's and Son's power to produce the Spirit would be the divine essence insofar as it is related to the Father's and Son's joint act of producing the Spirit.

11

Scotus against Henry

Scotus thinks that Henry's approach to divine power is entirely misguided. Hence, while Henry claims that the divine essence needs to be "determined" to its various activities, Scotus argues that the divine essence needs no determination at all; and while Henry claims that the divine essence must be "determined" by relationships, Scotus argues that relationships cannot do any "determining" whatsoever. For Scotus, the divine essence is the most potent entity there is, so it is entirely capable, in and of itself and without the need for any further determination, to serve as the basis for all divine activities, and that includes the activity of producing another divine person. In this chapter, I want to look at Scotus's arguments for these claims in more detail.

11.1. THE DIVINE ESSENCE DOES NOT NEED ANY DETERMINATION

As I explained in section 10.2, Henry maintains that in and of itself, the divine essence is indifferent to the various activities that are based on it, and for this reason, it must be "determined" to specific activities by its relationship with each of them. Scotus rejects this, claiming instead that the divine essence needs no determination whatsoever to be the source of all divine activity. Scotus levels a number of arguments against Henry on this point, but there is one argument that is particularly illuminating for our purposes.

Scotus begins by claiming that there are two ways powers can be indifferent: passive powers are indifferent in one way, and active powers are indifferent in another way. In the *Lectura*, Scotus describes the first kind of indifference as follows.

> A power can be indifferent in two ways... One way is the indifference
> of a passive power, and this is [an indifference with respect] to contra-
> dictory [states of affairs]. In order for it to be determined [to one or the
> other state of affairs], it must receive [something]. For instance, a log
> has the potential to be heated, but sometimes it is deprived of heat, so it
> only becomes actually [hot] when it receives heat. This is [the sort of
> indifference that belongs to] the passive power of matter.[1]

In this passage, Scotus explains that something with passive power is indifferent to contrary states of affairs, like how logs are indifferent to being hot or not being hot. After all, a log does not care, so to speak, whether it is one or the other, for there is nothing about a log that requires that it be hot, or that it not be hot. On the contrary, a log only becomes hot from the agency of something else (like a flame that acts on it and thereby causes it to receive heat).

As for the second sort of indifference, namely that of an active power, Scotus goes on to describe it like this:

> The other [kind of] indifference is that of active power, which is an
> indifference that follows from the unlimitedness of its causality and
> power [*virtutis*]. And this power [that exists] in natural things... is not
> [indifferent] to contradictory [states of affairs]. In order for such an
> indifferent power to be determined [to some activity], it does not need
> to receive a form. Rather, it only requires the presence of a recipient (if it
> requires a recipient at all). For instance, the sun is indifferent to the
> many effects [it can bring about] by an indifference and a certain
> unlimitedness that belongs to its active power. For this reason, in
> order for it to be determined [to some effect], it does not need to have
> some form imprinted in it.[2]

[1] Scotus, *Lectura* [= *Lect.*], 1.7.un., n. 26 (*Vat.* 16: 481.16–22): "duplex est potentiae indeterminatio... Una enim est indeterminatio 'potentiae passivae', et haec est ad contradictoria, quae ad hoc quod determinetur, oportet quod recipiat (sicut lignum est in potentia ad calefaciendum et privatur calore aliquando, et ideo non vadit in actum nisi recipiat calorem); et haec est potentia passiva, quae est 'materiae'."
[2] Scotus, *Lect.*, 1.7.un., n. 26 (*Vat.* 16: 481.22–482.5): "Alia est 'potentiae activae' indeterminatio, quae indeterminatio consequitur illimitationem suae causalitatis et suae virtutis, et haec potentia in naturalibus... non est ad contradictoria; et ista potentia indeterminata, ad hoc quod determinetur, non recipit aliquam formam, sed sufficit praesentia passi si requirat passum (sicut sol est indeterminatus ad multos effectus indeterminatione et illimitatione quadam suae virtutis activae; et ideo ad hoc quod determinetur, non requiritur quod aliqua forma sibi imprimatur)."

Here Scotus explains that some active powers have the capability to bring about more than one kind of activity, and for convenience, let us call these "super powers." These sorts of powers are indifferent not to contradictory states of affairs (i.e. being *F* vs. not being *F*), but rather to the various activities they empower. For instance, the sun can produce many effects: it can produce maggots in piles of rotting organic material, it can melt ice, it can illuminate the earth, and so on. But none of these are contradictory states of affairs. Rather, they are different *kinds* of activities that the sun has the power to bring about. Consequently, the sun does not need to receive anything to bring these effects about in the way that passive entities need to receive something.[3]

Of course, the sun can only bring about these effects when it is in the right circumstances. For instance, if a lump of ice stands in direct sunlight, the sun can melt it, and likewise if a pile of mud stands in direct sunlight, the sun can dry it out. The sun is "indifferent" to these various activities because it can do any of them. It does not care, so to speak, whether it melts some ice or dries out a pile of mud. It can (and will) do either, so long as there is some ice or mud to act upon.[4] But the point here is that the sun does not need to receive some further

---

[3] Scotus, *Ordinatio* [= *Ord.*], 1.7.1, n. 21 (*Vat.* 4: 115.7–12): "Confirmatur, quia talis indeterminatio activi licet sit ad disparata, non tamen est ad contradictoria, sed determinate ad alteram partem contradictionis respectu cuiuslibet illorum disparatorum; nulla autem indeterminatio prohibet ex se determinate agere, nisi quae aliquo modo esset ad contradictoria, ut ad agere et non-agere; ergo etc." *Reportatio I–A* [= *Rep. I–A*], 1.7.1, n. 18 (Wolter, 309): "Prima igitur indeterminatio, scilicet potentiae passivae, est ad contradictoria sive ad privative opposita; sed secunda ad disparata, ut sol sive potentia activa solis aeque indeterminata ad herbam sicut ad animal etc., et tamen ex se determinatur ad producendum quodlibet"; ibid., n. 19 (Wolter, 309–10): "quia indeterminatio quae est ad disparata et non ad contraria vel contradictoria non impedit agere. Sola enim illa indeterminatio quae est ad agere et non agere impedit unam partem nisi determinetur, non autem illa indeterminatio quae est ad disparata. Patet de sole, qui est causa aequivoca, indeterminatus ad plantam vel vermem, non tamen est indeterminatus ad producendum vel non producendum, sed indeterminatus est ad producendum hoc et illud, et posito passo determinato producit herbam, et tamen simul posito alio passo determinato potest producere vermem."

[4] Scotus, *Lect.*, 1.3.3.2–3, n. 415 (*Vat.* 16: 391.11–17): "Loquendo autem de causa effectiva primo modo [viz. ut causa efficiens est indeterminata ad producendum aliquem effectum quem tamen immediate producere potest], ad hoc quod determinetur ad agendum sufficit praesentia passi, sicut sol habet virtutem qua immediate potest dissolvere et constringere: ad hoc quod dissolvat sufficit praesentia dissolubilis, ut glaciei, et ad hoc quod constringat sufficit etiam praesentia passi, ut luti; unde causa effectiva non determinatur per hoc quod aliquam formam recipit."

form to do any of these things. It only needs to be in the right circumstances.

I want to emphasize that passive powers are indifferent to *contradictory* states of affairs (i.e. being *F*, or not being *F*), while active super powers are indifferent to different *kinds* of activities (i.e. doing *A*, or doing *B*). For this explains why a passive power must receive something in order to be "determined" to one or the other contradictory states of affairs. Even if a passive entity could "decide" whether it wanted to be *F* or *not-F*, it could still only *become F* if it actually received *F*. But an active super power does not need to receive anything to do *A* or *B*. On the contrary, it only needs to be in the right circumstances to bring about *A* or *B*.

Scotus's basic point here is that passive entities are *not sufficient* in and of themselves to bring about the activity in question. They need to receive something first (as logs can only become hot if they receive heat). But an active super power *is sufficient* in and of itself to bring about the activities in question, provided that it is in the right circumstances.[5] In short, passive entities are insufficient to do the job because they do not have enough power, but entities that can perform different kinds of activities are sufficient to do the job because they have so much power that they can bring about more than one kind of effect.[6]

With that distinction at hand, Scotus argues (against Henry) that while it is true that passive entities need to be "determined" by something (like how a log must receive heat), an entity that can perform more than one kind of activity does not need to be

[5] Scotus, *Ord.*, 1.7.1, n. 20 (*Vat.* 4: 114.5–11): "Quod est indeterminatum 'indeterminatione materiae' oportet quod recipiat formam ad hoc quod agat, quia non est in actu sufficiente ad agendum, sed quod est indeterminatum 'indeterminatione potentiae activae' est ex se sufficienter determinatum ad producendum quemcumque illorum effectuum: et hoc si passum-dispositum sit approximatum, ubi requiritur passum, vel ex se ipso ubi passum non requiritur"; *Rep. I–A*, 1.7.1, n. 20 (Wolter, 310): "potentia activa, si esset tantum huiusmodi producti, esset determinata ad productionem huiusmodi effectus; sed si habet virtutem activam sufficientem non solum ad hoc sed ad aliud producendum, nihil tollitur de causalitate eius respectu huiusmodi."

[6] Scotus, *Rep. I–A*, 1.7.1, n. 17 (Wolter, 309): "videatur differentia inter indeterminationem quae est ex parte potentiae passivae et quae est ex parte potentiae activae in entibus. Indeterminatio quae ex parte potentiae passivae est imperfectionis, ut indeterminatio materiae ad diversas formas. Et tale non est activum nisi determinetur, quia non est aliquod ens actu nisi per formas. Alia indeterminatio potentiae activae non est propter carentiam actus, sed est ex plenitudine perfectionis, et ista indeterminatio non exspectat aliquod formale determinans."

"determined" in this way at all.[7] Such entities have all the power they need to bring about the effects in question (provided that they are in the right circumstances).

To explain this idea further, Scotus argues that if we consider a single active cause that is entirely sufficient to bring about only one kind of effect (in the right circumstances), nobody would think that it needed to be "determined" in any way, for it has all the power it needs to actively bring about the effect in question. But now suppose that this entity can also produce another effect. Scotus maintains that this entity would not, as a consequence, lose any of its power for producing the first effect. On the contrary, it would simply have *more* power: it would have the power to produce the first effect, *and* it would have the power to produce the second effect. Consequently, this entity would be just as capable of bringing about both effects as two separate single causes would be.[8]

Scotus then claims that the divine essence has the sort of indifference that belongs to active super powers: the divine essence is the sort of thing that can empower more than one kind of activity, without the need to receive anything. The divine essence is "indifferent" to various activities not because it lacks or needs to receive "determination"

---

[7] Scotus, *Lect.*, 1.3.3.2–3, n. 415 (*Vat.* 16: 390.22–391.6): "dicendum quod indeterminatio duplex est: una est indeterminatio quae convenit causae materiali, et alia est indeterminatio quae convenit causae agenti universali et quodammodo illimitatae. Exemplum primi est de indeterminatione ligni respectu caloris vel alterius formae; exemplum secundi est de indeterminatione solis ad producendum hoc generabile vel illud; unde haec indeterminatio virtutis activae est ad agendum et non ad aliquam formam ab aliquo recipiendam. Quando igitur dicitur quod illud quod est indeterminatum requirit aliquam formam determinantem qua determinetur, verum est de potentia passiva."

[8] Scotus, *Lect.*, 1.7.un., n. 27 (*Vat.* 16: 482.6–17): "Ex his arguitur sic: principium indeterminatum 'indeterminatione activa', quod est totale principium naturale et non 'voluntarium indifferens ad contradictoria', est de se determinatum ad producendum. Ista propositio iam manifesta est in exemplo praedicto [viz. solis], et iterum probatur ratione: quia si talis causa limitaretur ad unum effectum tantum, determinaretur sufficienter ad illum; sed per hoc quod talis causa ponitur illimitata respectu aliorum effectuum, non aufertur determinatio ad istum effectum nec tollitur comparatio eius ad istum effectum, unde nihil eius perfectionis tollitur per comparationem ad istum effectum; igitur potentia naturalis quae est indeterminata illimitatione suae naturae, determinatur ex se"; *Ord.*, 1.7.1, n. 20 (*Vat.* 4: 114.11–115.2): "probatio: si tale activum esset de se determinatum ad unum effectum, posset de se sufficienter producere illum,—sed si est indeterminatum ad hoc et ad aliud, ex tali illimitatione non tollitur perfectio causalitatis eius respectu talis effectus, sed tantum additur causalitas respectu alterius; ita ergo potest istud producere, sicut si tantum esset istius, et ita non requiritur aliquod determinans."

from something, but rather because it has so much power that it can empower *any* of those activities. And since the divine essence does not need to be "determined" by anything, it cannot be "determined" by relationships (or anything else, for that matter), as Henry claims.[9]

11.2. RELATIONSHIPS CANNOT
DETERMINE POWERS

Now, on the face of it, the argument I discussed in the last section begs the question against Henry. For Henry would agree that the divine essence is not indifferent in the manner of a passive power (at least not exclusively). On the contrary, Henry would agree that the divine essence is indifferent in the manner of an active super power. Henry's point, though, is that the divine essence only counts as the basis of power for one activity rather than another insofar as it is *related* to the one rather than the other.

However, Scotus argues against this aspect of Henry's thought in his *Questions on Metaphysics*, book 9, question 5.[10] Scotus agrees, of course, than when a power actively empowers some sort of activity, that power stands in a certain relationship with that activity.[11] But

---

[9] Scotus, *Rep. I–A*, 1.7.1, n. 16 (Wolter, 309): "quando aliquid est indeterminatum ad aliqua indeterminatione potentiae activae, ex se est sufficienter determinatum ad quodcumque illorum, circumscripto omni alio determinativo; sed essentia divina, si sit indeterminata respectu productionis Filii et Spiritus Sancti, hoc est indeterminatione potentiae activae; ergo etc."; *Lect.*, 1.7.un., n. 27 (*Vat.* 16: 482.17–22): "Cum igitur essentia divina sit indeterminata non indeterminatione passiva, sed indeterminatione quae est virtutis activae illimitatae, ipsa non requiret aliquam formam ipsam determinantem; si igitur essentia divina sit principium generationis aut spirationis, ipsa non determinatur ad producendum per aliquam proprietatem respectivam"; *Ord.*, 1.7.1, n. 21 (*Vat.* 4: 115.3–7): "Ad propositum. Essentia divina non est principium indeterminatum 'indeterminatione materiae': ergo si est indeterminatum indeterminatione alterius quasi principii activi, erit simpliciter determinatum determinatione quae requiritur ad agendum, et ita non requiritur aliquid aliud."

[10] The question Scotus poses in his *Quaestions on Metaphysics* (henceforth: *Meta.*), 9.5 is explicitly directed at this issue (*OPh* 4: 559.4–5): "Quaeritur an potentia activa sive passiva, in quantum prior est naturaliter principiato, includat essentialiter aliquem respectum." And of course, Scotus's main target here is Henry of Ghent. See the discussion of Henry's view and Scotus's response at *OPh* 4: 560.6–562.16.

[11] Scotus, *Meta.*, 9.5, n. 12 (*OPh* 4: 562.19–22): "Ideo dicitur aliter ad quaestionem quod cum relatio, quam importat hoc nomen 'potentia' ... simul sit natura cum relatione principiati actu, actu, et potentia, potentia"; ibid., 9.3–4, n. 19 (*OPh* 4:

Scotus also maintains that relationships are naturally posterior to the
things they relate, and for Scotus, one thing will be naturally posterior
to another if the former cannot exist without the latter, but not
vice versa:[12]

> (T34) For any *x* and *y*,
>> *x* is naturally prior to *y* if
>>> (i) *x* can exist without *y*, and
>>> (ii) *y* cannot exist without *x*.

Hence, an *A* and a *B* simply could not be related if one (or both) of
them were absent. Any relationship between *A* and *B* presupposes
that there already is an *A* and a *B* to relate in the first place. Likewise
for powers: if a power is related to an activity, that presupposes that
the activity is already going on.[13]

542.13–14): "Patet itaque quod principium importat essentialiter relationem princi-
piationis"; ibid., n. 20 (*OPh* 543.9–10): "Consimiliter omnino dicendum est de
potentialitate, potentia et potente, quod eandem relationem important"; ibid., n. 25
(*OPh* 4: 545.3–5): "Sciendum tamen, secundo, quantum ad istum articulum, quod
principium non tantum habet relationem ad principiatum, et tale principium ad tale
principiatum . . ." See also ibid., n. 19 (*OPh* 4: 542.1–543.8).

[12] Scotus, *De Primo*, 1.8 (Wolter, 5): "Secundo modo prius dicitur, a quo aliquid
dependet, et posterius, quod dependet. Huius prioris hanc intelligo rationem, quam
etiam Aristoteles 5° Metaphysicae testimonio Platonis ostendit: Prius secundum
naturam et essentiam est quod contingit esse sine posteriori, non e converso. Quod
ita intelligo, quod, licet prius necessario causet posterius et ideo sine ipso esse non
possit, hoc tamen non est quia ad esse suum egeat posteriori, sed e converso; quia si
ponatur posterius non esse, nihilominus prius erit sine inclusione contradictionis.
Non sic e converso, quia posterius eget priore, quam indigentiam possumus depen-
dentiam appellare, ut dicamus omne posterius essentialiter a priore necessario de-
pendere; non e converso, licet quandoque necessario posterius consequatur istud";
Ord., 2.1.4–5, n. 262 (*Vat.* 7: 129.12–17): "quia impossibilitas quod *a* sit sine *b* aut est
propter identitatem *b* ad *a*, aut propter prioritatem, aut simultatem in natura; igitur si
b non sit prius naturaliter quam *a*, nec necessario simul natura, et *a* non potest esse
absque *b*,—sequitur quod *a* sit idem *b*: si enim sit aliud et posterius eo, non est
verisimile quod naturaliter non possit esse sine eo absque contradictione." Note,
however, that some *a*'s being able to exist without some *b* but not vice versa is only
a sufficient condition (not a necessary condition) for *a*'s being naturally prior to *b*.
This is important, because for Scotus, some entities in the Godhead are naturally prior
to others, even though everything in the Godhead is necessary.

[13] Scotus, *Meta.*, 9.5, n. 10 (*OPh* 4: 562.2–6): "nam illa [viz. relatio principii
principiantis in actu] simul natura est cum principiato in quantum principiatum,
cum sint correlativa, et posterior est natura eo quod est principiatum, hoc est, illo in
quo fundatur relatio principiati; quia relatio principiati, quae simul est cum relatione
principiantis in actu, posterior est eodem, quod scilicet est principiatum"; ibid., n. 13
(*OPh* 4: 563.11–14): "Sed ab absoluto [principio], sine omni respectu praecedente, est
effectus absolutus; quo posito, posterius natura sequitur relatio actualis mutua

For Scotus then, relationships show up on the scene too late, as it were, to "determine" a power to its activity. Whatever it is that makes something a power for the activity in question, it must be naturally prior to any relationship the power might have with its activity.[14] (This does not mean that a power must exist for a period of time before it is exercised, for Scotus admits that some powers are coeval with their exercise. A power only needs to be *naturally* prior to its exercise.[15])

To help illustrate Scotus's point, consider a generator that is switched off. Would this generator still have the power to provide electricity? As Scotus sees it, Henry would have to say no. For Henry thinks a power consists in a relationship with its activity, but if no activity were going on, there could not be any relationship with that activity either. Thus, Henry would have to say that a switched-off generator would have no power to provide electricity.

But for Scotus, that would be absurd. A switched-off generator is still capable of providing electricity even when at rest. So whatever it is that makes a generator capable of generating electricity, that must be present in the generator prior to being switched on. Or more precisely, even if the generator were always running, its relationship with its activity depends on it being the sort of thing that can provide electricity in the first place. And the same goes for any power.

Scotus thus insists that in this context, when we ask about whatever it is that makes something a power, we are not asking about its

---

principiati ad principium, quae in neutro esse potuit, altero extremo non posito"; ibid., n. 12 (*OPh* 4: 562.22–23): "ac per hoc illa relatio nullo modo sit prior naturaliter principiato."

[14] Scotus, *Meta.*, 9.5, n. 9 (*OPh* 4: 561.22–24): "Manet autem in principio quando principiat quidquid est de ratione eius in quantum est prius naturaliter principiato"; ibid., n. 10 (*OPh* 4: 562.6–8): "Oporteret autem relationem intrinsecam potentiae activae esse priorem natura illo quod est principiatum [si relatio determinaret potentiam activam, sed tale est impossibile]. Ergo omnino nulla relatio invenitur talis [in principio priore naturaliter principiato]"; ibid., n. 13 (*OPh* 4: 563.7–11): "Hoc modo intelligendo quaestionem, dicitur quod nihil est de ratione potentiae nisi absoluta aliqua essentia, in qua immediate fundatur aliquis respectus ad principiatum, ita quod nullus respectus praecedit in actu ipsam principiationem per quam quasi determinetur ad principiandum."

[15] Scotus, *Meta.*, 9.5, n. 14 (*OPh* 4: 564.1–6): "Nec potest dici quod una tantum praecedat aliam tempore, quia patet quod agens, habens actionem coaevam sibi, ita determinatur ad agendum et habet quidquid requiritur ad talem determinationem sicut agens praecedens tempore suam actionem. Ergo relatio determinans—si qua est—non oportet quod praecedat tempore, sed tantum natura."

relationship with any activity. Rather, we are asking about the absolute entity that serves as the basis for that activity.[16] And presumably, the reason is (again) that relationships show up too late to explain anything.

Indeed, as Scotus argues in the *Lectura*, if you asked me why two white things are similar, it would not help much if I said "because they have a similarity relationship." But it would help if I said "because they are both white." And the same goes for powers.[17] To call on the famous example from Molière, I cannot explain why opium makes me sleepy by saying that it has the power to make me sleepy,[18] if by "power" I mean the relationship that opium has with sleepiness. For Scotus would say that I need to appeal to something that is naturally prior to opium's relationship with sleepiness.

So even though Henry would agree that the divine essence is "indifferent" to a variety of activities in the manner of an active (super) power rather than a passive power, Scotus could still argue that Henry is wrong to think that relationships somehow constitute powers. On the contrary, for Scotus, relationships cannot play any constitutive role at all here. According to Scotus, an active super power (such as the divine essence) just cannot be "determined" by relationships.

---

[16] Scotus, *Meta.*, 9.3–4, n. 20 (*OPh* 4: 543.14–16): "ita frequenter quando dicimus 'potentiam', non intelligimus de respectu, sed de illo in quo fundatur respectus"; *Lect.*, 1.7.un., n. 34 (*Vat.* 16: 485.7–8): "Potentia igitur activa et passiva sunt nomina concreta non quoad subiecta, sed quoad fundamenta"; *Ord.*, 1.7.1, nn. 30–2 (*Vat.* 4: 119.13–22): "hoc nomen 'potentia' potest sumi pro eo quod per se significat [viz. relationem], vel pro eo quod denominat—quod est 'proximum fundamentum talis relationis'. Primo modo accipiendo dico quod potentia significat relationem, sicut potentialitas sive principiatio,—et hoc modo quaestio non habet difficultatem ... Secundo modo est difficultas quaestionis, inquirendo quid sit illud 'absolutum', quod est fundamentum 'proximum istius relationis'."
[17] Scotus, *Lect.*, 1.7.un., n. 35 (*Vat.* 16: 485.9–21): "Unde, quando quaerimus in quo sunt aliqui similes, non quaerimus in quo sunt similes per se primo modo, quia sic similitudine sunt similes, sed quaerimus in quo sunt similes secundo modo per se, utrum sint similes albedine vel alia forma; unde quaerimus de fundamento similitudinis. Similiter quando quaeritur quid sit potentia animae, non quaeritur de respectu quem potentia importat, sed quaeritur de fundamento" (on this, cf. *Meta.*, 9.3–4, n. 19 (*OPh* 4: 543.1–8)).
[18] Molière, *Le Malade Imaginaire* (in *The Dramatic Works of Molière*, 3 volumes, translated by Henri van Laun (Philadelphia: Gebbie & Barrie, Publishers, 1879), 3: 567): "Mihi à docto doctore. Domandatur causam et rationem quare Opium facit domire. A quoi respondeo; Quia est in eo Virtus dormitiva, Cujus est natura Sensus assoupire."

11.3. RELATIONSHIPS ARE REQUIRED
FOR DIVINE PRODUCTION

Thus far, we have seen that for Scotus, the divine essence is the basis for all divine activity. To put it another way, the divine essence is the power source for anything a divine person might do, and that includes the Father's act of producing a Son. However, one might wonder: why doesn't the divine essence itself produce the Son?

This is an issue that Scotus must deal with, for Scotus maintains that if a power source were to exist all by itself (per se), then it could also act all by itself (per se). For instance, if God caused the heat in a flame to exist all by itself, without the flame, Scotus would say that this free-floating bit of heat could still heat a nearby pot of water.[19]

Now, any of the authors I am considering here would insist that the divine essence cannot exist without the divine persons, and consequently, the divine essence could never be a detached, free-floating entity in the way that a detached bit of heat would be. But Scotus does think the divine essence is an individual all by itself (per se) "before" it exists in the divine persons, where "before" has the sense of natural priority that I defined above (T34).

Moreover, Scotus talks about naturally prior and posterior entities as if they exist in prior and posterior "instants of nature" (rather than instants of time).[20] We do not need to go into the details of this doctrine here, but the important point to note is this: Scotus believes that in the first divine "instant of nature," the divine essence exists all by itself, without the divine persons. The persons only enter the picture at later "instants of nature." As Scotus himself puts it:

> By starting with the first 'instant of nature', what occurs entirely first is that the divine essence exists by itself (*per se*) and from itself (*ex se*) . . . Therefore, *per se* existence belongs to the divine essence as it is considered in the most abstract way, and this is prior to any personal characteristics. In this first 'instant of nature', all of this occurs not as the divine essence is something that is receptive of any perfection, but

---

[19] Scotus, *Lect.*, 1.7.un., n. 13 (*Vat.* 16: 13–17): "quidquid est principium formale agendi in aliqua actione, et perfectum, si potest per se esse, potest et per se operari,— sicut si calor sit per se principium calefaciendi, si ponitur calorem separari, adhuc erit principium calefaciendi."

[20] For a more detailed discussion of Scotus on "instants of nature" (as well as Ockham's criticisms), see Adams, *Ockham*, 2: 1042–8.

rather as it is infinitely perfect, able in the second 'instant of nature' to be shared with . . . a divine person.[21]

Thus, although the divine essence may not be a *detached* power source in that first "instant of nature," it sure looks like an *independent* power source. But if a detached bit of heat can heat a pot of water, then why shouldn't the divine essence produce the Son in that first "instant of nature" as well?[22]

The answer to this problem, says Scotus, is that the divine essence is not in the right *circumstances* in that first "instant of nature." In order to be in the right circumstances, the divine essence needs the personal properties (such as fatherhood and sonship). And the reason here is this: Scotus maintains, like Henry and Ockham, that a producer and its product must be *really distinct*:

(T35) For any *x* and *y*,
        if *x* produces *y* by a production *P*,
        x and *y* are really distinct.

Now, in the divine case, a producer and its product cannot be distinguished by their shared essence, for in the Godhead, the producer and the product have the divine essence in common (see T8 in section 1.4), and no two things are distinguished by their commonalities. Consequently, in order to qualify as a distinct producer and product, the producer and the product must be distinguished by other features that they do not share. Thus, there cannot be a production in any "instant of nature" that lacks such distinguishing features. As Scotus puts it:

Although there are no recipients or impediments here [viz. in the Godhead], nevertheless, the form [of deity] (which is the basis for

---

[21] Scotus, *Ord.*, 1.5.2.un., n. 131 (*Vat.* 4: 74.13–75.3): "Incipiendo a primo signo naturae, omnino primo occurrit essentia divina ut est esse per se et ex se . . . Isti ergo essentiae, abstractissime consideratae, ut prior omnibus personalibus, competit esse per se, et in isto primo occurrit non ut aliquid receptivum alicuius perfectionis, sed ut infinita perfectio, potens quidem in secundo signo naturae communicari . . . supposito."

[22] Scotus nicely explains the problem at *Ord.*, 1.7.1, n. 74 (*Vat.* 4: 140.4–10): "quod illa maior [viz. quod omne quod per se est, si posset agere, per se agit] habet hic [viz. in divinis] maiorem probabilitatem quam in creaturis, quia ista forma sic per se est quod illi correspondet proprium 'quod', potens agere,—puta 'hic Deus', qui quodammodo praecedit relationes et sic agit: patet, quia sic primo intelligit et vult; ergo videtur quod possit in omnem actionem cuius suum 'quo' est proprium principium formale, et ita 'hic Deus' generat primo."

reproduction) would not act if it existed all by itself (*per se*) and not in
some person, for it would not have what belongs to an agent person,
who is a person that is distinct [from another person] and who does not
have the divine essence through reproduction. And for this reason,
although the divine essence is [naturally] prior [to the persons], since
it does not have what belongs to an agent person in that first [instant of
nature], it cannot reproduce, even though 'this deity' [viz. the divine
essence in the first 'instant of nature' before it exists in the divine
persons] can be understood as an [individual] thing. For this reason,
then, one should say . . . that something which exists by itself (*per se*)
can act by itself (*per se*) if it has whatever is required for action. But if
the divine essence were considered as it is [naturally] prior [to the
persons], in this way it would not be considered as it exists in the
person to which action belongs, and for this reason, it could not act
[in that first 'instant of nature'].[23]

Thus, although the divine essence, taken in itself, is the sort of thing
that *can* provide one divine person with the power to produce

---

[23] Scotus, *Lect.*, 1.7.un., n. 87 (*Vat.* 16: 504.3–13): "Sic in proposito: licet hic non sit
passum et impedimentum, tamen forma quae est hic principium generandi, si per se
esset et non in supposito, non ageret, quia deficeret sibi convenientia suppositi agentis,
quod est suppositum distinctum et non habens per generationem essentiam, et ideo
licit essentia prius sit, quia tamen in illo priore non habet convenientiam suppositi
agentis, ideo non potest generare, licet 'hic Deus' possit reri et intelligere. Per hoc
dicendum est . . . quod per se ens potest per se agere si potest habere ea quae
conveniunt actioni; nunc autem si essentia consideratur ut praecedit [personae], sic
consideratur non ut in supposito conveniente actioni, et ideo nec sic ageret." See also
Ord., 1.7.1, n. 75 (*Vat.* 4: 140.11–141.15): "De principio autem elicitivo falsa est,
quando principium elicitivum—si per se exsistit—non potest esse propinqua potentia
ad operandum. Exemplum: species—si ponatur principium elicitivum operationis
videndi in oculo—si per se exsisteret, non posset esse principium illius operationis,
et ratio esset, quia non posset esse in potentia propinqua ad agendum quia non posset
habere passum approximatum, quia approximatio—ut dictum est prius—requiritur
ad rationem potentiae propinquae. Sicut autem approximatio in creaturis vel amotio
impedimentorum requiritur, ita dictum est quod in proposito requiritur suppositum
conveniens ad agendum. Ergo forma, quae esset principium actionis in supposito
distincto, si esset per se exsistens, non esset suppositum nec principium distinctum,
nec in supposito distincto convenienti generationi, et ex quo illud suppositum requiritur ad potentiam propinquam agendi, non poterit talis forma per se agere. 'Essentiale'
autem si per se exsistat in aliquo instanti naturae antequam intelligatur esse in
supposito vel persona, in illo priore non est suppositum agens in potentia propinqua
ad agendum; ista enim actio distinctionem requirit aliquorum in ista natura, quae non
potest esse nisi suppositorum. Ergo suppositum conveniens huic actioni, est suppositum distinctum, exsistens in ista natura: in nullo tali est natura in quantum intelligitur per se esse, etsi per se sit aliquo modo antequam in persona,—et ideo non poterit
'per se agere' ista actione."

another, the divine essence is not in the right circumstances in that first "instant of nature" to do any reproducing itself. After all, although the divine essence is an individual all by itself, it cannot be multiplied, so if we consider just the divine essence itself, there is nothing that qualifies as a distinct producer and product. Consequently, the divine essence will not generate a Son all by itself.[24]

This is true for creatures too, for producers are always distinct from their products, irrespective of whether we are talking about creatures or divine persons. A free-floating bit of heat, for example, cannot do anything if there is nothing to heat. Imagine if a bit of heat existed in a world all by itself. It could not heat itself, for it would already be hot, but nor could it heat something else, for there would be nothing to heat.[25] Similarly, the divine essence cannot be multiplied, but since every production requires a distinct producer and product (by T35), the divine essence cannot produce another copy of itself in that first "instant of nature."

Scotus therefore admits that although the divine essence cannot be "determined" by relationships, relationships still play a role here, for they are required to constitute a distinct producer and product. That

---

[24] Scotus, *Lect.*, 1.7.un., n. 66–7 (*Vat.* 16: 496.25–497.13): "ideo absolutum [viz. essentia divina], ad hoc quod fiat potentia proxima generandi, requirit aliquid aliud quam sunt illa quae inveniuntur in creaturis. Quid igitur est illud? Dico sic, quod omnis forma quae est principium agendi aliquam actionem requirentem distinctionem suppositorum, est forma agendi in supposito, si non potest esse distinctio nisi suppositorum; sed in natura divina non potest esse distinctio nisi suppositorum, et productio requirit distinctionem suppositorum, quia nihil producit se; igitur forma quae est principium generandi in divinis, requirit esse in supposito conveniente huic actioni. Sicut igitur in creaturis potentia proxima agendi includit approximationem passi et exclusionem impedimenti, ita in divinis forma—ut est potentia proxima agendi—includit esse in supposito conveniente huic actioni; ista autem convenientia suppositi est: ut sit suppositum habens formam et essentiam divinam, ut non habuerit eam per actionem adaequatam,—et illud est suppositum conveniens huic actioni; absolutum igitur cum proprietate suppositi, qua conveniens est actioni, est potentia proxima generationis Filii."
[25] Scotus, *Lect.*, 1.7.un., n. 86 (*Vat.* 16: 503.21–25): "dico quod si principium elicitivum esset separatum in creaturis nec haberet passum sibi approximatum nec impedimenta essent amota, non ageret per se exsistens, et si in subiecto haberet ista, ageret,—et tamen est ibi vera potentia, modo dicta, licet sit separatum"; *Lect.*, 1.7.un., n. 37 (*Vat.* 16: 486.7–13): "Unde, si totus mundus esset ignis, ignis non calefaceret nec esset in potentia proxima ad calefaciendum, quia deficeret passum. Similiter si calefactibile esset et non esset praesens, ignis non esset in potentia proxima ad calefaciendum. Similiter si calefactibile esset approximatum, sed esset ibi aliquod impedimentum, ignis non calefaceret nec esset in potentia proxima ad calefacere."

is, relationships are not "determiners," but they are part of the right circumstances for divine production.[26]

As we have seen then, Scotus disagrees almost entirely with Henry's account of divine power. For one thing, relationships show up on the scene too late, as it were, to do any "determining," but perhaps more importantly, Scotus thinks the divine essence is so awesome that it is absurd to suggest that it needs any sort of determination. As I put it at the beginning of this chapter (and as we will see in more detail in the following chapter), Scotus believes the divine essence is the most potent entity in existence, so it is perfectly capable of sourcing all divine activity in and of itself without the need for any further determination, and that includes the activity of producing another divine person.

---

[26] As Scotus puts it in an argument against Henry at *Ord.* 1.7.1, n. 24 (*Vat.* 4: 116.11–117.4): "natura ut natura ponitur principium elicitivum illius actionis. Ipsa autem 'ut natura' non est determinabilis, secundum Damascenum cap. 50: «Proprietates determinant hypostases, non naturam» 'ut natura'. Ergo nullum est determinativum principii 'quo' ut est principium 'quo', sed tantum principii agentis."

12

Scotus on Power and Perfection

According to Scotus, the divine essence is the sole power source for all divine activity, and it needs no determination by relationships or anything else. But Scotus also discusses certain issues that have to do with the *perfection* of the divine essence in its role as a power source, and that is the topic of this chapter.

12.1. SUBORDINATIONISM

In addition to the arguments I discussed in the last chapter, Scotus also argues that the divine essence must be the source of the Father's reproductive activity in order to avoid subordinationism. In order to explain why Scotus thinks subordinationism is lurking in the background here, I need to say a few things about how Scotus understands the relationship between causation and perfection.

Scotus believes there are two basic ways that various entities in the universe can be ordered with respect to one another.[1] On the one hand, some things are more perfect than others, and they can be ordered according to the more and less perfect. Scotus calls this

---

[1] Scotus, *De Primo*, 1.5 (Wolter, 2–3): "Accipio autem ordinem essentialem, non stricte—ut quidam loquuntur, dicentes posterius ordinari sed prius vel primum esse supra ordinem—sed communiter, prout ordo est relatio aequiparantiae dicta de priori respectu posterioris, et e converso, prout scilicet ordinatum sufficienter dividitur per prius et posterius. Sic igitur quandoque de ordine, quandoque de prioritate vel posterioritate fiet sermo." For a fuller discussion of Scotus's ideas with regards to these kinds of essential ordering, see Peter King, "Scotus on Metaphysics," in *The Cambridge Companion to Duns Scotus*, ed. Thomas Williams (Cambridge: Cambridge University Press, 2003), 38–42.

the order of "eminence." On the other hand, some things depend on others, and they can be ordered accordingly. Scotus calls this the order of "dependence."[2]

Scotus then goes on to subdivide these two kinds of orders further, but in this respect there are two points that concern us here. As for the order of eminence, Scotus thinks that one of the ways things can be ordered by perfection is according to *kind*. That is, Scotus maintains that no two kinds are equal in perfection, and so all kinds are ranked as either more or less perfect than another.[3] Thus, if we take any two kinds and compare them (e.g. horse-kind vs. human-kind), one is more perfect than the other.

(T36) For any kinds K_1 and K_2,
      K_1 and K_2 are equal in perfection iff
      K_1 and K_2 are the same kind.

As for the order of dependence, the subdivision that concerns us here is that of efficient causality. Effects depend on their (efficient) causes, and so efficient causes and their effects can generally be ordered into chains of causes and effects, where such causes are naturally prior to their effects.

However, Scotus also maintains that producers cannot produce anything beyond the scope of their powers. That is, they can produce effects that are equal or lesser than they are, but not effects that are greater.[4] More precisely, Scotus holds that the *formal terminus* (i.e.

---

[2] See Scotus, *De Primo*, 1.6 (Wolter, 4–5): "Prima Divisio: Dico ergo primo quod ordo essentialis videtur primaria divisione dividi, sicut aequivocum in aequivocata, scilicet, in ordinem eminentiae et in ordinem dependentiae"; *De Primo*, 1.7 (Wolter, 4–5): "Primo modo prius dicitur eminens, et posterius, quod est excessum. Ut breviter dicatur, quidquid est perfectius et nobilius secundum essentiam est sic prius"; *De Primo*, 1.8 (Wolter, 4–5): "Secundo modo prius dicitur, a quo aliquid dependent, et posterius, quod dependent . . . Prius secundum naturam et essentiam est quod contingit esse sine posteriori, non e converso. Quod ita intelligo, quod, licet prius necessario causet posterius et ideo sine ipso esse non possit, hoc tamen non est quia ad esse suum egeat posteriori, sed e converso."

[3] Scotus, *De Primo*, 3.25 (Wolter, 56–7): "Duae naturae sub eodem communi non habent gradum aequalem. Probatur per differentias dividentes genus; si sunt inaequales, ergo et esse unius erit perfectius esse alterius."

[4] Scotus, *Reportatio I–A* [= *Rep. I–A*], 1.7.1, n. 30 (Wolter, 313): "omne principium formale producendi aliquid aequivoce est perfectius producto termino, et si sit productio univoca, est aeque perfectum termino producto."

the form produced in the product) must be equal to or lesser than the *power source* of the producer.[5] Hence:

(T37) For any producer x and product y,
if x produces y by a production P,
the formal terminus G in y
cannot be more perfect than
the power source F in x.

But if we combine T36 and T37, it follows that if a power source and its corresponding formal terminus are different in kind, then the formal terminus must be less perfect than the power source. After all, if no two kinds are equal in perfection (by T36), then the only way for a power source and a formal terminus to be equal in perfection is if they are the same in kind. Thus:

(T38) For any producer x and product y,
if x produces y by a production P,
the power source F in x and
the formal terminus G in y
are equal in perfection iff
F and G are the same in kind.

On the other hand, T36 and T37 entail that if a power source and its corresponding formal terminus are different in kind, then the formal terminus must be less perfect than the power source. After all, no two kinds are equal in perfection (by T36), so if the power source and the formal terminus are different in kind, then they must be different in perfection too. However, no power source can produce a formal terminus that is greater in kind (by T37), so the formal terminus cannot be a member of a more perfect kind. Thus, it must belong to a lesser kind:

---

[5] Scotus, *Lectura* [= *Lect.*], 1.7.un., n. 49 (*Vat.* 16: 489.24–7): "omnis terminus formalis in producto requirit aliquam formam in producente, perfectiorem si sit generatio aequivoca, vel aeque perfectam si sit generatio univoca, et hoc loquendo de totali causa producente"; ibid., n. 57 (*Vat.* 16: 493.17–19): "si sit generatio univoca, requiritur forma aeque perfecta,—si aequivoca, perfectior"; ibid., n. 95 (*Vat.* 16: 506.19–20, 23–4): "dico quod generans generat forma aeque perfecta cum forma producti, vel forma perfectiore...unde nullo modo est concedendum quod generatum sit perfectius sua totali causa"; *Ordinatio* [= *Ord.*], 1.7.1, n. 38 (*Vat.* 4: 122.19–123.1): "quia illud quo producens producit, si non est eiusdem rationis cum forma producti, continet eam virtualiter et est perfectior ea."

(T39) For any producer x and product y,
       if x produces y by a production P,
       the formal terminus G in y is less perfect than
       the power source F in x iff
       F and G are different in kind.

Now, in the Godhead, Scotus maintains that the personal properties are different in kind. As he explains:

> But I well concede that fatherhood and sonship are relationships that belong to different species and have different natures . . . for fatherhood and sonship are more different than fatherhood and fatherhood.[6]

Thus, for Scotus, any given personal property (such as fatherhood) is different in kind from any other personal property (such as sonship):

(T40) For any of God's personal properties F and G,
       F and G are different in kind.

Further, Scotus believes that the personal properties are all different in kind from the divine essence, for being divine is not the same thing as, say, being a father (though divinity and fatherhood are compatible, since a divine being can be a father, as indeed the Father is):

(T41) For any personal property F and the divine essence E,
       F and E are different in kind.

Scotus also holds that the personal properties are less perfect than the divine essence. According to Scotus, the divine essence is infinitely perfect, and anything that is so perfect must belong to *all* the divine persons (otherwise the persons would not be equally perfect). The personal properties, however, clearly do not belong to all the persons, for they are unique constituents which distinguish the persons from each other, so each personal property belongs to one and only one divine person. Thus, the personal properties cannot be infinitely

---

[6] Scotus, *Ord.*, 1.7.1, n. 51 (*Vat.* 4: 129.3–7): "Sed bene concedo quod paternitas et filiatio sunt relationes alterius speciei et alterius rationis, . . . magis etiam distinguitur paternitas a filiatione, quam paternitas a paternitate." Ockham too, in *Ordinatio* 1.9.2 (*OTh* 3: 281.13–14): "sicut conceditur quod paternitas et filiatio sunt alterius rationis"; ibid. (*OTh* 3: 280.11–13): "Sed paternitas in Patre, quae est sibi essentialis, non tantum assimilatur filiationi quae est Filio essentialis quantum assimilaretur si essent duae paternitates in divinis."

perfect, and consequently, they must be less perfect than the divine essence:[7]

(T42) For any personal property F and the divine essence E,
         E is more perfect than F.

With all that said, we can now turn to Scotus's worry about subordinationism. The starting point is this: what is the source of the Father's reproductive activity? Since there are only two constituents in the Father, namely fatherhood and the divine essence, it must be one of those.

Suppose, then, that fatherhood were the power source. If that were so, what would the formal terminus be? Since there are also only two constituents in the Son, namely sonship and the divine essence, it must be one of those. It cannot be the divine essence, for the divine essence is more perfect than fatherhood (by T42), and it is impossible for the formal terminus to be more perfect than the power source (by T37).[8]

That leaves sonship. But sonship cannot be the formal terminus either, for fatherhood and sonship are different in kind (T40), and since the formal terminus cannot be more perfect than the power

---

[7] Scotus, *Ord.*, 1.13.un., n. 39 (*Vat.* 5: 85.7–9): "probatio, quia nec relatio realis est formaliter perfectio infinita, quia tunc aliqua persona in divinis non haberet omnem perfectionem infinitum formaliter"; *Ord.*, 1.7.1, n. 42 (*Vat.* 4: 125.3–5): "in divinis autem nihil est perfectius absoluto, quia 'absolutum' [viz. essentia divina] est formaliter infinitum, relatio autem non"; *Quod.*, 5, n. 13 (*Wad.* 12: 128; *AW*, 118–19, n. 5.30): "Omnis perfectio simpliciter est communicabilis; omne infinitum intensive est perfectio simpliciter; ergo, etc. Nulla autem proprietas personalis est communicabilis, quia est formalis ratio incommunicabiliter existendi; ergo nulla proprietas personalis est infinita intensive."

[8] Scotus, *Lect.*, 1.7.un., n. 49 (*Vat.* 16: 490.3–5): "Sed nihil est perfectius illo absoluto communicato Filio [viz. essentia divina], nec formaliter aeque perfectum, quia illud absolutum formaliter infinitum est [viz., essentia divina]"; *Rep. I–A*, 1.7.1, n. 32 (Wolter, 313): "in divinis nihil est aeque perfectum formaliter quod non est essentia, relatio enim non est perfecta formaliter; ergo [relatio sicut paternitas] non potest esse principium communicandi essentiam"; *Ord.*, 1.7.1, n. 47 (*Vat.* 4: 127.1–6): "Ad ista respondeo, quod sive generatio ponatur aequivoca sive univoca, ratio non impingitur, quia in generatione aequivoca oportet principium productivum esse perfectius forma terminante; nihil autem est perfectius absoluto, et specialiter nulla relatio est perfectior: absurdissimum enim videtur dicere quod relatio contineat virtualiter essentiam divinam."

source (by T37), sonship would therefore have to be less perfect than fatherhood (by T39).[9] By extension then, the Son would turn out to be less perfect than the Father, and that would amount to subordinationism.

Thus, there simply could not be any formal terminus if fatherhood were the Father's power source for reproduction, and that is clearly absurd. Scotus therefore concludes that the divine essence must be the relevant power source, for apart from fatherhood, the only other constituent in the Father is the divine essence.

That, Scotus thinks, guarantees that there will be no subordinationism in divine reproduction, for as we saw in section 4.1, Scotus maintains that the formal terminus of the Son's production is the divine essence itself. And since the very same divine essence is both the power source in the Father and the formal terminus in the Son, there is no chance that one could be less perfect than the other.

Still, one might object that Scotus's own view should be susceptible to the same criticisms he levels against Henry. For according to Scotus, the personal properties are different in kind, and since no two kinds can be equal in perfection, it follows that fatherhood and sonship (for example) cannot be equal in perfection either. Thus, it would seem that Scotus should admit that since the Father and Son are constituted by constituents that are unequal in perfection, the Father and Son must be unequal in perfection as well.

In response, Scotus argues that although fatherhood and sonship are different in kind, they are not shareable in the way that most common natures are. On the contrary, fatherhood belongs only to the Father, sonship belongs only to the Son, and passive spiration belongs only to the Spirit. For that reason, Scotus maintains that a personal property like fatherhood does not contribute to the Father's *kind*. Rather, it only *distinguishes* him from the Son and Spirit. Hence, by Scotus's reckoning, fatherhood does make the Father any more

---

[9] Scotus, *Ord.*, 1.7.1, n. 38 (*Vat.* 4: 123.1–3): "ergo, si paternitas est quo Pater agit, et non est eiusdem rationis cum filiatione, continet filiationem virtualiter et est perfectior ea"; *Lect.*, 1.7.un., n. 45 (*Vat.* 16: 488.28–489.6): "si paternitas sit principium generandi Filium, tunc generatio Filii a Patre esset aequivoca; sed impossibile est productionem esse aequivocam nisi formalis ratio producendi contineat virtualiter ipsum productum et eius rationem; si igitur paternitas sit ratio generandi Filium, paternitas virtualiter continebit filiationem, et non e contra, nisi per circumincessionem, quia effectus non continet virtualiter suam causam, et sic filiatio non esset ita perfecta formaliter sicut paternitas."

or less perfect than the Son or Spirit. It only makes him distinct from them.[10]

Before I close this section, I want to make one final point. Scotus, I think, would see his view as superior to Henry's in precisely this respect. For as we saw in section 3.2, Henry argues that when it comes to divine production, the divine essence plays the role of matter and the personal properties play the role of forms. Hence, on Henry's view, the Father and Son will have different "forms." However, by many medieval accounts of reproduction, the power source and the formal terminus are the respective (substantial) forms of the producer and the product. Thus, as Scotus sees it, Henry would have to say that the power source in the Father and the formal terminus in the Son are different in kind, and by T39, that would mean the Son would have to be less perfect than the Father. So Scotus would think that Henry's view leads directly into subordinationism in the way I just explained.

In other words, Scotus thinks that Henry's view does not solve the subordination problem I outlined in section 1.3: how can one divine person produce another without producing a lesser deity? As far Scotus is concerned, the only way to avoid subordinationism is to say that the very same divine essence is both the power source in the producing person and the formal terminus in the produced person.

12.2. THE DIVINE ESSENCE IS A PERFECT POWER SOURCE

Still, one might wonder how one and the same thing (like the divine essence) could be both the power source for activity and the formal terminus of that activity. Surely the power source for any activity is, in a certain sense, the *starting point* of that activity, and surely that disqualifies it from serving as the terminus or end point too.

---

[10] For a more detailed analysis of Scotus's response to this objection, see my "Are the Father and Son Different in Kind? Scotus and Ockham on Different Kinds of Things, Univocal and Equivocal Production, and Subordination in the Trinity," *Vivarium* 48 (2010): 302–26.

According to Scotus, this is not really a problem. The divine essence can still function as the Father's power source, even though it is shared with the product. In fact, for Scotus, this makes divine production an *ideal case* of production, not a problem case that needs to be explained away.

To show this, Scotus begins with a general claim about power sources: perfection does not prevent a power source from functioning as a power source.[11] For instance, if I improve my ability to sculpt clay statues, I do not lose any of my sculpting ability. On the contrary, I become much better at it. As Scotus sees it, this goes for all power sources. The more perfect a power source is, the better it is. Let me formulate this idea as follows:

(T43)   For any power source *F*,
         F's perfection does not prevent *F*
         from functioning as a power source.

With this notion at hand, Scotus then identifies what he considers to be two marks of perfection for power sources. The first is sharability, and the second is what Scotus calls "adequate expression." I will say more about "adequate expression" in a moment, but first I want to talk about how Scotus understands sharability.

12.2.1. Sharability

To say that sharability is a mark of perfection for power sources means that a power source which can be shared with the product is more perfect than one which cannot. Now, Scotus maintains that the producer and the product share the numerically same form in the divine case, but this is not so when it comes to creatures. For example, when one flame produces another (as when I use a lighter to ignite some dry kindling), both the producer and the product are flames, but there are two forms there: the producer-flame has one, and the produced-flame has the other. In the divine case though, the producer

---

[11] Scotus, *Lect.*, 1.7.un., n. 62 (*Vat.* 16: 495.5–7): "illud quod est perfectionis in principio productivo, non aufert ab aliquo principium productionis"; *Ord.*, 1.7.1, n. 39 (*Vat.* 4: 123.8–9): "Quod est perfectionis in principio productivo, non tollit ab aliquo rationem principii productivi"; *Rep. I–A*, 1.7.1, n. 33 (Wolter, 313): "illud quod ponit perfectionem in principio productivo non tollit ab aliquo quod sit principium productivum, si sibi conveniat."

shares its own form with the produced person, so there is only one form shared by the two of them.[12]

The reason for this turns on how Scotus understands the way that natures are shared. According to Scotus, both the divine essence and created natures can be shared by multiple individuals, but in different ways. A created nature is shared by being multiplied, but the divine essence cannot be multiplied, so it must be numerically the same in both the producer and the product.[13]

As Scotus sees it, a created nature does not have enough being or entity to be an individual *this* something-or-other, so some "thisness" (*haecceity*) must be added to it in order to get an individual. Consequently, in order for one instance of a created nature to produce another instance of the same nature, the nature must be individuated into another "this," at which point the nature is thereby multiplied. The divine essence, on the other hand, has so much being or entity— in fact, it has an infinite "amount," so to speak—that it is, in itself, a "this." Thus, no more actuality or "thisness" can be added to it in order to complete it, so the divine essence cannot be multiplied when it is shared.[14]

Note that for Scotus, the divine essence is shareable in this way precisely because it is *so perfect*, i.e. precisely because there is so much being or entity to it that it cannot be multiplied. Created natures, on

---

[12] For a more detailed discussion of sharability in Scotus, see Richard Cross, "Divisibility, Communicability, and Predicability in Duns Scotus's Theories of the Common Nature," *Medieval Philosophy and Theology* 11 (2003): 43–63, and "Duns Scotus on Divine Substance and the Trinity," *Medieval Philosophy and Theology* 11 (2003): 181–201.

[13] Scotus, *Ord.*, 1.5.1.un., n. 10 (*Vat.* 4: 14.12–21): "Istud secundum in opinione Ioachim est haereticum, scilicet quod Pater et Filius et Spiritus Sanctus non sint aliqua una res, quia sicut arguitur cap. praeallegato, 'Pater gignendo dedit essentiam suam Filio' (nullam enim aliam potuit dare qua Filius esset Deus), et simili ratione ambo dederunt essentiam suam Spiritui Sancto: 'non enim erat illa communicatio partis essentiae, quia essentia est simplex et indivisibilis,—ergo totius essentiae; ergo tota eadem essentia, quae est in Patre, est in Filio et in Spiritu Sancto, et propter simplicitatem divinam quaelibet persona est illa res, et omnes tres personae sunt illa res'." See also *Ord.*, 1.2.2.1–4, nn. 377–87 (*Vat.* 2: 344–9).

[14] Scotus, *Rep. I–A*, 1.2.4, n. 214 (Wolter, 182): "Primo ex communicabilitate naturae in creaturis, ubi perfectionis est quod natura potest pluribus suppositis communicari, sed quod non possit eis communicare sine sui divisione, hoc est imperfectionis in ea. Auferendo igitur quod est imperfectionis in creatura, et attribuendo Deo quod est perfectionis, erit natura divina pluribus suppositis indivisibiliter communicata, supposito prius quod natura posset quantum est ex se esse in pluribus suppositis et communicari eis per identitatem."

the other hand, are not shared in this way precisely because they are *not perfect enough*, i.e. precisely because they do not have enough being or entity to be shared without being multiplied.[15] This is why Scotus sees complete sharability as a mark of perfection, for only the most perfect sort of entity can be shared in this way.

But according to T43, such sharability would not prevent a shared entity from functioning as a power source. That is, the fact that a producer completely shares one of its constituents *F* with a product gives us no reason to deny that *F* is the power source for that production. On the contrary, such sharability would make it an ideal candidate for the power source.

To illustrate this idea further, Scotus provides a hypothetical example. Consider, he says, a case where a flame produces some heat in a dry log. As Scotus sees it, everybody would agree that the flame's heat is the relevant power source, and everybody would agree that the flame produces a second bit of heat in the log by exercising that power.

But now suppose that we add Scotus's mark of perfection to the picture. That is, suppose that the flame makes the log hot by completely sharing its own heat with the log. In this case, what would the source of the flame's heating power be? Scotus sees no reason why it wouldn't still be the same thing, namely the flame's heat. If the flame's heat is the power source under normal circumstances, how much more could it be the power source if it were so perfect that it could be shared completely with the produced effect?[16]

---

[15] Scotus, *Rep. I–A*, 1.7.1, n. 33 (Wolter, 313): "multo perfectius est si aliquid communicaret se in identitate numerali quam si in specifica, quia prima est adaequata communicatio; unde ignis uno calore habet plures calefactiones et hoc est imperfectionis in eo, quia non potest se tantum communicare unica calefactione, sicut pluribus, quia non adaequate communicat se."

[16] Scotus, *Ord.*, 1.7.1, n. 41 (*Vat.* 4: 124.4–20): "Exemplum istius est, si calor in igne communicaret se eundem numero ligno, et communicatione adaequata, ita quod iste calor non posset esse principium alterius calefactionis, non negaretur calorem ignis esse principium productivum caloris in ligno, cum modo de facto ponatur calor esse principium illius, et hoc cum duplici imperfectione, opposita duplici perfectioni hic suppositae (quia nunc est ibi diversitas caloris communicati et communicatio non adaequata, tunc autem esset identitas caloris communicati et communicatio adaequata); et tamen—illa hypothesi posita—lignum calore non posset calefacere: non enim se, quia accipit calorem calefactione quae est ab hoc calore, et tunc prius haberet calorem quam haberet calorem,—nec aliud, quia ista calefactio ligni ponitur adaequata illi calori in ratione principii activi.—Ita intelligendum est in proposito, quod illud quod poneretur esse principium alterius calefactionis si communicatio fieret in

Similarly, says Scotus, suppose (counterpossibly) that God could produce another, numerically distinct God. What would be the first God's power source? As Scotus sees it, most everybody would agree that it would be the (first God's) divine essence, not some personal property (like fatherhood). But now imagine if the first divine being were to produce a second by completely sharing its own essence with the second. What would the power source be then? Again, Scotus sees no reason why it wouldn't be the same thing.[17]

For Scotus, sharability is a mark of perfection, and therefore it in no way prevents a power source from functioning as a power source. On the contrary, as Scotus sees it, if a producer shares its power source with a product, that is a mark of just how perfect that power source is.

12.2.2. Adequate expression

The second mark of perfection that Scotus talks about is what he calls "adequate expression." According to Scotus, there is something about each kind of power that can be expressed by its product(s), and a product is an adequate expression of a power when it completely and perfectly expresses that "whatever-it-is" of the power that can be expressed. Thus, when a product adequately expresses a power, it expresses everything about the power that could possibly be expressed, and it does this in the most excellent way possible.[18]

---

diversitate numerali et non adaequata, idem debet modo poni principium quando fit communicatio eisdem, adaequata principio productivo."

[17] Scotus, *Ord.*, 1.7.1, n. 39 (*Vat.* 4: 123.12–22): "Sed si Deus per incompossibile generaret alium deum, et ille alius tertium, deitas poneretur principium productivum alterius et non relatio; et tunc deitas non communicaret se in identitate numerali, nec communicaret se communicatione adaequata sibi in ratione principii productivi, quia deitas posset esse principium alterius communicationis, puta factae—per incompossibile—a secundo deo. Ergo cum modo deitas communicetur in identitate numerali et communicatione adaequata sibi, ita quod deitate non potest esse alia communicatio numero, eiusdem rationis cum ista,—sequitur quod multo magis nunc ponetur 'absolutum' esse principium productivum quam tunc poneretur."

[18] Note, though, that Scotus thinks a power is not exhausted or "all used up," so to speak, by giving rise to an adequately expressive product. Scotus, *Ord.*, 1.7.2, n. 93 (*Vat.* 4: 148.10–149.2): "Ponitur quod non [viz. quod possint esse plures Filii in divinis], quia tota fecunditas exhauritur in uno actu; igitur non est ad alium. Contra. Exhauriri in corporalibus significat illud non manere in illo unde exhauritur; sic non potest hic intelligi, sed non manet ad alium actum. Ergo praemissa impropria,—et ut est vera, est eadem conclusioni"; *Rep. I–A*, 1.2.3, n. 187 (Wolter, 175): "Illud autem

By way of contrast, consider a case where a power is not adequately expressed by the product(s). Consider, for instance, God's power to create birds. God expresses this power by creating eagles, woodpeckers, hummingbirds, and so forth, but none of these completely expresses God's bird-making power. For one thing, lots of species are needed to express all the ways God can create birds (e.g. birds with big wings for gliding high in the sky, birds with tiny wings for hovering in front of flowers, and so on). Further, birds are finite creatures that come into being and pass away, so they can be replaced and multiplied. Birds, then, cannot completely express God's bird-making power, because when a product completely and perfectly expresses a power, no aspect of that power goes unexpressed in the product, and it does not need to be replaced. An adequately expressive product must be a permanent, perfect expression of the power.[19]

As I noted already, Scotus holds that adequate expression is also a mark of perfection, just like sharability. After all, a power that can result in an adequately expressive product must be a very potent power indeed. Of course, for Scotus, the Son is an adequate expression of the Father's power to beget a Son, but since perfection does not prevent a power source from functioning as a power source (by T43), Scotus again infers that the fact that the Son is an adequate expression of the Father's reproductive power does not entail that the divine essence cannot be the *source* of that power. On the contrary, the divine essence is all the more perfect precisely because it provides the Father with the power to beget an adequately expressive Son.[20]

---

vocabulum 'exhauriri' accipitur a corporalibus ubi aliquid dicitur exhauriri ab alio quando extrahitur ab alio et non manet in eo, sicut quando aqua exhauritur de puteo et non manet in eo, dicitur exhauriri. Sic non potest intelligi in divinis quod fecunditas alicuius principii productivi sit totaliter exhausta. Ergo si similitudo sit in aliquo vera, hoc est quia principium productivum habens unam productionem non manet fecundum vel productivum respectu alterius actus, sed tunc nihil probat quia petitur conclusio in praemissa."

[19] For further reflections on Scotus's theory of adequate expression in the Godhead, see Cross, *Duns Scotus on God*, 146–8.

[20] Scotus, *Lect.*, 1.7.un., n. 63 (*Vat.* 16: 495.11–16): "nam imperfectionis est in principio communicativo communicare aliud a se et non se, et similiter imperfectionis est in principio communicativo quod non communicat communicatione adaequata; igitur opposita istorum erunt perfectionis in principio communicativo, scilicet communicare se ita perfecte sicut est, et hoc est communicare perfectione adaequata"; *Ord.*, 1.7.1, n. 39 (*Vat.* 4: 123.9–11): "sed communicare se in identitate numerali, et adaequata communicatione sibi, ponit perfectionem in principio productivo"; *Rep. I–*

Similarly, Scotus believes that the Father and Son have the power to produce a Spirit, and of course, the Spirit adequately expresses that power just as well. But again, Scotus would say that even though the Spirit so fully and completely expresses that power, this gives us no reason to think that the divine essence cannot be the source of that power either. Indeed, as we saw in section 11.1, Scotus maintains that the divine essence is so awesome that in and of itself, it can provide the persons with *all* their powers, and in this case, that means it provides the Father with his power to beget a Son, *and* it provides the Father and Son with their power to produce a Spirit. Nevertheless, the fact that the Son and Spirit so adequately express those powers just goes to show how perfect the Son's and Spirit's respective productions actually are, and by T43, that just goes to show how potent the divine essence is insofar as it is the source of those powers.

Finally, it is worth noting that for Scotus, such adequate expression explains why there can be only one Son and one Spirit in the Godhead. After all, since the Son so fully and completely expresses the power to beget a divine Son, there cannot be a second divine Son, for if there were, the first Son would obviously not have adequately expressed the power to beget a divine Son in the first place, and the same goes for the Spirit. According to Scotus then, there can only be one Son and one Spirit, for each arises from a power that so fully and completely expresses itself in its product that it need not, and indeed cannot, express itself again.[21]

A, 1.7.1, n. 33 (Wolter, 313): "communicare autem se in identitate numerali et adaequate est principium perfectionis in Patre producente."

[21] Scotus, *Ord.*, 1.2.2.1–4, n. 303 (*Vat.* 2: 308.3–309.4): "Ulterius sequitur: si non sint nisi duo principia productiva alterius rationis, ergo sunt tantum duae productiones numero. Probatio, quia utrumque principium productivum habet productionem sibi adaequatam et coaeternam; ergo stante illa, non potest habere aliam"; *Ord.*, 1.2.2.1–4, n. 358 (*Vat.* 2: 337.11–13, 15–18): "Ulterius, quod non possint esse plures personae productae quam istae duae probo sic: non possunt esse nisi duae productiones intra . . . hoc ergo nunc sit certum, quod tantum duae sunt productiones intra. Nulla autem istarum potest terminari nisi ad unam personam, quia persona producta est terminus adaequatus illi productioni; igitur etc."

13

Ockham against Henry

In this chapter, I want to look at Ockham's arguments against Henry. Like Scotus, Ockham rejects Henry's view that the divine essence needs to be "determined" to activities by relationships, for Ockham agrees with Scotus that relationships show up on the scene too late, as it were, to do any "determining." Ockham also agrees with Scotus that fatherhood cannot be the source of the Father's reproductive activity, though Ockham rejects Scotus's argument for this conclusion, as we shall see.

13.1. RELATIONSHIPS CANNOT DETERMINE ANYTHING'S ACTIVITY

As we saw in section 10.2, Henry argues that although the divine essence is the sole basis for all divine activity, it is "determined" to specific divine activities by the relationships it has with each of them. Like Scotus, Ockham takes issue with this claim. For as he sees it, relationships just cannot affect anything's activity in any way.

To make his case, Ockham asks us to consider the sun. According to medieval Aristotelians, the sun can bring about a variety of effects. For instance, it heats and illuminates the earth, it generates maggots in rotting carcasses, etc. Even so, says Ockham, the sun does not need any "determining" relationships to perform these various activities, for if it did, one would wonder: are these relationships supposed to be mere conceptual relationships, drawn only in the mind, or are they supposed to be real relationships?[1]

If they were mere conceptual relationships, they would not be able to influence the sun's activity in any way, for conceptual relationships only exist in someone's mind, and nature is generally not affected by what you or I or anyone else thinks of it. For instance, I can imagine any number of connections between the sun and other things, but merely drawing such connections in my mind would not cause the sun to act in some particular way.[2]

This is not to say that conceptual relationships never affect the course of events, for thinking beings can obviously be influenced by their thoughts (as for instance when Hamlet killed Polonius after getting it into his head that the man behind the curtain was Claudius). But of course, the sun is not a thinking being, so it cannot have anything "in mind" that might affect its activity. Clearly then, mere conceptual relationships can have no bearing on the sun's activity.[3]

One might point out that the Father is a thinking being, so unlike the sun, the Father could be influenced by mere conceptual relationships. But Ockham denies this, for as he sees it, the Father produces the Son naturally, and natural activities do not involve any premedi-

---

[1] Ockham, *Ordinatio* [= *Ord.*], 1.7.1 (*OTh* 3: 108.22–26): "nullus respectus est sic requisitus ad hoc quod actus diversi eliciantur. Primo, quia sol causat diversa sine tali variatione respectuum. Probatio: quia si sint tales respectus in sole ad diversa causabilia, aut sunt respectus reales aut tantum rationis."

[2] Ockham, *Ord.*, 1.7.1 (*OTh* 3: 110.5–7): "Quia nullum ens reale respicit aliud tamquam principium eius reale per aliquid rationis, nec multo magis inclinatur per ens rationis"; *Ord.*, 1.7.1 (*OTh* 3: 111.9–112.3): "nihil debet attribui enti reali propter fabricationem intellectus, nisi praedicata importantia tales fabricationes vel operationes intellectus vel aliqua sequentia ex talibus operationibus intellectus. Verbi gratia, quamvis propter operationem intellectus circa aliquod obiectum . . . possit dici quod ista res intelligitur vel est praedicatum vel subiectum . . . tamen quod propter quamcumque operationem intellectus circa hominem et albedinem . . . homo dicatur albus . . . est impossibile. Nunc autem elici, causari, movere vel moveri, . . . et sic de aliis, non important actus intelligendi . . . sicut intentiones logicae important. Igitur propter nullum actum intelligendi circa aliquid debet dici ipsum movere—nisi forte ad actum intelligendi—vel elici ab aliquo."

[3] Ockham, *Ord.*, 1.7.1 (*OTh* 3: 109.14–16): "Si autem respectus sint entia rationis, et ad actionem agentis naturalis, quod agit sine cognitione, nihil facit ens rationis, igitur isti respectus in nullo determinant solem ad effectus suos"; *Ord.*, 1.7.1 (*OTh* 3: 114.11–14): "nullus respectus rationis potest esse principium elicitivum vel determinativum alicuius actionis realis, sicut nec ens aliquod rationis. Et hoc maxime est verum quando agens non praecognoscit illud quod debet operi."

tated thought. Thus, the Father does not foreknow the Son before producing him. For Ockham, the Father's activity cannot be determined by mere conceptual relationships anymore than the sun's activity can.[4]

But what if Henry's proposed "determining relationships" were real relationships? To this, Ockham points out that the sun cannot be related to any effect *before* it brings that effect about, for relationships cannot exist without the things they relate, and an alleged relationship with something non-existent would not be a real relationship at all. Consequently, the sun can only have real causal relationships with its effects while it is actually causing them.[5]

However, like Scotus, Ockham takes this to mean that these relationships must be naturally *posterior* to, not prior to, the sun's effects, and like Scotus, Ockham holds that one thing is naturally prior to another if it can exist without the other but not vice versa.[6] As I put it in section 11.2:

(T34) For any *x* and *y*,
   x is naturally prior to *y* if
   (i) *x* can exist without *y*, and
   (ii) *y* cannot exist without *x*.

This applies to the sun and its activity, for some of the sun's effects can continue to exist after they have been produced (as maggots can survive after the sun has set), but the sun cannot have a causal relationship with any of its effects without the effects in question. Consequently, the sun's causal relationships are naturally posterior to its effects, and that means they show up on the scene too late, as it were, to do any "determining." For Ockham then, the sun produces

---

[4] Ockham, *Ord.*, 1.7.1 (*OTh* 3: 114.13–15): "Et hoc maxime est verum quando agens non praecognoscit illud quod debet operari, qualiter in divinis, quia Pater non ante cognoscit Filium quam producit eum."

[5] Ockham, *Ord.*, 1.7.1 (*OTh* 3: 109.1–6): "Si reales [respectus], contra: aut manent ante productionem effectuum aut non. Si sic, hoc est impossibile, quia termini illorum respectuum non possunt esse nisi illi effectus sint. Sed respectu non-exsistentis nullus est respectus realis. Igitur sol non habet diversos respectus respectu diversorum effectuum producibilium qui nondum sunt."

[6] Ockham, *Ord.*, 1.7.1 (*OTh* 3: 109.6–7): "Si [respectus] non sunt nisi dum sunt effectus, igitur effectus sunt priores naturaliter"; *Ord.*, 1.7.1 (*OTh* 3: 109.8–9): "quia 'prius naturaliter' est illud quod potest esse alio non-exsistente, et non e converso."

its effects without any "determining" relationships, and if this is so for the sun, then it is so all the more for a divine person.[7]

Ockham also makes the same point with regard to matter. As Ockham understands it, Henry thinks that a lump of matter's relationship with a form somehow makes it receptive to that form. But for Ockham, this cannot be, for relationships are naturally posterior to the things they relate, not vice versa. Besides, a lump of matter cannot be related to a form before it exists, and mere conceptual relationships will obviously have no affect on matter's real capabilities either, so a relationship simply cannot affect matter's receptivity anymore than it can affect the sun's activity.[8]

Ockham levels another argument against Henry that is worth mentioning here as well: if relationships were determiners, says Ockham, then we would end up with an infinite regress. After all, if the divine essence were so "indeterminate" that it would need to be determined by a set of relationships, then it would also be "indeterminate" with respect to those relationships, in which case it would need a second set of relationships determining it to the first set, and a third set determining it to the second set, and so on ad infinitum. And if Henry wished to say that the divine essence were not indeterminate with respect to its relationships, then we could just as easily say it is not indeterminate with respect to its activities either.[9]

It is easy to see how all of this applies to Henry's theory of powers. According to Henry, a power is constituted by its relationship with

---

[7] Ockham, *Ord.*, 1.7.1 (*OTh* 3: 109.9–12): "Sed isti effectus . . . possunt manere sine illis respectibus illius agentis, et ipsi respectus non possunt manere sine illis effectibus"; *Ord.*, 1.7.1 (*OTh* 3: 109.12–13): "Igitur isti respectus sunt posteriores naturaliter, igitur non determinant agens ad istos effectus"; *Ord.*, 1.7.1 (*OTh* 3: 109.17–18): "Si igitur sol sine talibus respectibus potest in plures operationes, multo fortius in Deus."

[8] Ockham, *Ord.*, 1.7.1 (*OTh* 3: 110.9–14): "Praeterea, quod [Henricus] dicit de materia, quod ipsa habet tales diversos respectus, est simpliciter falsum, quia materia non habet tales respectus reales, sicut nec activum naturale, quia termini, qui ponerentur illorum respectuum, sunt simpliciter non-existentes. Nec respectus rationis faciunt aliquid ad hoc quod materia recipiat vel non recipiat."

[9] Ockham, *Ord.*, 1.7.1 (*OTh* 3: 128.19–129.5): "sive relatio sit principium elicitivum sive non, non est principium determinativum, quia vane et superflue ponuntur tales respectus determinantes. Si enim tales respectus ponantur, adhuc essentia est indeterminata ad illos respectus, cum illa secundum se et absolute sit unica et respectus sint plures. Igitur oportet quod determinetur ad illos respectus per alios respectus, et sic in infinitum"; *Ord.*, 1.7.1 (*OTh* 3: 129.5–7): "Vel si [essentia divina] potest ex se determinari ad illos respectus, eadem ratione poterit ex se determinari ad illos actus, et ita superflue ponuntur tales respectus."

the activity for which it is a power. But as Ockham sees it, this cannot be, for relationships are naturally posterior to the things they relate, and so any relationship between a power and its activity already *presupposes* that power and its activity. Thus, Ockham agrees with Scotus that relationships show up too late in the order of explanation to actually determine or constitute powers in any way.

13.2. FATHERHOOD IS NOT THE SOURCE OF THE FATHER'S REPRODUCTIVE ACTIVITY

Ockham goes even further than this, however, for in addition to arguing that a relationship like fatherhood cannot *determine* the Father's reproductive power, he also claims that fatherhood cannot be the *source* of that power either. To make this point, Ockham begins by asserting that the Father's fatherhood *just is* his act of producing the Son:[10]

(T44) The Father's fatherhood F
     is identical to his reproductive act A.

This claim might have some intuitive appeal, for we could point out that (successfully) fathering a child is precisely what makes someone a father. Consequently, when we talk about the "fatherhood" of the Father, we are simply talking about his reproductive activity that results in a Son. But over and above this intuitive appeal, Ockham provides his own argumentation in support of T44. In fact, he argues for it at length in another context,[11] but in the texts I am considering here, Ockham offers what he calls a "persuasive" (rather than a demonstrative) argument in support of this claim.

According to Ockham, we should always assume that any two entities in God are formally the same in every way unless one of them can exist in some divine person without the other. Consider, for example, the divine essence and the Father's fatherhood: the divine essence belongs to the Son, but fatherhood does not, so the divine essence can exist in at least one divine person without

---

[10] Ockham, *Ord.*, 1.7.1 (*OTh* 3: 113.11–12): "sed proprietas personalis ipsius Patris et ipsa generatio activa sunt idem omnibus modis ex natura rei."
[11] Ockham, *Ord.*, 1.26.2 (*OTh* 4: 174.8–178.18).

fatherhood. Consequently, fatherhood cannot be the same as the divine essence, formally speaking.[12]

Now compare the Father's reproductive activity and his fatherhood. Could one of these exist in a divine person without the other? Ockham says no, and indeed, it is hard to imagine how (successful) reproductive activity could exist without fatherhood, no matter who or what we are talking about. For if someone or something—be it a creature or a divine person—successfully begets a son, then surely that makes him a father.

But since the Father's reproductive activity and fatherhood always exist together, Ockham concludes that they must be the very same thing, formally speaking.[13] For Ockham then, the Father's fatherhood is nothing other than his reproductive activity, as T44 claims. In other words, to say that the Father is a father and that he produces a Son are two ways of expressing the very same thing.

Given that, Ockham argues: if T44 is true, then fatherhood cannot be the power source for the Father's reproductive activity, for they are the very same thing, and nothing can be the source of itself.[14] After all, it would be absurd to say that producing a son gives someone the power to reproduce, for that would put the cart before the horse. Thus, fatherhood cannot be the power source for the Father's reproductive activity. On the contrary, it *just is* his reproductive activity, so the power source for that activity must be sought elsewhere.

As I explained in section 12.1, Scotus also argues that fatherhood cannot be the power source for the Father's reproductive activity. To

---

[12] Ockham, *Ord.*, 1.7.1 (*OTh* 3: 113.13–16): "Potest tamen hoc modo persuaderi, quia nihil ponendum est esse non-idem in divinis cum aliquo in divinis, nisi quod potest esse in aliqua persona in qua non est aliud vel e converso"; *Ord.*, 1.7.1 (*OTh* 3: 113.16–18): "Propter hoc enim quod essentia est in Filio et non paternitas, vel quia essentia est Filius et Pater non est Filius, ideo non sunt idem formaliter essentia et Pater." Ockham also points out that the same argument could be used to show that active spiration is not formally the same as fatherhood either. *Ord.*, 1.7.1 (*OTh* 3: 113.18–19): "Idem argumentum est de spiratione active et de paternitate."

[13] Ockham, *Ord.*, 1.7.1 (*OTh* 3: 113.19–23): "Sed nihil est proprietas personalis Patris quin sit generatio activa nec e converso, nec in aliqua persona est proprietas personalis Patris quin in eadem sit generatio activa et e converso. Igitur sunt idem omnibus modis ex natura rei propter identitatem realem cum essentia."

[14] Ockham, *Ord.*, 1.7.1 (*OTh* 3: 113.10–12, 23–4): "nihil est principium elicitivum sui ipsius; sed proprietas personalis ipsius Patris et ipsa generatio activa sunt idem omnibus modis ... Igitur unum non est principium elicitivum alterius"; cf. *Ord.*, 1.7.1 (*OTh* 3: 110.17–19): "illud quod est idem omnibus modis ex natura rei cum essentia non potest elici ab essentia; tunc enim idem eliceretur a se, quod est impossibile."

summarize briefly, Scotus maintains that the formal terminus of a production cannot be more perfect than the power source for that production (see T37 in section 12.1), and he maintains that the divine essence is more perfect than the personal properties (see T42 in section 12.1). Consequently, fatherhood cannot be the power source for the Father's reproductive activity, for if it were, the divine essence could not be the formal terminus of the Son's production (since the divine essence is more perfect than fatherhood), nor could sonship be the formal terminus (since that would make the Son inferior to the Father—a possibility Scotus rejects).

Ockham thinks Scotus's argument here is unsuccessful. According to Ockham, there simply cannot be any differences of perfection within the Godhead, for everything in God is perfectly identical to—and hence just as perfect as—the divine essence. Thus, there is just no way that anything in God could be inferior to anything else in God, so Scotus cannot base any conclusions on different levels of perfection within the Godhead.[15]

This deserves some comment. As I explained in section 5.4, Scotus agrees that everything in God is perfectly identical to the divine essence, but Scotus also believes that the personal properties are *formally distinct* from the divine essence.[16] One of the things this means for Scotus is that the divine essence and the personal properties can (and do) have different levels of perfection. Indeed, as I explained in section 12.1, Scotus explicitly argues that although

---

[15] Ockham, *Ord.*, 1.7.1 (*OTh* 3: 126.17–20): "Similiter sequeretur [ex ratione Scoti] quod essentia [divina] esset perfectior relatione [e.g. paternitate vel filiatione], quod est manifeste falsum, quia tunc relatio esset imperfectior essentia, quod est falsum, quia nihil est imperfectius in Deo"; *Ord.*, 1.5.2 (*OTh* 3: 61.15–16): "in Deo nullus est ordo perfectionis. Similiter, Pater est prior Filio origine, et tamen non est prior eo perfectione"; *Ord.*, 1.7.1 (*OTh* 3: 127.7–10): "Dico ergo quod sive paternitas sit principium elicitivum generationis sive non, non est perfectior filiatione, propter identitatem realem utriusque cum eadem essentia numero."

[16] Scotus, *Ord.*, 1.2.2.1–4, n. 403 (*Vat.* 2: 357.3–6): "Et ideo potest concedi quod ante omnem actum intellectus est realitas essentiae [divinae] qua est communicabilis, et realitas suppositi [i.e. personae] qua suppositum est incommunicabile; et ante actum intellectus haec realitas formaliter non est illa, vel non est formaliter eadem illi"; *Ord.*, 1.5.2.un., n. 118 (*Vat.* 4: 69.15–17): "unum simplicissimum [est constituta] ex istis [viz. ex essentia divina et proprietate personale, puta ex essentia et paternitate], quia una ratio est perfecte—immo perfectissime—eadem alteri, et tamen non formaliter eadem"; *Ord.*, 1.5.2.un., n. 138 (*Vat.* 4: 78.11–13): "Dico igitur breviter quod relatio [e.g. paternitas vel filiatio] et essentia [divina] ita sunt in persona [divina] ... sed sunt perfecte idem, licet non formaliter."

the divine essence is infinitely perfect, fatherhood and sonship are not. So Scotus clearly believes that the perfection of the divine essence does not transfer over to fatherhood and sonship, formally speaking, despite the fact that they are perfectly identical with the divine essence. Of course, Scotus would admit that the Father and Son can be denominated as infinitely perfect in virtue of the fact that they possess the divine essence, but the point is that this perfection does not transfer over *formally*.[17]

As for Ockham, it is fairly well known that on the one hand, he vigorously rejects Scotus's teaching on the formal distinction, while on the other hand, he says the personal properties are "formally distinct" from the divine essence. Now, one might take this to imply that although Ockham very much dislikes Scotus's formal distinction, he begrudgingly accepts it in the divine case.[18] But that assessment would be inaccurate, for Ockham simply uses the label "formally distinct" for cases where the scriptures or church doctrine force him to deny the transitivity of identity. That is precisely how Ockham sees the Trinity: although fatherhood and sonship are perfectly identical to the divine essence, the scriptures and church doctrine require that he say they are not perfectly identical to each other. And for lack of a better term, Ockham adopts "formally distinct" as a label for this very situation. As he himself puts it:

> Generally speaking, I say that one should never say that [two things which are really the same] are formally distinct, unless . . . one of them is truly said to be the same as some other thing while the other of them is not truly said to be the same as that thing. For instance, a relation and the divine essence—fatherhood and the divine essence, say—are formally distinct, because the divine essence is the same as sonship but fatherhood is not . . . Indeed, to be formally distinct, as I understand it, is nothing but a label for the following: when one of the two is the same as some other (absolute or relative) thing while the other of the two is not . . . When such a scenario can be found, then we should postulate a formal distinction, for that is all I mean by being formally distinct. But

---

[17] For more on this, see Richard Cross, *Duns Scotus on God*, 245–8.
[18] See, for instance, Philotheus Boehner, *Collected Articles on Ockham*, second edition, ed. Eligius Buytaert (St. Bonaventure, New York: The Franciscan Institute, 1992), 365ff.

when such a scenario is not possible, we should not postulate a formal distinction.[19]

So even though Ockham adopts Scotus's terminology, he has something very different in mind, and thus whereas Scotus maintains that perfection does not transfer from one formally distinct entity to another, Ockham thinks it does. For Ockham then, we cannot use different levels of perfection to conclude that fatherhood is not the power source for the Father's reproductive activity, for there simply are no differences of perfection within the Godhead.

Nevertheless, as we have seen, Ockham does accept Scotus's conclusion, for according to Ockham, fatherhood just is the Father's reproductive activity, and nothing can be the source of itself. Hence, in addition to agreeing with Scotus (contra Henry) that relationships cannot "determine" divine activity, Ockham also agrees that a personal property (like fatherhood) cannot be the power source for divine production.

---

[19] Ockham, *Ord.*, 1.2.1 (*OTh* 2: 19.3–18): "universaliter dico quod nunquam de aliquis verificatur distingui formaliter nisi . . . quando scilicet de uno illorum vere dicitur quod est aliqua res et de reliquo vere dicitur quod non est illa res, sicut relatio et essentia [in divinis] distinguuntur formaliter, puta essentia et paternitas, quia videlicet essentia est filiatio et paternitas non est filiatio . . . Immo distingui formaliter non est aliud, sicut ego teneo distinctionem formalem, et hoc est quid nominis ipsius, scilicet quod unum illorum est aliqua res absoluta vel relativa et alterum non est illa res . . . Et quando est hoc possibile invenire, tunc est ponenda distinctio formalis, quia nihil aliud voco distingui formaliter; et quando non est possibile, tunc non est ponenda." See also *Ord.*, 1.2.11 (*OTh* 2: 371.5–10) and *Quod.*, 1.3 (*OTh* 9: 20.1–3). For more on the formal distinction in Ockham, see Adams, *Ockham*, 1: 46–52 and 2: 1001–3.

14

Ockham on the Source of Divine Production

Having discussed Ockham's critique of Henry (and Scotus, to some extent) in the last chapter, I want to turn now to Ockham's own position on the matter. As we shall see, Ockham ends up with a view that is similar to Scotus's, but Ockham gets to his conclusions in his own way. Indeed, as I will show below, Ockham's argumentation for his conclusions relies on his distinctive views of efficient causality.

14.1. THE SOURCE OF PRODUCTIVE ACTIVITY

Ockham claims that we should identify the power source for any activity—and that includes productive activity—in the same way that we identify the causal source of any effect. According to Ockham though, we identify the causal source of an effect as follows:

> Setting aside everything that is not a cause of the effect in question, the basis [or source] for causing [the effect] is that which, either existing by itself or in something else, can be the cause of that effect or is required for the existence of the other [viz. the effect], and which is not constituted by the causation or the effect itself.[1]

This passage needs some unpacking, and there are three points I want to highlight. First, Ockham says at the very end of this quotation that the source of an effect cannot be constituted by the causation (i.e. the

---

[1] Ockham, *Ordinatio* [= *Ord.*], 1.7.1 (*OTh* 3: 114.19–23): "dico quod sicut ratio causandi est illud quod exsistens in aliquo vel in se potest esse causa effectus, omni illo quod non est causa eiusdem effectus circumscripto, vel quod requiritur ad esse alterius et quod non constituitur ex ipsa causatione seu causato."

causal activity) or the effect itself. Presumably, the idea here is that causes *result* in effects, not the other way around, so the source we are seeking cannot be the effect itself, nor can it be the activity that brings the effect about (as we saw in section 13.2), nor can it be anything that is constituted by or otherwise results from that effect or activity.

Second, Ockham says at the beginning of this passage that we should set aside everything which is not a cause of the effect in question. This, I take it, is meant to rule out anything that is merely a required circumstance for causal activity. For instance, my stove can only heat a pot of water when the pot is close enough to be heated, but nobody would think that "being close enough" is the source of the water getting hotter. It is, rather, just part of the required circumstances.

Of course, certain types of effects can come about in different circumstances. For example, water can be heated on the stove, in the microwave, in an electric kettle, and so on. Consequently, alternative sets of circumstances might be possible for certain types of effects. But the point here is that any given effect can only happen in the right circumstances, where "the right circumstances" ranges over *any* set of appropriate circumstances.

Third and finally, Ockham says in the middle of the above passage that the source of an effect is that which can cause the effect or is required for the existence of the effect. This makes it clear that Ockham thinks the source of an effect is just its (efficient) cause— or in cases where the source does not produce the effect (which, as we shall see, happens in the Godhead), the source is at least some absolute thing that must exist if the effect is to exist too.

To appreciate this last point, we need to briefly consider Ockham's views on efficient causality.[2] The issues are complicated, but for our purposes here, the relevant point is this: Ockham is fond of saying that an efficient cause is the absolute thing which, assuming an appropriate set of circumstances, must be posited in order to also posit the effect (and, conversely, no matter what else is posited, when that absolute thing is not posited, the effect cannot be posited either).[3]

---

[2] For a thorough discussion of the texts and issues, see Adams, *Ockham*, 2: 741–98.

[3] Ockham, *Ord.*, 1.45.un. (*OTh* 4: 664.20–665.3): "quamvis non intendam dicere universaliter quid sit causa immediata, dico tamen quod istud sufficit ad hoc quod aliquid sit causa immediata, scilicet quod illa re absoluta posita ponatur effectus, et ipsa non posita,—omnibus aliis concurrentibus quantum ad omnes condiciones et dispositiones consimiles—, non ponitur effectus. Unde omne quod est tale respectu

In other words, the cause of an effect is that which is required for the existence of the effect, given an appropriate set of circumstances.

So, for instance, suppose that after placing a pot of water over a flame on my stove, the water begins to heat up. What would the cause of this be? One might be tempted to think it is the flame, for apart from the pot of water and its proximity to the flame, the only thing left is the flame itself, and without the flame, the water presumably would not get warmer.

But Ockham's view takes us in a different direction, for Ockham would say it is the *heat* in the flame (rather than the flame itself) that is required for the water to get warmer. In fact, the flame does not seem to be required at all here, for if God destroyed the flame but preserved the heat, that free-floating bit of heat could heat the water just as well.

In other words, the flame does not satisfy the conditions that are required for it to be the cause of the water's getting warmer. For on Ockham's view, the cause of any effect is that which, given an appropriate set of circumstances, must be posited in order to also posit the effect, and conversely, if it is not posited, the effect cannot be posited either. But in this case, the flame does not need to be posited at all, for the heat (rather than the flame) explains the fact that the water gets warmer. Thus, as Ockham sees it, the heat (rather than the flame) must be the cause of the water's getting warmer.

What role does the flame play then? To explain this, Ockham employs a traditional distinction derived from Aristotle between proper and incidental causes (or, as Ockham puts it, *per se* and *per accidens* causes). According to Aristotle, the proper cause of a statue is a sculptor, but if that sculptor also happens to be a musician, then we might say something like, "did you know that musician sculpted this statue?" Yet the fact that our sculptor is a musician is incidental to the fact that she sculpted the statue, for her musicality plays no causal role in her producing the statue.[4]

---

alicuius est causa illius." Note, however, that Ockham formulates this claim in a variety of ways throughout his works, some of which are more compatible than others. For fuller discussion, see Adams, *Ockham*, 2: 746–50.

[4] Aristotle, *Physics*, 2.3, 195a32–b2 (*AL* 7.1: 60.6–11; cf. *Iunt.* 4: 61vM-62rA): "Amplius autem sicut accidens et horum genera, ut statue aliter Policlitus et aliter statuam faciens, quoniam accidit statuam facienti Policliti esse. Et continentes autem accidens, ut si homo causa sit statue et omnino animal. Sunt autem et accidentium alie aliis longius et magis propius, ut si albus et musicus causa dicantur statue."

Ockham takes this to mean that a proper cause produces its effects through its own power, not through something else. For instance, as I just explained, when a flame heats a pot of water, Ockham would say the flame's heat is what directly warms the water. Similarly, when I think, Ockham would say that my mind (my intellectual soul) is what directly generates my thoughts.[5]

But when the proper cause exists in a subject (as heat exists in a flame), or when it is a part or constituent of a larger whole (like the intellectual soul in a human), Ockham thinks we can denominate the proper cause by pointing to that subject or whole, for anything can be denominated by the various qualities or constituents that pick it out. Nevertheless, although we can denominate the cause of the water's getting warmer by pointing to the flame itself, the real cause of the water's getting warmer is the flame's heat.[6]

Taking all of these points together, we can formulate the following as Ockham's criterion for identifying the cause or source of an effect:[7]

---

[5] Ockham, *Ord.*, 1.2.10 (*OTh* 2: 345.15–24): "Sed causa per se est illud quod causat non per aliquid aliud realiter distinctum sed per se, ita quod ipso posito, omni alio circumscripto quod non est causa in alio genere causae, poterit sequi effectus. Et isto modo ipse calor est causa per se caloris, quia ipso posito, et omni alio amoto quod non habet rationem causae, poterit sequi calor in passo disposito et approximato; et ideo calor per se causat calorem, quia non per aliud. Et isto modo ipsa anima intellectiva per se causat intellectionem et volitionem, quia non per aliud, nisi secundum quod ly per notat circumstantiam causae partialis concurrentis."

[6] Ockham, *Ord.*, 1.2.10 (*OTh* 2: 344.21–345.14): "Et ideo potest dici quod causa per accidens est illud quod agit per aliquid aliud ab eo; sed tale non est nisi subiectum vel totum habens partem qua agit. Et isto modo potest dici quod ignis per accidens calefacit, et eodem modo quod calidum per accidens calefacit. Et isto modo potest dici quod homo per accidens ratiocinatur; et similiter totum per accidens agit, quando actio sibi non convenit nisi mediante parte sua. Et ratio istius est quia illud dicitur per accidens competere alicui quo amoto nihil minus potest esse, sed igne destructo et reservato calore nihilominus poterit sequi calefactio, quia, sicut ostendetur in quarto, accidens actu separatum ita potest agere sicut coniunctum. Eodem modo illa actio quae competit homini mediante anima intellectiva poterit ita elici ab anima separata sicut a coniuncta; et ideo actio quae primo convenit parti, dicitur convenire toti per accidens, quia convenit sibi per aliud. Similiter actio primo competens accidenti dicitur convenire suo subiecto per accidens, quia per aliud. Et ita large accipiendo 'per accidens,' secundum quod est idem quod 'per aliud realiter distinctum,' sic potest concedi tam de subiecto accidentis quam de toto, cuius parti primo convenit actio, quod est agens per accidens, et eodem modo quod est causa per accidens."

[7] Ockham does not, so far as I know, ever offer a formal definition for a cause (though he does say that a cause is that which has the power to bring about its effect, see *Quaestiones in Librum Quartum Sententiarum*, 4.1 (*OTh* 7: 17.14–16): "dico quod de ratione causae est quod possit virtute propria ad eam sequi effectus ex natura rei et naturaliter"). Hence, T45 is not a *definition* for a cause. But Ockham would regard

(T45) For any effect y that is produced by a causal act A,
there is an x such that x is the causal source of y iff
(i) given an appropriate set of circumstances,
then no matter what else is posited,
if x is posited then y is posited, and
if x is not posited then y is not posited,
(ii) x is neither A nor y,
(iii) x is constituted by neither A nor y, and
(iv) x is not part of the appropriate circumstances
for causing y.

With all that said, Ockham then points out that we should identify the source of *activity* in the same way that we identify the source of an *effect*. In other words, *power sources* should be identified in the same way that efficient *causes* are identified. Hence, just as the causal source of an effect is that which is required for the existence of the effect in the way just explained,

> so also is the elicitive [i.e. power] source of some activity, undergoing, or production that which is necessarily and by itself required for that production, and which is not constituted by the production or the product.[8]

Thus, like the cause of any effect, the power source for any productive activity cannot be a mere circumstance for that activity, nor can it be the activity, the product, or anything constituted by the activity or product. Rather, it is just the absolute thing which, given an appropriate set of circumstances, then no matter what else is posited, it must be posited in order to also posit the productive activity in question (and, conversely, when it is not posited, that activity cannot be posited either).

T45 as the best *criterion* for identifying a cause. Hence, *Ord.*, 1.45.un. (*OTh* 4· 665.3–10)· "Quod autem illud sufficiat ad hoc quod aliquid sit causa alterius, videtur esse manifestum. Quia si non, perit omnis via ad cognoscendum aliquid esse causam alterius immediatam. Nam si ex hoc quod hoc posito sequitur effectus, et hoc non posito non ponitur effectus, non sequitur illud esse causam illius effectus, nullo modo potest cognosci quod ignis sit causa caloris in ligno, quia potest dici quod est aliqua alia causa illius caloris, quae tamen non agit nisi in praesentia ignis." For more discussion on this, see Adams, *Ockham*, 2: 750–4.

[8] Ockham, *Ord.*, 1.7.1 (*OTh* 3: 114.23–6): "ita principium elicitivum alicuius actionis vel passionis vel productionis est illud quod necessario et per se requiritur ad illam productionem et non constituitur nec ex productione nec ex producto."

14.2. THE POWER SOURCE FOR THE FATHER'S REPRODUCTIVE ACTIVITY

What, then, is the power source for the Father's reproductive activity? That is, assuming that the right circumstances are present in God, what must be posited in order to also posit the production of the Son? To this, Ockham points out that since all activities ultimately stem from the power of absolute things, the Father's reproductive activity must stem from something absolute too. But of course, the only absolute thing in the Godhead is the divine essence itself, so at the very least, the divine essence is required for the Son's production.[9]

But is anything else required? As Ockham sees it, the answer is no, for apart from the divine essence, the only other constituent in the Father is his fatherhood. But that cannot be the source of his reproductive activity, for as we saw in section 13.2, Ockham believes that fatherhood just is the Father's reproductive activity, and nothing can be the source of itself. Besides, as we saw in section 13.1, Ockham maintains that no relationships are needed to empower activity.[10] By Ockham's reckoning then, the only thing that could possibly be the source of the Father's reproductive activity is the divine essence itself.

However, this might lead one to wonder: if the divine essence is all we need to posit in order to also posit the production of the Son, then wouldn't the divine essence itself directly produce the Son? Indeed, Ockham's T45 typically identifies that which actually *produces* the effect in question (e.g. the heat in a flame). So wouldn't T45 identify the divine essence as the Son's *producer*?

Again, Ockham says no, for like Scotus, Ockham maintains that the producer and product of any given production must be really distinct (for if a product were the very same thing as its producer, the producer would not need to produce it in the first place):

---

[9] Ockham, *Ord.*, 1.7.1 (*OTh* 3: 114.26–115.4): "Et quia sola essentia divina requiritur ad generationem activam et passivam, et spirationem activam et passivam, vel saltem solum aliquid absolutum, isto modo, ideo praecise aliquid absolutum est ratio eliciendi istas productiones tam activas quam passives."

[10] Ockham, *Ord.*, 1.7.1 (*OTh* 3: 114.11–18): "nullus respectus rationis potest esse principium elicitivum vel determinativum alicuius actionis realis . . . Nec etiam respectus realis potest esse principium elicitivum vel determinativum, sicut prius probatum est. Igitur, nullum respectus est ibi [viz. in divinis] principium elicitivum vel determinativum."

(T35) For any x and y,
       if x produces y by a production P,
       x and y are really distinct.

The divine essence, however, is not really distinct from the Son, nor his sonship. In fact, the divine essence is not really distinct from anything in God, so the divine essence cannot produce anything in the Godhead. Consequently, the divine essence merely provides the *power* to reproduce; it cannot reproduce itself.[11]

But if the divine essence does not produce the Son, then who or what does? The answer we are looking for, obviously, is a divine person, namely the Father. However, this might lead one to think that the Father must come to exist *before* he produces the Son—not prior in time, but prior at least in the order of explanation.[12]

Unfortunately, Ockham does not think this line of reasoning is open to him. As he sees it, apart from the divine essence, there is nothing in God except internal productive activity (i.e. the activities that result in the Son and Spirit). Consequently, a distinct producer and product in God can only be constituted by the divine essence and that productive activity, for those are the only available constituents.[13]

Ockham believes, though, like any good medieval Aristotelian, that there is an active and passive side to any given production, and these are distinct (for producing another is not the same thing as being produced yourself). So, thinks Ockham, the active and passive sides of a divine production must be what constitute, along with the divine

---

[11] Ockham, *Ord.*, 1.7.1 (*OTh* 3: 115.4–7): "Sed quia ista essentia [divina] a nulla istarum [productionarum] realiter distinguitur—et semper inter principium et principiatum est realis distinctio—ideo essentia non est quod agit, sed est quo agit"; ibid., (*OTh* 3: 132.11–13): "dico quod omnis productio est a principio distinctivo tamquam ab illo quod producit, non tamquam ab illo quo producit "

[12] As Ockham puts it on behalf of an objector, *Ord.*, 1.7.1 (*OTh* 3: 117.11–12, 14–16): "quod non est principium formale nisi ex hoc quod est aliquid suppositi . . . Sed essentia divina non est principium formale elicitivum generationis nisi ex hoc quod est aliquid suppositi Patris."

[13] For instance, when speaking of the Father, Ockham explains in *Ord.*, 1.7.1 (*OTh* 3: 130.15–20) that "quando dicitur quod 'essentia non est principium formale nisi ut est aliquid suppositi', ista propositio potest intelligi bene et male. Si enim intelligatur quod requiritur aliquod suppositi tamquam praevium supposito vel generationi, sic est simpliciter falsa. Quia nihil est praevium, nec aliquid quocumque modo distinctum a supposito et a generatione illa, nisi essentia praecise."

essence, distinct persons, one of whom will be the producer, and the other of whom will be the product.[14]

For Ockham then, we should not think that the Father is constituted naturally prior to the Son's production. Indeed, besides the divine essence, there is nothing else that could constitute the Father, apart from that very production. Hence, the Father must come to exist simultaneously (or better: eternally) with his reproductive activity, as must the Son.[15] When it comes to divine reproduction, there is just the divine essence and reproductive activity, and all together that constitutes a distinct producer and a distinct product (namely, the Father and the Son).

14.3. PRODUCTIVE ACTS ARE NOT PRODUCED

Still, where does God's internal productive activity come from, if not a person? Ockham maintains that God's productive activity does not "come from" anything, as if it were *produced* in some way. This comes out most clearly when Ockham discusses a particular view of Peter Aureol.

Peter argues that productive acts are not "elicited" in God at all.[16] As he sees it, if a productive act were to come forth from a divine person, then that act would itself have to be produced. But this, Peter argues, is a mistake. We should not think that, say, the Father first

[14] Ockham, *Ord.*, 1.7.1 (*OTh* 3: 115.7–10): "Et quia, non obstante identitate reali inter essentiam [divinam] et istas productiones [e.g. generationem activam et passivam], tamen propter distinctionem realem istarum productionum inter se [essentia] constituit cum ipsis supposita distincta realiter, ideo unum illorum erit producens et aliud productum"; ibid., (*OTh* 3: 132.9–10): "propter distinctionem realem paternitatis et filiationis, et quia cum ipsis essentia constituit distincta supposita."

[15] Ockham, *Ord.*, 1.7.1 (*OTh* 3: 130.8–14): "dico quod, posito quod essentia non esset principium formale nisi ex hoc quod est aliquid suppositi, bene requireretur aliquid aliud ad hoc quod essentia esset principium formale, non tamen tamquam determinativum et praevium generationi, sed tamquam actio vel productio cuius illud principium formale deberet esse principium elicitivum, quia nihil est in supposito nisi essentia et illa generatio cuius est principium elicitivum."

[16] Peter Aureol, *Sent.*, 1.5.17, nn. 90–1 (ed. Buytaert, 2: 793.1–4): "considerandum est quod communis imaginatio circa istam materiam decipit opinantes propter duo. Primum quidem quia omnes imaginantur quod generatio in divinis sit aliquid elicitum."

causes a reproductive act to come forth, and then, secondly, that this act results in the Son.[17]

Now, one might think that Peter is worried about an infinite regress. Indeed, one could easily argue that if a productive act were itself produced, then that act would also have to be produced by a further productive act, and so on ad infinitum. But this is not Peter's concern, at least not in this context.

Like all his contemporaries, Peter maintains that each divine person includes two constituents: the divine essence and a personal property. Like Ockham though, Peter believes that the Father's fatherhood is nothing more than his reproductive activity.[18] That is, fatherhood is just the act of producing a son, so on Peter's view, the Father is constituted by (i) the divine essence, and (ii) his reproductive activity.

Suppose then, that the Father's reproductive act were itself produced. If that were so, then one of the Father's constituents would be produced, and as Peter sees it, that would mean that the Father himself would be produced. After all, the Father is a father, formally speaking, in virtue of his fatherhood, so if his fatherhood were to come into being by being produced, then the Father would come into being by being produced too. But of course, the Father is not produced, so by Peter's reckoning, the Father's reproductive activity cannot "come forth" from anything in any way.[19]

Perhaps we can recast Peter's reasoning roughly as follows. Peter is thinking that the Father is constituted by his reproductive activity, so if that activity were to "come forth," then *before* it came forth, there

[17] Peter Aureol, *Sent.*, 1.5.17, n. 101 (ed. Buytaert, 2: 796.123–7): "Imaginantes autem, quod generare eliciatur et profluat ab essentia [divina] tanquam a ratione formali . . . et idcirco omnes opinantes inde sumunt causam discedendi a vero"; ibid., 1.7.19, n. 53 (ed. Buytaert, 2: 850.13–18): "Sed in divinis generare et spirare non sunt productiones elicitae. Pater enim nihil habet elicitum aut entitatem accipiens . . . apparet impossibile quod generare et spirare sint productiones elicitae."
[18] Peter Aureol, *Sent.*, 1.7.19, n. 54 (ed. Buytaert, 2: 850.27–30): "Sed eadem est potentia qua potest generare et qua potest esse Pater. Idem est enim actus cum actu. Generare enim et paternitas eadem res sunt qua pater est actu pater. Et patet in omnibus quod eadem potentia qua quis potest generare, potest se facere patrem."
[19] Peter Aureol, *Sent.*, 1.5.17, n. 91 (ed. Buytaert, 2: 793.5–11): "Res quidem paternitatis non potest esse res quae capiat suam realitatem aliunde. Si enim caperet, tunc Pater constitueretur formaliter per rem productam et elicitam ac capientem aliunde originaliter entitatem; et per consequens Pater erit aliquid originatum et productum, cum sua forma sit originata; quod omnino erroneum est et absurdum. Impossibile est ergo quod realitas paternitatis sit aliunde originata, aut capiat suam realitatem ab aliquo causative."

would be no Father. But when that reproductive activity comes into being, it would then constitute the Father. Thus, the Father would "come forth" as that reproductive activity "comes forth." But of course, the Father does not "come forth" from anything, so his reproductive activity cannot "come forth" from anything either.[20]

In response, Ockham points out that "coming forth" can have two meanings. Sometimes, says Ockham, we talk about products "coming forth" from their producers, as for instance when we say that the heat in a pot of water comes forth from the heat source that warms it. But other times we talk about actions "coming forth" from their agents, as when we say that an act of heating comes forth from a flame. In the first sense, that which "comes forth" really is produced, but this is not so in the second sense, for when we talk about actions, we are simply talking about the activity by which one thing produces another.[21]

Ockham then claims that the Father's reproductive activity "comes forth" only in the second sense, not the first. That is, when we talk about the Father's reproductive activity, we are not talking about something that is produced; we are simply talking about the activity *by which* the Son is produced.[22]

Peter, on the other hand, is clearly thinking of "coming forth" in the first sense, for he assumes that if any reproductive activity were to "come forth" at all, then it would have to "come forth" as a product.[23]

---

[20] Peter Aureol, *Sent.*, 1.7.19, n. 66 (ed. Buytaert, 2: 854.165–70): "Praeterea, si generare proflueret ab aliqua potentia productiva, Pater esset quoddam possibile produci in quantum generare facit ipsum esse Patrem; et iterum Pater ageret in se causando in se generationem et spirationem, et infinita impossibilia quae sequuntur. Non igitur potest poni generare profluere a generativa potentia, tamquam a principio productivo formaliter."

[21] Ockham, *Ord.*, 1.7.1 (*OTh* 3: 118.5–15): "Ad primum istorum dico quod aequivocatio est de elicito. Aliquid enim dicitur elicitum quia est aliquid vere productum ab aliquo. Et sic dicimus quod calor est elicitus ab igne, quamvis hoc non sit communiter. Unde non dicimus communiter quod ignis elicit ignem, sed producit ignem, et elicit actum producendi ignem. Similiter, calor in igne est principium producendi calorem in ligno, et est principium eliciendi calefactionem qua calefacit lignum. Aliter dicitur aliquid elicitum esse illud quod denominat aliquid producere aliud, sicut calefactio dicitur elicita ab igne quia ignis calefactione denominatur calefacere lignum."

[22] Ockham, *Ord.*, 1.7.1 (*OTh* 3: 118.16–20): "Et quia Pater generatione activa dicitur generare Filium, ideo dicitur generatio activa 'elicita' isto secundo modo. Sed non primo modo, quia generatio activa non est aliqua realitas producta, sed est simpliciter improducta. Est tamen illud quo formaliter aliquid dicitur generare, et hoc est eam esse elicitam."

[23] Peter Aureol, *Sent.*, 1.7.19, n. 54 (ed. Buytaert, 2: 850.22–6): "posse esse patrem non est posse potentiae productivae . . . Si enim posse esse patrem caderet sub aliqua

But Ockham simply denies that. For Ockham, the act of producing the Son does indeed "come forth," but only in the way that actions are that by which agents bring about effects, and actions are not products.[24]

Yet even though Ockham disagrees with Peter's argumentation, he agrees with the basic conclusion, namely that God's internal productive activity is not produced in any way. Rather, it is just "there," so to speak, as the activity by which a divine person is produced. For Ockham then, there is just the divine essence and God's internal productive activity, and that constitutes distinct producers and products.

Still, one might think that Ockham's account here is rather unsatisfying. For Ockham maintains that reproductive activity *constitutes* the Father, and surely constituents are prior in some way to what they constitute. But that makes it looks as if *first* there is some kind of reproductive activity in God, without a reproducer, and then *second* that this activity constitutes the Father.

But surely it should be the other way around: surely there must *first* be a producer, and *then* productive activity. After all, it is hard to imagine any activity at all without someone or something to enact it. Again, though, Ockham does not think this line of reasoning is open to him, for he would say, "Look, there is nothing in God except the divine essence and productive activity, so those are the only entities that could possibly constitute the divine persons. We just have to make due with that."

And indeed, like all his contemporaries, Ockham has no choice but to accept this. For by any standard Aristotelian analysis of the sort that Ockham and his contemporaries employ, agents are normally constituted naturally prior to their activities, but in the Godhead, it is the other way around: the persons are constituted by their (productive) activities. Thus, anyone in Ockham's shoes has to either reject the Aristotelian analysis, or modify it in some way.

---

potentia productiva, necessario pater produceretur in esse Patrem in divinis, quod erroneum est."

[24] Ockham, *Ord.*, 1.7.1 (*OTh* 3: 119.9–14): "Igitur eodem modo potest dici quod generatio activa est elicita, quamvis non sit producta. Per hoc patet ad argumenta recitata [Petris]. Et eodem modo dicendum est ad alia quae fiunt, quod procedunt ac si poneretur quod paternitas vel generatio activa esset producta vel originata. Quod tamen non ponitur, sed dicitur actio elicita, modo exposito."

14.4. CONCLUSION

According to Ockham then, the source of the Father's reproductive power is that which is required for the existence of the Son, and that is just the divine essence. Nevertheless, the divine essence cannot produce the Son, for any producer must be distinct from its product, and the divine essence is not distinct in the Father and Son. Hence, the mutually opposed active and passive sides of divine begetting are required to constitute a distinct producer and a product, and the same applies to the Spirit's production.

Still, as we have seen, Ockham believes that the active and passive sides of divine production simply distinguish the producer and product. They are not produced, and they do not "determine" the divine essence in any way. So although Henry, Scotus, and Ockham all agree that the divine essence is the absolute basis for all divine activity, Henry argues that the source of the Father's reproductive activity (and likewise the source of the Father's and Son's act of producing the Spirit) consists in the divine essence plus its relationship with that activity, while Scotus and Ockham maintain that it consists simply in the divine essence itself.

15

Conclusion

As I pointed out in the Introduction, Christians believe not only that there are three divine persons in the Godhead (namely the Father, Son, and Spirit), they also believe that there is an internal process of origination that gives rise to these three persons. To borrow some metaphors from the Latin tradition, the Father "begets" the Son, and then the Father and Son together "breathe" the Spirit.

But the question is: how exactly is this sort of divine production even possible, and how exactly is it supposed to work? Here, in this final chapter, I want to summarize what Henry, Scotus, and Ockham have said about this, and I want to conclude with some observations about the relationship between philosophy and orthodoxy in the context of this issue.

15.1. HOW A DIVINE PERSON IS PRODUCED

In the first part of this book, I considered the following question: when one divine person produces another, what are the ingredients, so to speak, that go into the produced person? For instance, when the Father begets the Son, what are the basic ingredients that go into the Son, and what role do they play in the productive process that brings the Son into being?

According to Henry, the Father produces the Son analogous to the way that terrestrial beings construct things out of materials. When we produce something, we transform pre-existing materials into the desired product by giving those materials a new form. Henry thinks that much the same applies to the Son's production, where the divine essence plays the role of the materials, and sonship plays the role of the new form. Thus, the Father "constructs" the Son, as it were, by taking the divine essence and giving it the form of sonship.

Henry justifies this analogy by pointing out that the Father does not produce the divine essence in the Son, much as we do not produce the materials in our products. But the Son's sonship does get produced as a result of the Father's productive activity, much as the forms of our products get produced as a result of our productive activities. So the divine essence is like a lump of "matter" insofar as it is not produced, and sonship is like a "form" insofar as it is produced in the product.

The same applies to the Spirit's production. When the Father and Son produce the Spirit, Henry believes that the divine essence plays the role of the materials (for it does not get produced in the Spirit), and passive spiration plays the role of the form (for it does get produced in the Spirit). In this way then, the Spirit is "constructed" from the divine essence in much the same way that the Son is.

But as we have seen, Scotus entirely rejects Henry's theory. After all, Scotus reasons, everybody agrees that the divine essence provides the Son with his divine nature, whereas sonship provides the Son with his distinction from the other divine persons. So at the very least, the divine essence must be like a kind-bestowing constituent, whereas sonship must be like a distinguishing constituent.

But if that is right, then the divine essence cannot be anything like matter. Indeed, terrestrial beings do not derive their kind-natures from the materials they are made from, for all of the earth's inhabitants are ultimately made from the same basic matter. On the contrary, it is the *form* of a thing that makes it what it is. Humans are humans because of their human forms, cows are cows because of their bovine forms, and so on.

So Scotus concludes that the divine essence cannot play the role of some shared material from which the divine persons are made. Rather, it must be more like a shared form that provides each person with their divine nature. To put it as Scotus does, the divine essence must be the "formal terminus" of the Son's production, where the formal terminus of any procreation is the ultimate substantial form of the offspring that provides it with its kind-nature.

Ockham rejects the views of both Henry and Scotus. As for Henry's view, Ockham argues that the divine essence cannot literally be a lump of matter, for obvious reasons. But nor can it be *like* a lump of matter, for the divine essence is "like" a lot of things, and that means we have no reason to think that the divine essence is more like matter than anything else.

Indeed, Ockham recognizes that the only reason Henry has to say that the divine essence is like a lump of matter is this: it is not produced in the Son or Spirit. But Ockham points out that it is logically possible for the form of a thing to be unproduced as well, so the mere fact that a constituent of something is not produced gives us no reason to think that it must therefore play the role of matter.

As for Scotus's view, Ockham rejects that too. As Ockham sees it, the divine essence cannot be the "formal terminus" of production, for to say that anything is the "terminus" of a production means that it comes to exist through that production. The divine essence, however, does not come to exist through any production whatsoever. On the contrary, it is simply shared with the Son and Spirit, and that is all there is to it.

Further, Ockham maintains that sonship is not the "terminus" of the Son's production either, at least not in any strict sense. After all, Ockham believes that sonship is just an abstract label for the fact that the Son is produced by the Father. In other words, "sonship" denotes the causal relationship *by which* the Son comes to exist, but it does not denote any actual product. And the same goes for passive spiration.

For Ockham then, the only thing that comes to exist as a result of divine production is a produced person, namely the Son or Spirit. Thus, the Father produces the Son, and then the Father and Son together produce the Spirit, but in each case, the producer(s) share(s) the divine essence with the product, and the respective causal relationships that are involved in those productions constitute distinct producers and products. But in all of this, neither the divine essence nor the personal properties need to be construed as the "matter" or the "forms" of the products.

15.2. HOW A DIVINE PERSON IS A PRODUCER

In the second part of this book, I turned my attention to a different question: when one divine person produces another, do any of the producing-person's ingredients play some role in the productive process? If so, what exactly is their function?

According to Henry, if one thing produces another, it must have the power to do so, for agents can only perform activities that fall within the scope of their powers. Further, the sorts of powers an agent has depends on the sorts of constituents it has. Just as a flame derives its heating power from its own heat, so also does any agent derive its power from some absolute part or constituent within itself.

Henry thinks this is true of the divine persons as well. Since the Father produces the Son, he must have the power to do so, and he must derive that power from some absolute constituent within himself. But the only absolute constituent in the Father (or any other divine person, for that matter) is the divine essence, so the Father must derive his reproductive power from the divine essence itself.

However, Henry also believes that having a particular power involves more than just having the right parts or constituents. For as Henry sees it, powers are defined with reference to the activities for which they are powers. After all, we do not say "Jane has power" without specifying (or at least implying) what Jane has the power for. So far as Henry is concerned, this means that powers are essentially *relational* in character: they involve a connection with their corresponding activities.

Henry maintains that the same holds true in the Godhead. To say that the Father has the power to produce a Son implies not only that the Father has the right sort of parts or constituents (which in this case is just the divine essence), it also implies a connection with the activity of producing a Son. Thus, the Father's power to produce a Son is constituted by (i) the divine essence, and (ii) its connection with the Father's reproductive activity.

This makes perfect sense within the context of Henry's theory of powers. Indeed, the divine essence is shared by all three of the divine persons, so in and of itself, it is indifferent to the various activities the persons perform. Consequently, says Henry, the divine essence is "determined" to one activity rather than another by its connection with the one activity rather than the other.

Scotus rejects Henry's theory on this front as well. As Scotus sees it, the divine essence is the most potent entity in existence, so it is absurd to suggest that the divine essence needs to be "determined" in any way. On the contrary, the divine essence is so potent that it is perfectly capable (in and of itself) of providing the power to produce a divine Son and Spirit, entirely apart from its connections with the productive activities that bring about the Son and Spirit.

In this sense, Scotus thinks the divine essence is like the sun. The sun can illuminate the earth, it can help plants grow, and it can generate maggots in a rotting carcass, for the sun is potent enough to bring about all of these activities in and of itself. Similarly, thinks Scotus, the divine essence is entirely capable of providing the power to produce a Son or Spirit, and it does not need any further "determination" to do so.

Besides, Scotus believes that any connection or relationship between two items is naturally posterior to those items, for two items cannot be related if either of them does not exist. But if powers require a connection with their corresponding activities (as Henry claims), then it would follow that there would be no power when the activity in question is not going on, for nothing can have a connection with a non-existent activity.

Scotus thinks that would be absurd, for surely I have the power to perform certain activities even when I am not actually doing so. Thus, Scotus reasons, whatever it is that constitutes a power, it cannot involve a connection with its corresponding activity. Of course, Scotus believes that there is such a connection when the activity is actually going on, but the point here is that this connection cannot *constitute* the power, for it shows up on the scene too late, as it were, to play any constitutive or determining role.

Likewise in the Godhead: the Father, for instance, gets his reproductive power from the divine essence alone, entirely apart from its connection with the Father's reproductive activity. On Scotus's view, that connection is a consequence, not a constituent, of the Father's reproductive power. And the same goes for the Father's and Son's power to produce a Spirit: it comes from the divine essence alone, entirely apart from its connection with their spirative activity.

Ockham takes a similar line to Scotus here. As Ockham sees it, the relationship between a cause and its effect presupposes the existence of the effect. After all, a cause cannot be related to a non-existent effect, at least not in any real sense. So Ockham believes, like Scotus, that relationships show up on the scene too late, as it were, to do any "determining."

Thus, the divine essence cannot be "determined" by any relationships. On the contrary, the divine essence must have everything it needs, in and of itself, to provide the Father with his power to produce a Son, and the same goes for the Father's and Son's power to produce a Spirit. For Ockham, the divine essence is entirely sufficient to source the Father's reproductive power, as well as the Father's and Son's spirative power.

15.3. SOLVING THE CREATION AND SUBORDINATION PROBLEMS

How does any of this solve the creation and subordination problems I discussed in section 1.3? For if the Son or Spirit are produced without materials—and that is certainly a plausible hypothesis—how could they *not* be created from nothing? Further, if it turns out that the Son and Spirit are created, how would they *not* be lesser deities?

Henry solves the creation problem by insisting that when it comes to divine production, the divine essence plays the role of matter. For as Henry sees it, if the Son or Spirit were produced without any materials whatsoever, they would be produced from nothing, in which case they would be created. But since that contradicts the Nicene Creed, Henry concludes that the Son and Spirit *must* be produced from materials, at least in some sense or other. And that is precisely why Henry thinks the divine essence must play the role of matter.

One could also see this as a solution to the subordination problem. After all, the worry of subordinationism arises from the creation problem: if the Son and Spirit were created, they would then be lesser deities, for creatures are typically inferior to their creators. But if it turns out that the Son and Spirit are *not* created, which is just what Henry claims, then the Son and Spirit would obviously not be inferior creatures (especially considering that they share the very same divine essence). So by solving the creation problem in the way that he does, Henry also relieves the worry of subordinationism, at least in principle.

Scotus, however, believes that Henry does not solve the subordination problem. On the contrary, he falls straight into it. On Henry's view, it looks as if the persons are different in kind, for they all have different forms (i.e. different personal properties). But as any good Aristotelian knows, when like produces unlike, the product is typically inferior to its producer. So far as Scotus is concerned then, Henry would have to admit that the Son is inferior to the Father, and that the Spirit is inferior to both the Father and the Son. As

Scotus sees it, Henry ends up with a subordinationist account of divine production after all.

This provides Scotus with yet another reason to insist (against Henry) that the divine essence must play the role of a shared substantial form rather than some sort of shared material. Indeed, all of the earth's inhabitants are made of the same basic matter, but all of the earth's inhabitants are not equal. The only terrestrial beings that are intrinsically equal, at least with respect to one another, are those that have the same kind of substantial form. Likewise in the divine case: the only way the persons will be intrinsically equal is if they have the same form as well. So Scotus concludes again that the divine essence must play the role of a shared substantial form, not some shared material.

Ockham, on the other hand, argues that neither Scotus nor Henry have to worry about subordinationism at all. As Ockham sees it, the fact that the divine essence is perfectly identical to everything else in the Godhead means that everything in God will be equal in perfection. Since everything in the Trinity is identical to the divine essence (which is infinitely perfect), everything in the Trinity will be infinitely perfect as well. Consequently, it does not matter whether we construe the divine essence as a shared form, some sort of shared material, or anything else. However we explain divine production, everything in God will always turn out to be infinitely perfect.

Still, as we have seen, Ockham agrees with Scotus that the divine essence is not like some sort of shared material that the Father, Son, and Spirit are made from. One might wonder then, how Scotus and Ockham solve the creation problem. After all, if the Son and Spirit are produced without materials of any sort, as Scotus and Ockham both claim, then wouldn't the Son and Spirit be created from nothing?

According to Scotus and Ockham, the answer is no. They agree that if a product is produced without any "pre-existing ingredients" whatsoever, then of course it will be created from nothing. But a "pre-existing ingredient" does not need to be some sort of material. On the contrary, it could be a form or any other sort of constituent that is not produced in the product. So for Scotus and Ockham, a product will be uncreated so long as it includes at least one unproduced constituent, whatever sort of constituent that might be.

Scotus and Ockham then point out that this is precisely what happens in divine production. Because the divine essence is not produced in the Son and Spirit, it counts as a "pre-existing ingredient," as it were. And since the Son and Spirit each include at least one unproduced constituent (the divine essence), it follows that they are not created *ex nihilo*. By Scotus's and Ockham's reckoning then, the creation problem gives us no reason to construe the divine essence as some sort of shared material. All we need to say is that the divine essence is an unproduced constituent in the Son and Spirit, and that is a claim that virtually every late thirteenth- and early fourteenth-century Christian schoolman would agree with.

15.4. SCHOLASTIC PHILOSOPHY AND THEOLOGICAL ORTHODOXY

One of the most striking features of this whole debate is Henry's claim that the divine essence is (or at least plays the role of) some sort of shared material from which the divine persons are made. This is so striking precisely because the late thirteenth and early fourteenth centuries fall squarely within the tradition of high scholasticism, where God is supposed to be the most perfect conceivable being. As Anselm famously put it a few centuries earlier: God is that than which nothing greater can be conceived.

Now, one of the things we typically think this means for the schoolmen is that God is not material in any way. Indeed, material beings are limited by space and time, but since God is the greatest conceivable being, surely God is not limited in these ways. God is not restricted to, say, the right-hand corner of the universe, and for such-and-such a period of time. God is supposed to transcend space and time, so surely he cannot be material in any sense.

Given that, one might wonder how Henry could ever have proposed that the divine essence plays the role of matter in divine production. Indeed, with a claim like that, we would not be surprised in the least if Henry had been condemned flatly as a heretic.

But this was not the case. Scotus does point out that no one since the days of Augustine had ever heard of a theory like Henry's, but even if this were just rhetorical propaganda on the part of Scotus, the more important point is that it simply accuses Henry of going against the traditional grain. It does *not* accuse Henry of heresy. In fact, I know of no place where Scotus or Ockham accuse Henry of being heretical with respect to this particular issue. Scotus and Ockham saw Henry's view here as being *philosophically* untenable, but they did not see it as a form of heresy.

Moreover, as I pointed out in Part I, Henry garnered a healthy group of followers on this particular point. That is, a number of highly competent Christian scholastics in the late thirteenth and early fourteenth centuries thought not only that Henry's theory was not heretical, but also that it was essentially *correct*. How, then, could Henry propose the theory that he did, but not tread on the toes of the established orthodoxy?

I suggest the following: in the context of divine production, the only claims in the late thirteenth and early fourteenth centuries that fell under the umbrella of unquestionable orthodoxy were those that were derived directly from the Creeds or accepted Church doctrine (and crucially, as I pointed out in section 1.4, that includes the Fourth Lateran Council of 1215). Everything else was up for grabs, so to speak, and a Christian scholastic was free to make what he could of it, so long as he did not contradict something derived from the Creeds or accepted Church doctrine.

That would be one way to explain why Henry, Scotus, and Ockham did not question the ideas that (i) the Son or Spirit are not created from nothing, and (ii) that the Son or Spirit are equal to the Father. Those are claims made by the Nicene Creed (at least as it was traditionally understood), so *of course* those claims would go unquestioned.

But the idea that the persons cannot be described as being produced with materials—that was a notion that the schoolmen (namely, Henry and his followers) could and did question, as we have seen. Thus, the idea that the persons cannot be described as being produced with materials could not have been seen as a piece of received orthodoxy. Rather, it must have been seen as just a very plausible claim that one could accept or reject on philosophical grounds. And that may very well explain why Henry could propose the theory that he did so successfully.

Of course, the schoolmen were concerned with the *intelligibility* of Christian doctrine, so they were not going to accept just anything. In this case, the critique against Henry that we find in Scotus and Ockham ultimately amounts to a critique about the intelligibility of Henry's theory. As Scotus and Ockham see it, Henry's theory of divine production does not provide an intelligible account of the

Son's and Spirit's productions, and that is the grounds on which Scotus and Ockham reject it. In short, theirs was not purely a theological critique. It was a philosophical critique as well.

All of this suggests that late thirteenth- and early fourteenth-century theologians were allowed a great deal of philosophical creativity when they tried to work out various aspects of Christian doctrine. This does not mean that such theologians didn't have to be careful about what they said, but I want to propose that so long as such theologians proceeded carefully, they could offer creative and original hypotheses in the realm of philosophical theology.

References

Adams, Marilyn McCord. "Ockham on Identity and Distinction." *Franciscan Studies* 36 (1976): 25–43.

——. *William Ockham*, 2 volumes. Notre Dame, Indiana: University of Notre Dame Press, 1989.

——. "The Metaphysics of the Trinity." *Franciscan Studies* 66 (2008): 112–40.

Aristotle. *Aristoteles Latinus*. Edited by G. Vuillemin-Diem, et al. Bruges, Paris, Leiden, Köln, et al., 1953–.

Aristotle and Averroes. *Aristotelis Opera cum Averrois Commentariis*. Edited by Johannes Franciscus Bagolinus, et al. Venice: Giunta, 1562–1574.

Augustine. *De Trinitate. Corpus Christianorum, Series Latina*, volumes 50–50A. Edited by W. J. Mountain and F. Glorie. Turnhout: Brepols, 1968.

Aureol, Peter. *Scriptum super Primum Sententiarum*, 2 volumes. Edited by Eligius Buytaert. St. Bonaventure, NY: St. Bonaventure University Press, 1952–1956.

Avicenna. *Liber de Prima Philosophia sive Scientia Divina, V–X*. Edited by S. van Riet. Leiden: Brill, 1980.

Boehner, Philotheus. *Collected Articles on Ockham*, second edition. Edited by Eligius Buytaert. St. Bonaventure, New York: The Franciscan Institute, 1992.

Brower, Jeffrey. "Abelard on The Trinity." In *The Cambridge Companion to Abelard*. Edited by Jeffrey Brower and Kevin Guilfoy. Cambridge: Cambridge University Press, 2004, 223–57.

Caffarena, José Gómez. "Cronología de la *Suma* de Enrique de Gante por relación a sus *Quodlibetos*." *Gregorianum* 38 (1957): 116–33.

——. *Ser participado y ser subsistente en la metafísica de Enrique de Gante*. Roma: Pontificia Università Gregoriana (Analecta Gregoriana, 93), 1958.

Chatton, Walter. *Reportatio super Sententias*, volume 1. Edited by Joseph Wey and Girard Etzkorn. Toronto: Pontifical Institute of Medieval Studies, 2002.

Cross, Richard. *Duns Scotus*. Oxford: Oxford University Press, 1999.

——. "Divisibility, Communicability, and Predicability in Duns Scotus's Theories of the Common Nature." *Medieval Philosophy and Theology* 11 (2003): 43–63.

——. "Duns Scotus on Divine Substance and the Trinity." *Medieval Philosophy and Theology* 11 (2003): 181–201.

——. "Scotus's Parisian Teaching on Divine Simplicity." In *Duns Scotus à Paris: Actes du colloque de Paris, 2–4 septembre 2002*. Edited by Olivier Boulnois et al. Turnhout: Brepols (Textes et Etudes du Moyen Age, 26), 2004, 519–62.

———. *Duns Scotus on God*. Aldershot, England and Burlington, Vermont: Ashgate, 2005.

———. "Accidents, Substantial Forms, and Causal Powers in the Late Thirteenth Century: Some Reflections on the Axiom '*actiones sunt suppositorum*'." In *Compléments de substance: Etudes sur les propriétés accidentelles offertes à Alain de Libera*. Paris: Vrin, 2008, 133–46.

Dales, Richard. *Medieval Discussions of the Eternity of the World* (Leiden: Brill, 1990).

Davidson, Herbert. *Alfarabi, Avicenna, and Averroes on Intellect: Their Cosmologies, Theories of the Active Intellect and Theories of Human Intellect*. Oxford: Oxford University Press, 1992.

Dumont, Stephen. "William of Ware, Richard of Connington, and the *Collationes Oxoniensis* of John Duns Scotus." In *John Duns Scotus: Metaphysics and Ethics*. Edited by Ludger Honnefelder, Rega Wood, and Mechthild Dreyer. Leiden: E. J. Brill, 1996, 59–85.

Friedman, Russell. *Medieval Trinitarian Thought from Aquinas to Ockham*. Cambridge: Cambridge University Press, 2010.

Gelber, Hester. "Logic and the Trinity: A Clash of Values in Scholastic Thought, 1300–1335." PhD dissertation, University of Wisconsin, 1974.

Ghent, Henry of. *Quodlibeta*. Edited by Jodicus Badius. Paris, 1518. Reprinted by Louvain: Bibliothèque S. J., 1961.

———. *Summa Quaestionum Ordinariarum*. Edited by Jodicus Badius. Paris, 1520. Reprinted by St. Bonaventure, NY: The Franciscan Institute, 1953.

———. *Henrici de Gandavo Opera Omnia*. Edited by Raymond Macken, et al. Leuven: Leuven University Press, 1979–.

Grajewski, Maurice. *The Formal Distinction of Duns Scotus*. Washington, D.C.: The Catholic University of America Press, 1944.

Grant, Edward. *Planets, Stars, and Orbs: The Medieval Cosmos, 1200–1687*. Cambridge: Cambridge University Press, 1996.

Henninger, Mark. *Relations: Medieval Theories 1250–1325*. Oxford: Clarendon Press, 1989.

King, Peter. "Scotus on Metaphysics." In *The Cambridge Companion to Duns Scotus*. Edited by Thomas Williams. Cambridge: Cambridge University Press, 2003, 38–42.

Little, Andrew. *The Greyfriars in Oxford*. Oxford: Clarendon Press, 1892.

Lombard, Peter. *Sententiarum Quatuor Libri*. Ad Claras: Quarrachi, 1882.

Macken, Raymond. "Les diverses applications de la distinction intentionelle chez Henri de Gand." In *Sprache und Erkenntnis im Mittelalter*, volume 2. Edited by Jan Beckmann, et al. Berlin: de Gruyter (Miscellanea Mediaevalia, 13), 1981, 769–76.

Merlan, P. "Aristotle's Unmoved Movers." *Traditio* 4 (1946): 1–30.

Molière. *Le Malade Imaginaire*. In *The Dramatic Works of Molière*, 3 volumes. Translated by Henri van Laun. Philadelphia: Gebbie & Barrie, Publishers, 1879.

Nasr, Seyyed Houssein. *An Introduction to Islamic Cosmological Doctrines*, revised edition. Boulder, Colorado: Shamhala, 1978.

Ockham, William. *Opera Theologica*. St. Bonaventure, NY: The Franciscan Institute, 1967–1986.

———. *Opera Philosophica*. St. Bonaventure, NY: The Franciscan Institute, 1974–1988.

Paasch, JT. "Are the Father and Son Different in Kind? Scotus and Ockham on Different Kinds of Things, Univocal and Equivocal Production, and Subordination in the Trinity." *Vivarium* 48 (2010): 302–26.

Rea, Michael. "Sameness without Identity: An Aristotelian Solution to the Problem of Material Constitution." *Ratio* 11 (1998): 316–28.

Rea, Michael and Jeffrey Brower. "Material Constitution and the Trinity." *Faith and Philosophy* 22 (2005): 57–76.

Schmaus, Michael. *Der Liber Propugnatorius des Thomas Anglicus und die Lehrunterschiede zwischen Thomas von Aquin und Duns Scotus*, volume 2. Münster Westfalen: Verlag der Aschendorffsche Verlagsbuchhandlung, 1930.

Scotus, John Duns. *Opera Omnia*. Civitas Vaticana: Typis Polyglottis Vaticanis, 1950–.

———. *A Treatise on God as First Principle*, second revised edition. Translated and edited by Allan Wolter. Chicago: Franciscan Herald Press, 1966.

———. *Opera Omnia*. Edited by Luke Wadding. Lyons, 1639. Reprinted by Hildesheim: Georg Olms Verlagsbuchhandlung, 1968.

———. *God and Creatures: The Quodlibetal Questions*. Edited and translated by Felix Alluntis and Allan Wolter. Princeton, NJ: Princeton University Press, 1975.

———. *B. Iohannis Duns Scoti Opera Philosophica*. St. Bonaventure, NY: St. Bonaventure University Press, 1997–2006.

———. *The Examined Report of the Paris Lecture (Reportatio I–A)*, volume 1. Edited by Allan Wolter and Oleg Bychkov. St. Bonaventure, NY: The Franciscan Institute, 2004.

Tanner, Norman (editor). *The Decrees of the Ecumenical Councils*, 2 volumes. London: Sheed and Ward, and Washington, D.C.: Georgetown University Press, 1990.

Teske, Roland. "Distinctions in the Metaphysics of Henry of Ghent." *Traditio* 61 (2006): 227–45.

Theissing, Hermann. *Glaube und Theologie bei Robert Cowton, OFM*. Münster: Aschendorffsche Verlagsbuchhandlung, 1970.

Wetter, Friedrich. *Die Trinitätslehre des Johannes Duns Scotus*. Münster Westfalen: Aschendorffsche Verlagsbuchhandlung, 1967.

Wolfson, Harry. "The Plurality of Immovable Movers in Aristotle and Averroes." *Harvard Studies in Classical Philology* 63 (1958): 233–53.

Index